Selfish Routing and the Price of Anarchy

Selfish Routing and the Price of Anarchy

Tim Roughgarden

The MIT Press
Cambridge, Massachusetts
London, England

This book was set in Times Roman by the author using the LATEX document preparation system.

Library of Congress Cataloging-in-Publication Data

Roughgarden, Tim.
  Selfish routing and the price of anarchy / Tim Roughgarden.
      p.   cm.
  Includes bibliographical references and index.
   ISBN 978-0-262-18243-0 (hardcover)
   ISBN 978-0-262-54932-5 (paperback)
   1. Computer networks–Design and construction. 2. Computational complexity. I. Title.

TK5105.5.R697 2005
004.6'5–dc22

                                        2004051172

Contents

Preface

The last several years have seen a tremendous surge of activity at the interface of computer science and economics. This book is a brief introduction to two intertwined facets of this emerging research area, *the price of anarchy* and *selfish routing*.

The price of anarchy measures the extent to which competition approximates cooperation. It is a rendezvous between the idea of an equilibrium, an idea fundamental to game theory, and the concept of approximation, which is ubiquitous in theoretical computer science. Selfish routing refers to a mathematical model of traffic in a congested network, and it is the price of anarchy's biggest success story so far. This model is interesting in its own right and has a long history and a wide array of applications. In addition to serving as an introduction, this book provides sufficient preparation for original research in these two areas.

Intended Audience

This is a research monograph, not a textbook. Nevertheless, I have endeavored to keep the discussion at a level accessible to an eager first- or second-year doctoral student in a mathematical discipline. Some parts of the book may fall short of this goal, but I hope they are few and far between.

Realistically, I expect that researchers and graduate students in theoretical computer science or in optimization will have the easiest time understanding and appreciating this book. On the other hand, I earnestly hope that readers coming from other parts of computer science and operations research, and from economics, electrical engineering, mathematics, and transportation science will find something that interests them. When I betray my roots as a theoretical computer scientist, be it with jargon, interminable discussions of NP-completeness, or an untreatable addiction to worst-case analysis, I have tried to be honest about it. I hope that readers from other fields will have little trouble looking past these biases.

Overview

Chapter 1 provides a nontechnical introduction to selfish routing. It includes an informal overview of the seminal examples of Pigou and Braess to motivate the analyses that follow. Chapter 2 is a clearinghouse for technical results of a preliminary nature, and it primarily serves as a reference for the other chapters. Chapter 3 is the heart of the book and is devoted to the price of anarchy of selfish routing, with Pigou's example playing a central role. This chapter covers only the most basic material on the topic. Chapter 4 surveys some of the many generalizations and variants of the work described in Chapter 3. Chapter 5 shifts the discussion to Braess's Paradox. This chapter studies both the worst-case severity of the paradox and the computational complexity of algorithmically detecting it. Chapter 6 concludes by describing Stackelberg routing, which is one way to reduce the price of anarchy of selfish routing using a modest degree of centralized control.

Chapter Notes

This book is an updated and slightly expanded revision of my doctoral thesis. As such, it is inevitably slanted toward my own research. I have, however, included work by other researchers when I felt that it was important and blended in well with the rest of the book. At the same time, I wanted the book to have a brisk pace, a goal that seemed to preclude careful discussions of who did what. As a compromise, in all of the chapters I have deferred all bibliographic references to a final section entitled "Notes." While not encyclopedic and written at a higher level than the rest of the book, I think these sections give a thorough and accessible review of the relevant literature. Indeed, one of the purposes of the chapter notes is to summarize the work of different research communities addressing a common problem. I hope that my efforts catalyze further cross-fertilization between these different fields.

I also have relegated to the chapter notes discussions that are of secondary importance or that do not fit naturally into the text proper. Examples include historical notes, references to topics that I view as prerequisite material or as outside the scope of this book, and extensions and refinements of the models and results in the preceding sections. The chapter notes can be skipped without interfering with the use of the rest of the book.

Acknowledgments

This book would not have been possible without a great deal of help from others. At the very least, the following individuals have provided advice, encouragement, comments, questions, and answers: Aaron Archer, Ben Atkin, Lou Billera, Avrim Blum, Dietrich Braess, Jennifer Chayes, Richard Cole, José Correa, Artur Czumaj, Yevgeniy Dodis, David Eppstein, Joan Feigenbaum, Lisa Fleischer, Rob Freund, Eric Friedman, Leslie Ann Goldberg, Anupam Gupta, Ramesh Johari, Hisao Kameda, George Karakostas, Howard Karloff, Michael Kearns, Frank Kelly, Jon Kleinberg, Stavros Kolliopoulos, Elias Koutsoupias, Harish Krishnan, Amit Kumar, V. S. Anil Kumar, Henry Lin, Mohammad Mahdian, Patrice Marcotte, Tom McCormick, Nimrod Megiddo, Anna Nagurney, Asu Ozdaglar, Christos Papadimitriou, David Parkes, Serge Plotkin, Satish Rao, Amir Ronen, Robert Rosenthal,

Steve Schneider, Leonard Schulman, Andreas Schulz, Scott Shenker, David Shmoys, Yoav Shoham, Emil Gun Sirer, Cliff Stein, Nicolás Stier Moses, Éva Tardos, Mike Todd, John Tsitsiklis, Vijay Vazirani, Adrian Vetta, Berthold Vöcking, Bernhard von Stengel, Dror Weitz, Tom Wexler, David Williamson, and Neal Young. I am sure that I have forgotten a few people, to whom I apologize.

Three of the above individuals deserve to be singled out: Éva, for supervising the doctoral thesis on which this book is based, and for collaborating on much of the research described herein; Leonard, for introducing me to selfish routing; and Christos, first for asking about the price of anarchy of selfish routing, and second for suggesting The MIT Press as a publisher for this book. Speaking of which, I thank Bob Prior, Mel Goldsipe, and everyone else at The MIT Press for their patience and professionalism.

I benefitted from the hospitable environments of Cornell University, IBM Almaden, and UC Berkeley during the research for and writing of this book. I am also indebted to the National Science Foundation, the Office of Naval Research, and Cornell University for financial support for these activities.

Finally, I am extremely grateful to Eve Donnelly for her support throughout this project.

I INTRODUCTION AND PRELIMINARIES

1 Introduction

1.1 Selfish Routing

What route should you take to work tomorrow? All else being equal, most of us would opt for the one that allows us to wake up at the least barbaric time—that is, most of us would prefer the shortest route available. As any morning commuter knows, the length of time required to travel along a given route depends crucially on the amount of traffic congestion—on the number of *other* commuters who choose interfering routes. In selecting a path to travel from home to work, do you take into account the additional congestion that you cause other commuters to experience? Not likely. Almost certainly you choose your route *selfishly*, aiming to get to work as quickly as possible, without regard to the consequences your choice has for others. Naturally, you also expect your fellow commuters to behave in a similarly egocentric fashion. But what if everyone cooperated by coordinating routes? Is it possible to limit the interference among routes, thereby improving commute times? If so, by how much?

This book studies the loss of social welfare due to *selfish routing*—selfish, uncoordinated behavior in networks. Part II of the book develops techniques for quantifying the worst-possible loss of social welfare from selfish routing, called *the price of anarchy*. Part III uses these techniques to evaluate different approaches to *coping with selfishness*—reducing the price of anarchy with a modest degree of centralized control.

1.2 Two Motivating Examples

This section motivates the questions studied in this book by informally exploring two important examples. These examples are treated rigorously in Chapter 2. Pigou discovered the first example in 1920; Braess discovered the second in 1968.

1.2.1 Pigou's Example

Posit a suburb s and a nearby train station t, connected by two noninterfering highways, and a fixed number of drivers who wish to commute from the suburb s to the train station t at roughly the same time. Suppose the first highway is short but narrow, with the time needed to drive along it increasing sharply with the number of drivers who use it. Suppose the second is wide enough to accommodate all traffic without any crowding, but it takes a long, circuitous route. For concreteness,

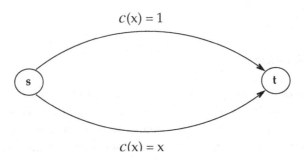

Figure 1.1
Pigou's example. A cost function $c(x)$ describes the travel time experienced by drivers on a road as a function of the fraction x of the overall traffic using that road.

assume that all drivers on the latter highway require 1 hour to drive from s to t, irrespective of the number of other drivers on the road. Further suppose that the time needed to drive using the short narrow highway is equal, in hours, to the fraction of the overall traffic that chooses to use it. Figure 1.1 shows this network pictorially. Call the functions $c(\cdot)$ *cost functions*; in this example they describe the travel time experienced by drivers on a road as a function of the fraction of the traffic that uses the road. The upper edge in Figure 1.1 thus represents the long, wide highway, and the lower edge the short, narrow one.

Assuming that all drivers aim to minimize the driving time from s to t, we have good reason to expect all traffic to follow the lower road and therefore, because of the ensuing congestion, to require one hour to reach the destination t. Indeed, each driver should reason as follows: the lower route is never worse than the upper one, even when it is fully congested, and it is superior whenever some of the other drivers are foolish enough to take the upper route.

Now suppose that, by whatever means, we can choose who drives where. Can the power of centralized control improve over the selfish routing outcome? To see that it can, consider assigning half of the traffic to each of the two routes. The drivers forced onto the long, wide highway experience one hour of travel time, and are thus no worse off than in the previous outcome. On the other hand, drivers allowed to use the short, narrow road now enjoy lighter traffic conditions, and arrive at their destination after a mere 30 minutes. The state of affairs has therefore improved for half of the drivers while no one is worse off. Moreover, the average travel time has dropped from 60 to 45 minutes, a significant improvement. The interested reader might want to ponder whether or not other outcomes are possible in which the

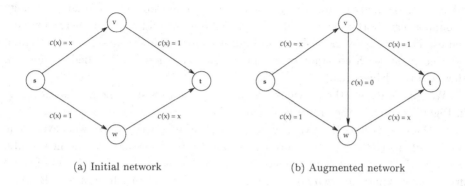

(a) Initial network   (b) Augmented network

Figure 1.2
Braess's Paradox. The addition of an intuitively helpful edge can adversely affect all of the traffic.

average travel time is less than 45 minutes.

Pigou's example demonstrates a well known but important principle:

selfish behavior need not produce a socially optimal outcome.

This observation motivates the work described in Part II, which analyzes the price of anarchy: *how much worse* can a selfish outcome be relative to a socially optimal one? As Part II shows, Pigou's example plays a crucial role in answering this question.

1.2.2 Braess's Paradox

Pigou's example illustrates an important principle: the outcome of selfish behavior need not optimize social welfare. However, it may not be surprising that the result of local optimization by many individuals with conflicting interests does not possess any type of global optimality. The next example, called *Braess's Paradox*, is decidedly less intuitive.

Begin again with a suburb s, a train station t, and a fixed number of drivers who wish to commute from s to t. For the moment, assume two noninterfering routes from s to t, each comprising one long wide road and one short narrow road as shown in Figure 1.2(a). The combined travel time in hours of the two edges in one of these routes is $1 + x$, where x is the fraction of the traffic that uses the route. The routes are therefore identical, and traffic should split evenly between them. In this case, all drivers arrive at their destination 90 minutes after their departure from s.

Now, an hour and a half is quite a commute. Suppose that, in an effort to

alleviate these unacceptable delays, we harness the finest available road technology
to build a very short and very wide highway joining the midpoints of the two existing
routes. The new network is shown in Figure 1.2(b), with the new road represented
by edge (v, w) with constant cost $c(x) = 0$, independent of the road congestion.
How will the drivers react?

We cannot expect the previous traffic pattern to persist in the new network. As
in Pigou's example, the travel time along the new route $s \to v \to w \to t$ is never
worse than that along the two original paths, and it is strictly less whenever some
traffic fails to use it. We therefore expect all drivers to deviate to the new route.
Because of the ensuing heavy congestion on the edges (s, v) and (w, t), all of these
drivers now experience two hours of travel time when driving from s to t. Braess's
Paradox thus shows that the intuitively helpful action of adding a new zero-cost
link can negatively impact *all* of the traffic!

Braess's Paradox raises several interesting issues. First, it furnishes a second
example of the suboptimality of selfish routing. Indeed, Braess's example demonstrates this principle in a stronger form than does Pigou's: all drivers would *strictly
prefer* the coordinated outcome—the original traffic pattern in the network of Figure 1.2(a)—to the one obtained noncooperatively. More importantly, Braess's Paradox shows that the interactions between selfish behavior and the underlying network
structure defy intuition and are not easy to predict. When we tackle algorithmic
approaches to coping with selfishness in Part III, the counterintuitive moral of
Braess's Paradox will be a persistent thorn in our side:

with selfish routing, network improvements can degrade network performance.

1.3   Applications and Caveats

Although this introduction to selfish routing uses the language of road networks, the
model has an array of interpretations and applications, some of which this section
discusses. (For more, see Section 1.5.) Also, like every mathematical model, this
model of selfish routing has made some concessions to the demands of mathematical tractability, at the expense of perfect verisimilitude. We discuss the primary
disconnects between selfish routing and reality in Section 1.3.4.

1.3.1   Transportation Networks

Our first interpretation of selfish routing—as road traffic—is consistent with the
chronology of its applications. Pigou described his 1920 example in terms of a road
network. The model has enjoyed a central position in theoretical transportation

research since the 1950's. Hundreds, if not thousands, of papers have studied it and its innumerable extensions. Sections 1.5 and 2.8 survey some of this work.

1.3.2   Computer Networks

More recently, researchers in computer science and electrical engineering discovered two connections between selfish routing and methods of routing information in computer networks, one obvious, the other less so. In order to emphasize the main ideas behind these connections and avoid consideration of a number of details, the following discussion is deliberately kept at a naive level.

The first interpretation of selfish routing for computer networks is for networks that employ so-called *source routing*. Source routing means that if one computer wants to send information to another, then the sender is responsible for selecting a path of data links between the two machines. This task would typically be performed by the computer's software, rather than manually by the actual computer user. In networks with source routing, cost minimization is a natural goal for end users. In this case, the road and computer network interpretations of selfish routing correspond directly.

While the idea of source routing has generated a fair amount of research in the computer networking community, for several reasons it is not common in real networks. Routing is instead usually accomplished in a *distributed* fashion. In distributed routing, a computer selects only a *single* link along which to send information. After the data crosses the link, it is then the next machine's responsibility to see that the information continues toward its destination. The choice of this link can depend on several factors, including the destination of the data and the current network conditions.

A serious problem with distributed routing is that traffic can travel in circles, never arriving at its destination. Ignoring a host of implementation challenges, the following is a solution to this problem. Each computer decides on a positive *length* for the links that emanate from it. Each such link could have a fixed length, or the lengths could be sensitive to the amount of congestion in the network. The length of a path is the sum of the lengths of its individual links, and a *shortest path* between two points is a path with length equal to or less than the length of every other path. Since edge lengths are positive, a shortest path will not cycle back on itself. Routing on shortest paths therefore avoids cycles. Moreover, practical distributed implementations of algorithms that compute shortest paths between all pairs of machines in a network exist, including some that form the basis of popular Internet routing protocols.

Shortest-path routing leaves a key parameter unspecified: the length of each edge. A direct correspondence between selfish routing and shortest-path routing exists if and only if the edge cost functions coincide with the lengths used to define shortest paths. In other words, when an x fraction of the overall network traffic is using an edge with cost function $c(\cdot)$, then the corresponding shortest-path routing algorithm should define the length of the edge as the number $c(x)$. If the cost function c is nonconstant, then this is a congestion-dependent definition of the edge length. In this case, shortest-path routing will route traffic exactly *as if* it is a network with selfish routing (or source routing). This establishes an equivalence between selfish routing and the distributed routing common in real-life computer networks. Section 1.5 gives pointers to rigorous proofs of this equivalence.

For example, the cost function $c(x)$ of an edge might model the average delay of traffic on the edge, given that an x fraction of the network traffic uses it. Selfish routing with these cost functions models networks in which users pick paths with minimum total delay. Shortest-path routing with these cost functions corresponds to computers defining the length of each outgoing edge as the current average delay experienced by data crossing the edge. The aforementioned equivalence implies that traffic is routed identically in these two different scenarios.

1.3.3 Mechanical and Electrical Networks

Selfish routing also can be relevant in systems that have no explicit notion of traffic whatsoever, as an analogue of Braess's Paradox (Section 1.2.2) in a mechanical network of strings and springs shows.

In the device pictured in Figure 1.3, one end of a spring is attached to a fixed support, and the other end to a string. A second identical spring is hung from the free end of the string and carries a heavy weight. Finally, strings are connected, with some slack, from the support to the upper end of the second spring and from the lower end of the first spring to the weight. Assuming that the springs are ideally elastic, the stretched length of a spring is a linear function of the force applied to it. We can therefore view the network of strings and springs as a traffic network, where force corresponds to traffic and physical distance corresponds to cost.

With a suitable choice of string and spring lengths and spring constants, the equilibrium position of this mechanical network is described by Figure 1.3(a). Perhaps unbelievably, severing the taut string causes the weight to *rise*, as shown in Figure 1.3(b)! An explanation for this curiosity follows. Initially, the two springs are connected in series, and each bears the full weight and is stretched out to great length. After cutting the taut string, the two springs are only connected in parallel. Each spring then carries only half of the weight, and accordingly is stretched to only half of its previous length. The rise in the weight is the same as the improvement

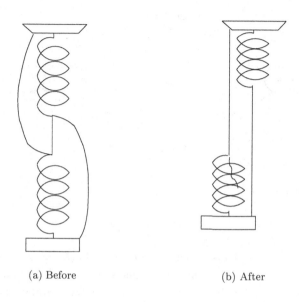

(a) Before   (b) After

Figure 1.3
Strings and springs. Severing a taut string lifts a heavy weight.

in the selfish outcome obtained by deleting the zero-cost edge of Figure 1.2(b) to obtain the network of Figure 1.2(a). Because such systems of strings and springs are essentially the same as networks with selfish routing, the bounds on the price of anarchy that Chapter 3 describes also limit the largest-possible magnitude of this counterintuitive effect.

Similarly, removing a conducting link from an electrical network can increase its conductivity. Electrical networks are again the same as networks with selfish routing, so bounds on the price of anarchy translate to limits on this increase of conductivity.

1.3.4 Caveats

This section has demonstrated that selfish routing is a versatile model that captures key features of a diverse collection of applications. The model does, however, possess some weaknesses, especially in the context of routing in Internet-like computer networks. Two of these follow, along with a critique of the price of anarchy. While this is not an exhaustive list of the model's flaws, these are arguably the most fundamental. Many other assumptions made by the model can be removed, as

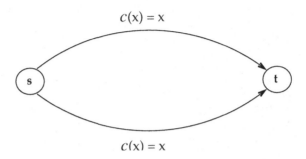

Figure 1.4
A possibly unstable network.

Chapter 4 shows.

The first criticism of selfish routing applies to both the road and computer network interpretations of the model: the model is *static*, while the world is *dynamic*. When we prove bounds on the price of anarchy, we will assume that the network has reached an "equilibrium." We already have an informal sense of what this means from the examples in Section 1.2; Section 2.2 defines the notion formally. Conceptually, the hope is that traffic will experiment over time and reach an equilibrium, but it is not clear that this will always occur, especially in networks where parameters such as the traffic rate are changing rapidly over time. For a contrived example, replace the long, wide highway in Pigou's example with a second short, narrow one (Figure 1.4). Imagine a computer at s that routes traffic using shortest-path routing with the cost functions c. Perhaps at first the computer routes all of the traffic on the upper route. Then, finding that the upper edge has cost 1 and the lower edge cost 0, the computer reconsiders and routes all of the traffic on the lower edge. This undesirable oscillation can continue unabated.

In defense of studying equilibria, a variety of reasonably weak conditions are known to be sufficient for a network with selfish routing to settle into an equilibrium. In the contrived example above, the obvious solution is to restrict the amount of traffic that can be rerouted at each time step.

Second, shortest-path routing in computer networks, and in the Internet in particular, poses a particular challenge for the model. A network like the Internet is volatile. Its traffic patterns can change quickly and dramatically, and data links and machines are constantly failing. The assumption of a static model is therefore particularly suspect in such networks. Indeed, early versions of the Internet used variants of delay-based distributed routing and suffered from unstable behavior.

Moreover, routing in the Internet today is often not sensitive to congestion. In addition to its relative stability, this naive routing is common because economic factors tend to overwhelm performance-based ones: cheap links are used even when they are very congested. Of course, there is little hope of proving anything about performance-ignorant routing. Indeed, recent experiments have demonstrated that current routing in the Internet is highly inefficient. Because of this, congestion-sensitive routing has been making a bit of a comeback, at least within the research community. If widely adopted, this would improve the accuracy of the correspondence between selfish routing and distributed routing in large, real-life networks. See Section 1.5 for references on these developments.

As a final critique, the price of anarchy—defined in Section 2.3 as the worst-possible ratio between the average travel time of a selfish solution and the smallest achievable average travel time—is by definition a worst-case measure. Worst-case analysis has long inspired heated debate. Worst-case bounds are of course compelling when they exist, but worst-case analysis can focus undue attention on contrived bad examples—akin to ignoring a lush forest for the sake of a few dead trees. On the other hand, alternatives to worst-case analysis usually must define what a "typical case" or an "average-case analysis" means, and no such definition is without its own controversy. Also, these alternatives are often less mathematically tractable than their worst-case counterparts.

Most of this book adopts the worst-case approach. Fortunately, interesting worst-case bounds can usually be established for the price of anarchy. Moreover, Part II demonstrates that worst-case examples are often similar to networks that can arise in practice. Nevertheless, the pursuit of alternatives to worst-case analysis remains an important and largely unexplored research direction.

1.4   How to Read this Book

1.4.1   Prerequisites

This book has few prerequisites, other than mathematical maturity. On occasion it assumes a bit more, as follows. A few proofs assume that the reader remembers some basic calculus and analysis, mostly to use derivatives to approximate a function, and to use the fact that a continuous real-valued function defined on closed and bounded subset of Euclidean space attains its minimum. The reader with no exposure to mathematical programming should skip the proofs in Sections 2.4 and 2.6 and that of Lemma 4.3.6. The reader is assumed to be familiar with the theory of NP-completeness only in Sections 5.3 and 6.6, although the language of

Table 1.1
Prerequisites needed for particular sections of the book.

Prerequisite	Needed for parts of...
Calculus/Analysis	Sections 2.4, 2.6, 3.2, 3.5 and 4.3
Convex Programming	Sections 2.4, 2.6, and 4.3
NP-Completeness	Sections 5.3 and 6.6

complexity theory also occurs in a few other places. To navigate these, the reader unfamiliar with computational complexity can simply translate "polynomial-time" as "computationally efficient," "NP-complete" and "NP-hard" as "computationally intractable," and take $P \neq NP$ as an axiom. See Table 1.1 for a summary of these prerequisites.

Prior exposure to the language of graphs, as provided by an undergraduate course in algorithms or in combinatorics, will also be very useful. Experience with network flow or combinatorial optimization is ideal. The presentation here is self-contained, but it will probably seem a bit terse to readers without this background. Finally, while the book sometimes uses the language of game theory, no prior knowledge of the field is required. The chapter notes also discuss some of the connections between the work described in this book and classical game theory.

1.4.2 Dependencies

Chapter 2 is a prerequisite for all that follows, though most of its sections are required only for a subset of the rest of the book. This breakdown is discussed in detail in the chapter's introduction. Chapters 3, 5, and 6 can be read independently of each other, although Chapter 5 uses some of the results from Chapter 3. Chapter 4 is meant to be read after Chapter 3.

1.5 Notes

Section 1.1

The term "selfish routing" is originally due to Roughgarden and Tardos [347], though the mathematical model that it refers to is much older. This model was discussed qualitatively by Pigou [320] and Knight [227] in the 1920s. In the 1950s, Wardrop [394] and Beckmann, McGuire, and Winsten [40] formalized the model, and selfish routing has been intensely studied ever since. Chapter 2 discusses this history in much greater detail. There have also been innumerable other applications of game theory to networks over the past several decades. See the end of Section 3.7; the papers by Shenker [360], Altman et al. [10], and Linial [258]; and the references therein for many examples.

The concept of the price of anarchy originated in Koutsoupias and Papadimitriou [239], where it was called the *coordination ratio*. Section 3.7 discusses in depth the model studied in [239]. The phrase "price of anarchy" was coined by Papadimitriou [303]. There were several precursors to this concept, however, as Section 2.8 discusses.

"Coping with selfishness" is meant to parallel the expression "coping with NP-completeness," which was popularized by Garey and Johnson [172] and refers to methods for evading the (presumed) worst-case computational intractability of important NP-complete problems. Part III of this book describes only two of the many known ways to reduce the price of anarchy; for example, the vast and important topic of economic incentives, such as taxes and subsidies, will be touched on only briefly in Sections 5.3 and 6.7.

Section 1.2

Pigou's example and Braess's Paradox first appeared in Pigou [320] and Braess [64], respectively. Murchland [285] was the first to describe Braess's Paradox in English. The quantitative details in Section 1.2, such as the network cost functions, are somewhat different than in Pigou's and Braess's original formulations. They are taken from Roughgarden and Tardos [348] and L. Schulman (personal communication, October 1999), respectively. Chapter 5 studies Braess's Paradox in depth.

The first moral of Section 1.2, that selfish behavior need not yield a socially optimal outcome, is arguably as old as economics itself. In the language of economics, this moral states that a selfish outcome can be *Pareto inefficient*—there can be a different outcome in which someone is better off while no one is worse off. Perhaps the most canonical example in game theory of the Pareto inefficiency of selfish behavior is the *Prisoner's Dilemma*. In the Prisoner's Dilemma, two prisoners have been captured and are to be interrogated separately by the authorities. Each prisoner has to plead guilty or not guilty to the charges and is aware of the following possible outcomes. If both prisoners plead not guilty, the authorities lack sufficient evidence to convict them, and they will both go free. If both plead guilty, then both receive moderate jail terms. If exactly one of them pleads guilty, then the confessor is set free and given a reward for the information, while the other prisoner is given a draconian jail sentence. If the prisoners could coordinate, they would both plead not guilty. In the absence of cooperation, however, the incentives are clear: each prisoner is strictly better off by confessing, no matter what the other prisoner says. We therefore expect selfish behavior to result in both prisoners confessing and serving time. As in Braess's Paradox, everyone suffers in the selfish outcome, relative to what can be achieved with cooperation. For more on the Prisoner's Dilemma and its history, see Raiffa [325] and the book by Rapoport and Chammah [326]. For further discussion of the Pareto inefficiency of selfish behavior, see Dubey [128] or Cohen [81].

Analogues of the second moral of Section 1.2 are also known in many different contexts; some of these are surveyed in Section 5.4.

Section 1.3

Selfish routing was originally introduced to model transportation networks, and Chapter 2 discusses this history in detail. Its application to computer networks, with both source and distributed routing, is somewhat more recent. Cantor and Gerla [72], Gallager [170], and Stern [375] are good early references on the topic. Bertsekas and Tsitsiklis [51]—especially Sections 3.5, 5.6, and 7.6—is a nice textbook treatment. Both [72] and [51], and more recently Friedman [164], give details on the equivalence between selfish and shortest-path routing discussed in Section 1.3.

Most networking textbooks contain far more details about the nuts and bolts of implementing a distributed routing protocol than are included in Section 1.3. Examples include Bertsekas and Gallagher [50], Keshav [224], Peterson and Davie [318], and Walrand [393].

The mechanical and electrical network examples of Section 1.3.3 were first given by Cohen and Horowitz [82]. Other connections between traffic equilibria and these physical networks were discussed earlier by Duffin [129] and Enke [134]. Penchina and Penchina [314] offer advice on realizing the strings and springs system of Figure 1.3.

Just as the applications of Sections 1.3.1–1.3.3 are intended to demonstrate that selfish routing is a useful and flexible mathematical model, the caveats of Section 1.3.4 are meant as a caution against overzealous interpretations of the results of this book. For example, despite the connotations of a recent *New York Times* article [26], there is no easy way to translate the theoretical work of this book into a better Internet. Nonetheless, the techniques described in this book should find use as a tool to analyze congestion-sensitive routing in a variety of network applications.

The first caveat of Section 1.3.4 is that the selfish routing model studied in this book assumes convergence to an equilibrium; the example shown in Figure 1.4 is essentially due to Friedman (see [26]). This issue is reasonably well understood for transportation networks. First, there are numerous more general models of selfish routing that explicitly account for dynamics; some of these are surveyed in Section 2.8. Second, convergence to the static equilibrium in such networks has been verified both experimentally and theoretically. See [146, 156, 165, 251, 262, 291, 368, 405], for example, for further details.

Khanna and Zinky [226] and the references therein describe how delay-based distributed routing was implemented in the early Internet, and discuss how these implementations can fail to converge to an equilibrium. See also Keshav [224, §11.7]. On the other hand, careful implementations can be proven to converge in networks that are not too volatile. See, for example, Bertsekas and Tsitsiklis [51] and the related research papers by Tsitsiklis and Bertsekas [385] and Tsai, Tsitsiklis, and Bertsekas [384]. Other ways to improve the stability of congestion-sensitive shortest-path routing are given by, among others, Khanna and Zinky [226] and Chen, Druschel, and Subramanian [76].

Savage et al. [352] describe experiments that demonstrate the inefficiency of current (congestion-insensitive) Internet routing and discuss some possible alternatives. The potential benefits of congestion-sensitive routing in the Internet are also mentioned in many other papers, including in [76, 226].

Worst-case analysis has long been central to theoretical computer science, dating back to an early obsession with the worst-case running time of computer algorithms (see e.g. [4]). For further discussion of its merits and drawbacks see, for example, Aho, Hopcroft, and Ullman [4], Ahuja, Magnanti, and Orlin [5], or Kozen [240]. Chapters 5 and 6 of this book consider approximation algorithms, which exemplify another type of worst-case analysis.

Prerequisites

The following are some favorite references for the topics that Section 1.4.1 discusses. The few facts from calculus and analysis used here are covered in Mardsen and Hoffman [268], Rudin [350], and Spivak [371]. Hillier and Lieberman [193] and Peressini, Sullivan, and Uhl [316] provide elementary introductions to mathematical programming. Garey and Johnson [172] and Papadimitriou [302] are good references for NP-completeness. Ahuja, Magnanti, and Orlin [5], Cook et al. [90], Papadimitriou and Steiglitz [306], and Tarjan [380] are among the many excellent texts on combinatorial optimization and network flow. Lastly, standard introductions to game theory include Fudenberg and Tirole [166], Mas-Colell, Whinston, and Green [270], Osbourne and Rubinstein [300], and Owen [301]. Also, Straffin [377] is good for a quicker, less technical introduction to game theory.

2 Preliminaries

This chapter presents the basic definitions and preliminary technical results needed in the rest of the book. Section 2.1 formally defines the traffic model discussed in Chapter 1. Section 2.2 defines flows at Nash equilibrium and proves some of their basic properties. Section 2.3 formally defines the price of anarchy. Section 2.4 gives a useful characterization of optimal flows. In Section 2.5, several concrete examples illustrate the definitions and propositions of Sections 2.1–2.4. Section 2.6 builds on the results of Section 2.4 to prove the existence and essential uniqueness of flows at Nash equilibrium. Section 2.7 proves several properties of flows at Nash equilibrium in networks where all traffic shares the same source and destination.

Different portions of the book depend on different subsets of this chapter. In particular, only the first three sections are essential for the rest of the book. On the first reading, the following strategy is recommended: read enough of this chapter to understand the examples in Section 2.5, then move on and return to this chapter only on a need-to-know basis. Table 2.1 summarizes how other chapters depend on this one.

2.1 The Model

All of the definitions and notation required to formally discuss networks are included in this section. Characteristic of graph theory, it includes a bewildering array of words to describe near-trivial concepts. Resist getting bogged down in formalities, and instead use this section mainly as a reference.

We will model a traffic network with a directed graph $G = (V, E)$, with a finite set V of *vertices* V and a finite set E of (directed) *edges* E. An edge is an ordered pair of distinct vertices, directed from the first vertex, the *tail*, to the second vertex, the *head*. As in Pigou's example (Section 1.2.1), we will allow parallel edges—distinct edges with the same head and tail. We will sometimes refer to vertices as *nodes* and to edges as *links*.

Several vertices $s_1, \ldots, s_k$ are deemed *sources*—vertices from which traffic emanates. All traffic embarking from the source vertex s_i intends to travel to the corresponding *destination* or *sink* vertex t_i. We will often refer to a source-destination pair $\{s_i, t_i\}$ as *commodity i*. Two commodities can share vertices, but there will be no loss of generality in assuming that no two commodities share both the same source and the same destination. We will call a graph with one or more source-destination pairs a *network*. A network is *single-commodity* if it is assumed to have

Table 2.1
How other chapters depend on Chapter 2.

Section	Prerequisite for...
2.1–2.3	everything
2.4	Sections 2.5–2.6, 3.2, 3.5, 4.2, 4.4
2.5	none
2.6	everything/Section 4.5
2.7	Sections 4.7 and 5.2

Section 2.5 is not logically necessary for what follows, but the examples described in it show up frequently in later chapters. The proof techniques of Section 2.6 are needed only in Section 4.5, but the results of the section will be assumed in the rest of the book.

one source-destination pair, and *multicommodity* otherwise. We will abuse notation and denote both graphs and networks by G.

A "path" is a route from one vertex to another that does not circle back on itself. For a more formal definition, first call a *walk* a sequence of edges in which the tail of each edge after the first coincides with the head of the previous edge. A walk is *closed* if it begins and ends at the same vertex. A closed walk is a *cycle* if no vertex belongs to more than two of its edges. A *path* is then a walk that contains no cycles.

By a *u-v path*, we mean a path that begins at the vertex u and terminates at the vertex v. For a network G, we denote the set of s_i-t_i paths by $\mathcal{P}_i$, and define $\mathcal{P} = \cup_i \mathcal{P}_i$. To avoid trivialities, we will always assume that $\mathcal{P}_i \neq \emptyset$ for every i. A *flow* is a nonnegative real vector, indexed by $\mathcal{P}$. We interpret a flow f as the aggregated routes chosen by a large number of individuals or *agents*, with f_P measuring the amount of agents that use the route P. Note that each individual is assumed to control only a negligible fraction of the overall traffic. The assumption is relaxed in Section 4.4.

A flow f induces a *flow on edges* $\{f_e\}_{e \in E}$, where $f_e = \sum_{P \in \mathcal{P}: e \in P} f_P$ is the amount of flow using paths that include edge e. If a flow f induces the flow on edges $\{f_e\}_{e \in E}$, we will sometimes call the flow f a *path decomposition* of $\{f_e\}_{e \in E}$. A flow induces a unique flow on edges, but a flow on edges can admit many different path decompositions; see Section 2.7 for more details.

We associate a finite and positive *traffic rate* r_i with each pair $\{s_i, t_i\}$, the amount of flow that needs to travel from the source s_i to the destination t_i. With respect to a network and a set r of traffic rates, a flow f is *feasible* if for all i,

$$\sum_{P \in \mathcal{P}_i} f_P = r_i.$$

Finally, we are interested in networks in which each edge $e \in E$ has a *cost*, which can depend on the amount of flow on the edge. We will denote the cost function of edge e by $c_e(\cdot)$. For each edge $e \in E$, we will assume that the cost function c_e is nonnegative, continuous, and nondecreasing. An *instance* is a triple of the form (G, r, c), where G is a network, and r and c are vectors of traffic rates and cost functions, respectively.

In the examples in Chapter 1, we implicitly assumed that the sum of all traffic rates is 1, and explicitly defined cost functions in terms of the *fraction* of the traffic using an edge. At several points in this book, we will find occasion to vary the traffic rates in a network while keeping the cost functions fixed. For this reason, allowing arbitrary traffic rates and defining cost functions in terms of the *amount* of traffic on an edge are more convenient. These two perspectives differ only by a change in the units used to measure traffic rates.

The *cost of a path P with respect to a flow f* is defined as the sum of the cost of the edges in the path, denoted by

$$c_P(f) = \sum_{e \in P} c_e(f_e). \tag{2.1}$$

We define the *cost $C(f)$* of a flow f in an instance (G, r, c) as the sum of all costs incurred by the traffic:

$$C(f) = \sum_{P \in \mathcal{P}} c_P(f) f_P. \tag{2.2}$$

By summing over the edges in a path P and reversing the order of summation, we can rewrite the right-side of (2.2) as follows:

$$\sum_{P \in \mathcal{P}} c_P(f) f_P = \sum_{P \in \mathcal{P}} \left(\sum_{e \in P} c_e(f_e) \right) f_P = \sum_{e \in E} \left(\sum_{P \in \mathcal{P} : e \in P} f_P \right) c_e(f_e) = \sum_{e \in E} c_e(f_e) f_e.$$

We therefore have an alternative definition of the cost of a flow f in an instance (G, r, c):

$$C(f) = \sum_{e \in E} c_e(f_e) f_e. \tag{2.3}$$

The cost of a flow differs from the *average* cost of traffic by a multiplicative factor equal to the sum $\sum_i r_i$ of all traffic rates. Again, we will usually work with the (total) cost because it is the more convenient quantity when increasing or decreasing the traffic rates of a network.

Now that we have settled on an objective function, which allows us to deem one flow superior to another, our aspirations are clear. Specifically, a flow feasible for an instance (G, r, c) is *optimal* if it minimizes $C(f)$ over the set of feasible flows. Such a flow must exist, as the space of all feasible flows is a closed and bounded subset of Euclidean space and the cost $C(\cdot)$ is a continuous function.

2.2   Flows at Nash Equilibrium

This section formulates a notion of an equilibrium. Intuitively, a flow should fail to be at equilibrium if some traffic can decrease its cost by switching paths, and it should be at equilibrium otherwise. For example, in Pigou's example (Section 1.2.1), the flow in which half of the traffic is routed on each of the two paths should not be at equilibrium because if a small amount of traffic switched from the upper path to the lower path, then the cost incurred by this traffic would decrease. On the other hand, if all traffic is routed on the lower path, then no traffic can benefit by switching to the upper path, and hence the flow should be at equilibrium.

The definition of an equilibrium simply formalizes these ideas. Specifically, a flow is an equilibrium if and only if whenever traffic switches paths, the cost incurred by that traffic can only increase. Since we are assuming that all network users control a negligible fraction of the overall traffic, the amount of traffic that switches paths can be arbitrarily small.

Definition 2.2.1 A flow f feasible for the instance (G, r, c) is at *Nash equilibrium*, or is a *Nash flow*, if for all commodities $i \in \{1, \ldots, k\}$, s_i-t_i paths $P_1, P_2 \in \mathcal{P}_i$ with $f_{P_1} > 0$, and all amounts $\delta \in (0, f_{P_1}]$ of traffic on P_1,

$$c_{P_1}(f) \leq c_{P_2}(\tilde{f}),$$

where the flow $\tilde{f}$ is obtained from f by moving δ units of flow from the path P_1 to the path P_2:

$$\tilde{f}_P = \begin{cases} f_P - \delta & \text{if } P = P_1 \\ f_P + \delta & \text{if } P = P_2 \\ f_P & \text{if } P \notin \{P_1, P_2\}. \end{cases}$$

Letting δ tend to 0, continuity and monotonicity of the edge cost functions give the following useful characterization of a flow at Nash equilibrium. The straightforward proof is left to the reader.

Proposition 2.2.2 *A flow f feasible for the instance (G, r, c) is at Nash equilib-*

rium if and only if for every $i \in \{1, \ldots, k\}$ and $P_1, P_2 \in \mathcal{P}_i$ with $f_{P_1} > 0$,

$$c_{P_1}(f) \leq c_{P_2}(f). \tag{2.4}$$

Briefly, Proposition 2.2.2 states that, in a flow at Nash equilibrium, all flow travels on minimum-cost paths. In particular, if f is at Nash equilibrium then all s_i-t_i flow paths—s_i-t_i paths to which f assigns a positive amount of flow—have equal cost.

Corollary 2.2.3 *If f is a flow at Nash equilibrium for (G, r, c), then for each commodity i, all s_i-t_i flow paths of f have a common cost $c_i(f)$.*

We can then use equation (2.2) to express the cost $C(f)$ of a flow f at Nash equilibrium in a particularly nice form.

Proposition 2.2.4 *Let f be a flow at Nash equilibrium for the instance (G, r, c). Let all s_i-t_i flow paths of f have common cost $c_i(f)$. Then,*

$$C(f) = \sum_{i=1}^{k} c_i(f) r_i.$$

This section concludes with two fundamental facts about Nash flows: existence and uniqueness.

Proposition 2.2.5 *Every instance (G, r, c) admits a Nash flow.*

While an instance can admit more than one Nash flow (see Remark 2.6.5), the next proposition states that all Nash flows of an instance have the same cost. Since we are only concerned with the cost of flows, Nash flows are therefore "essentially unique" in that we can view all Nash flows as equivalent.

Proposition 2.2.6 *If f and $\tilde{f}$ are flows at Nash equilibrium for the instance (G, r, c), then $C(f) = C(\tilde{f})$.*

Proofs of Propositions 2.2.5 and 2.2.6 are given in Section 2.6.

2.3   The Price of Anarchy

As mentioned in Chapter 1, the price of anarchy is the worst-possible ratio between the cost of a flow at Nash equilibrium and that of an optimal flow. A formal definition follows.

Definition 2.3.1

(a) Let (G, r, c) be an instance admitting an optimal flow f^* and a flow at Nash equilibrium f. The *price of anarchy* of (G, r, c), denoted $\rho(G, r, c)$, is defined as the ratio

$$\rho(G, r, c) = \frac{C(f)}{C(f^*)}.$$

(b) If $\mathcal{I}$ is a set of instances, then the *price of anarchy* of $\mathcal{I}$ is

$$\rho(\mathcal{I}) = \sup_{(G, r, c) \in \mathcal{I}} \rho(G, r, c).$$

Since all Nash flows of an instance have equal cost (Proposition 2.2.6), the ratio $\rho(G, r, c)$ of Definition 2.3.1(a) is well defined provided $C(f^*) > 0$. If f^* is a flow with zero cost, then $c_P(f^*) = 0$ whenever $f_P^* > 0$, and Proposition 2.2.2 implies that f^* is also at Nash equilibrium. In this case, we define $\rho(G, r, c)$ to be 1.

The price of anarchy can be defined much more generally; indeed, the concept makes sense for every application possessing an objective function and a notion of equilibrium. One subtlety in extending Definition 2.3.1 to a more general setting is that Proposition 2.2.6—stating that all equilibria have equal objective function value—fails in many applications, including in some of the variants of selfish routing studied in Chapter 4. In such contexts, the price of anarchy is traditionally defined as the ratio between the objective function value of the *worst* equilibrium and that of an optimal solution. See Section 2.8 for more details.

2.4   A Characterization of Optimal Flows

We now investigate the properties of optimal flows—flows with minimum-possible cost. The first half of this section assumes that the reader has some understanding of basic mathematical programming. On the other hand, the most important concepts in this section—the statements of Definitions 2.4.2 and 2.4.5, and Corollary 2.4.6— do not require this background.

This section assumes for simplicity that cost functions are continuously differentiable, though analogues of the following results also hold under weaker assumptions.

By the second definition (2.3) of the cost of a flow, we can model the problem of finding an optimal feasible flow for the instance (G, r, c) as the nonlinear program

$$\text{Min} \quad \sum_{e \in E} h_e(f_e)$$

subject to:

(NLP)

$$\sum_{P \in \mathcal{P}_i} f_P = r_i \qquad \forall i \in \{1, \dots, k\}$$

$$f_e = \sum_{P \in \mathcal{P}: e \in P} f_P \qquad \forall e \in E$$

$$f_P \geq 0 \qquad \forall P \in \mathcal{P},$$

with $h_e(f_e) = c_e(f_e)f_e$. In this formulation, we are identifying a flow feasible for (G, r, c) with a point in $(|\mathcal{P}| + |E|)$-dimensional Euclidean space in the obvious way. Since flows and such points enjoy a natural bijective correspondence, the rest of this section does not make any distinction between them.

Following standard mathematical programming terminology, we will call the function $\sum_e h_e(f_e)$ the *objective function* of (NLP). Similarly, we will call the points in Euclidean space that satisfy all of the constraints of (NLP) the *feasible region* of (NLP).

Remark 2.4.1 Readers sensitive to computational complexity issues will note that we have formulated the problem of finding an optimal flow via a nonlinear program in which the number of variables can be exponential in the size of the instance (G, r, c). It is straightforward to give an equivalent compact formulation that requires only polynomially many variables and constraints.

Next, we will characterize the optima of (NLP). This task will be relatively painless if we impose a little bit of convexity on the nonlinear program (NLP). To make this precise, we need some definitions. In what follows, $\mathcal{R}$ and $\mathcal{R}^+$ denote the reals and the nonnegative reals, respectively.

Definition 2.4.2

(a) If x and y are two points in the Euclidean space $\mathcal{R}^n$, then a *convex combination* of x and y is a point on the line segment between x and y—a point of the form $\lambda x + (1 - \lambda)y$ for some $\lambda \in [0, 1]$.

(b) A subset S of $\mathcal{R}^n$ is *convex* if it contains all of its convex combinations: whenever

x, y lie in S, so does $\lambda x + (1 - \lambda)y$ for all $\lambda \in [0, 1]$.

(c) A function $h : S \to \mathcal{R}$ defined on a convex subset S of Euclidean space is *convex* if all line segments between two points on h's graph lie above the graph:

$$h(\lambda x + (1 - \lambda)y) \leq \lambda h(x) + (1 - \lambda)h(y) \qquad (2.5)$$

for all $x, y \in S$ and $\lambda \in [0, 1]$.

(d) A function $c : \mathcal{R}^+ \to \mathcal{R}^+$ is *semiconvex* if the function $x \cdot c(x)$ is convex.

Parts (a)–(c) of Definition 2.4.2 are utterly standard. Part (d) is not a standard definition but is ideally suited for many results in this book. Examples of convex sets include balls and boxes. The corresponding surfaces, spheres and cubes, are not convex. Every twice differentiable function with a nonnegative second derivative is convex, so examples of convex functions on the real line include polynomials with nonnegative coefficients, and the exponential function e^x.

For the rest of this section, we will assume that our cost functions are semiconvex. Under this assumption, the cost $C(\cdot)$ is a convex function in the sense of Definition 2.4.2(c). Also, the feasible region of (NLP) is an intersection of halfspaces and is therefore convex. The nonlinear program (NLP) is thus a *convex program* when all cost functions are semiconvex.

Remark 2.4.3 Since we assume that cost functions are nondecreasing, semiconvexity is a strictly weaker assumption than convexity. For example, the function $\ln(1 + x)$, where ln denotes the natural logarithm, is semiconvex on $\mathcal{R}^+$ but is not convex. Semiconvex, or even convex, cost functions suffice to model most applications of interest, including delays in congested networks. The most notable example of a nondecreasing, continuous function that is not semiconvex is a continuous approximation of a step function.

Next is an important characterization of the optima of (NLP) when the objective function is continuously differentiable and convex. In the statement of this characterization, we will use h'_e to denote the derivative $\frac{d}{dx}h_e(x)$ of h_e and $h'_P(f)$ to mean $\sum_{e \in P} h'_e(f_e)$.

Proposition 2.4.4 *Let f^* be a feasible solution to a nonlinear program of the form (NLP) in which every function h_e is continuously differentiable and convex. Then, the following are equivalent.*

(a) The flow f^* is optimal.

(b) For every $i \in \{1, \ldots, k\}$ and $P_1, P_2 \in \mathcal{P}_i$ with $f_{P_1}^* > 0$,

$$h'_{P_1}(f^*) \leq h'_{P_2}(f^*).$$

(c) For every feasible flow f,

$$\sum_{P \in \mathcal{P}} h'_P(f^*) f_P^* \leq \sum_{P \in \mathcal{P}} h'_P(f^*) f_P.$$

(d) For every feasible flow f,

$$\sum_{e \in E} h'_e(f_e^*) f_e^* \leq \sum_{e \in E} h'_e(f_e^*) f_e.$$

Proof: Statements (c) and (d) are equivalent by the same reversal of summations that established the equivalence of the two definitions of cost, (2.2) and (2.3). To see that statements (b) and (c) are equivalent, define the function H by

$$H(f) = \sum_{P \in \mathcal{P}} h'_P(f^*) f_P.$$

Since f^* is fixed, $H(f)$ is effectively the cost of the flow f where the cost of each path P is the congestion-independent constant $h'_P(f^*)$. It should be clear that H is minimized by precisely the feasible flows that route, for each i, all the flow of commodity i on s_i-t_i paths that minimize $h'_P(f^*)$ over all such paths. Thus, $H(f^*)$ minimizes H over all feasible flows, and hence meets condition (c), if and only if condition (b) holds.

We will finish the proof by showing that property (a) implies property (b) and that property (d) implies property (a). To prove the first implication, suppose f^* is an optimal flow, and consider an s_i-t_i path $P_1 \in \mathcal{P}_i$ with $f_{P_1}^* > 0$ and another s_i-t_i path $P_2 \in \mathcal{P}_i$. Since every function h_e is assumed continuously differentiable, transferring a small $\lambda \in (0, f_{P_1}^*]$ amount of flow from P_1 to P_2 yields a feasible flow with objective function value equal to

$$\sum_{e \in E} h_e(f_e^*) + \lambda \left[\sum_{e \in P_2} h'_e(f_e^*) - \sum_{e \in P_1} h'_e(f_e^*) \right] \tag{2.6}$$

plus an error term that vanishes as $\lambda \downarrow 0$. This objective function value cannot be smaller than that of the optimal flow f^*, which is $\sum_e h_e(f_e^*)$. Once λ is sufficiently small, the estimate in (2.6) is sharp enough to imply that $h'_{P_1}(f^*)$ cannot be larger than $h'_{P_2}(f^*)$. Hence, property (b) holds.

We conclude by using the convexity assumption to prove that condition (d)

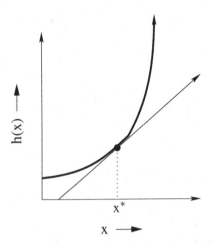

Figure 2.1
Using a linear approximation to lower bound a convex function. The thick line is the original
convex function h; the thin solid line is its linear approximation at the point x^*.

implies condition (a). Suppose that f^* satisfies property (d), and let f be a feasible
flow. Since every function h_e is convex, we can lower bound the objective function
value of f via a linear approximation of the objective function at f^* (see Figure 2.1):

$$\sum_{e \in E} h_e(f_e) \geq \sum_{e \in E} [h_e(f_e^*) + h_e'(f_e^*)(f_e - f_e^*)]$$

$$= \sum_{e \in E} h_e(f_e^*) + \sum_{e \in E} h_e'(f_e^*)(f_e - f_e^*). \qquad (2.7)$$

By assumption, f^* satisfies property (d) and hence the second term on the right-
hand side of (2.7) is nonnegative. It follows that the objective function value of f
is at least that of f^*. Since f was arbitrary, f^* is an optimal flow. ■

There is a striking similarity between Proposition 2.4.4(b), which characterizes
the optimal solutions to convex programs of the form (NLP), and Proposition 2.2.2,
which characterizes flows at Nash equilibrium. This similarity provides a useful
interpretation of an optimal flow:

optimal and Nash flows are the same thing, just with different cost functions.

To make this relationship precise, we require one further definition.

Definition 2.4.5 If c is a differentiable cost function, then the corresponding *marginal cost function* c^* is defined by

$$c^* = \frac{d}{dx}(x \cdot c(x)). \qquad (2.8)$$

Propositions 2.2.2 and 2.4.4(b) now yield the following corollary.

Corollary 2.4.6 *Let (G, r, c) be an instance with continuously differentiable, semiconvex cost functions and corresponding marginal cost functions c^*. Then, a flow f feasible for (G, r, c) is optimal if and only if it is at Nash equilibrium for the instance (G, r, c^*).*

Remark 2.4.7 Marginal cost functions have an appealing, classical economic interpretation. The defining equation (2.8) of a marginal cost function c^* implies that $c^*(x) = c(x) + x \cdot c'(x)$. If we ponder slightly increasing the amount of flow on an edge, we see that the corresponding marginal cost function c^* has one term $c(x)$ capturing the (per-unit) cost experienced by the new traffic, as well as a second term $x \cdot c'(x)$ accounting for the (per-unit) increased cost incurred by existing traffic due to the additional congestion. Essentially, the only difference between an optimal flow and a flow at Nash equilibrium is that the former accounts for this conscientious second term while the latter disregards it.

Remark 2.4.8 We will typically denote an optimal flow for an instance by f^*. The marginal cost functions are denoted by c^* since they are "optimal cost functions" in a sense made precise by Corollary 2.4.6: the optimal flow f^* arises as a flow at Nash equilibrium with respect to the cost functions c^*.

This section concludes with two facts about computing optimal flows. The first fact, which will be useful in Chapter 6, notes that since (NLP) is a convex program when all edge cost functions are semiconvex, an optimal flow of such an instance can be found efficiently.

Fact 2.4.9 *If (G, r, c) is an instance with semiconvex cost functions, then an optimal flow for (G, r, c) can be computed, up to an arbitrarily small error term, in time polynomial in the size of the instance and the number of bits of precision required.*

Fact 2.4.9 follows from existing polynomial-time algorithms for convex programming. A further discussion of this point, together with relevant references, is in the chapter notes (Section 2.8).

Remark 2.4.10 The term "polynomial-time algorithm" means that the running time of the algorithm is bounded by a polynomial function of the input size. We are using this term imprecisely because we have not specified how an instance (G, r, c) should be encoded for input to a (mathematical model of a) computer, and have therefore not formally defined the size of an instance. While a careful discussion of this issue is outside the scope of this book, there are several reasonable ways to make such encodings precise, and Section 2.8 lists several references on the topic.

Remark 2.4.11 The additive error term in Fact 2.4.9 arises because existing algorithms for solving convex programs output a rational solution, while an exact description of an optimal flow can require irrational numbers.

The final fact of this section implies that the semiconvexity assumption in Fact 2.4.9 cannot be completely removed, assuming that $P \neq NP$.

Fact 2.4.12 *If $P \neq NP$, then there is no algorithm for computing an approximation of an optimal flow in arbitrary instances (G, r, c) that always runs in time polynomial in the size of the instance and in the number of bits of precision in the approximation.*

Fact 2.4.12 remains true even in networks of parallel links.

2.5   Examples

This section illustrates the definitions and propositions of the previous sections with several concrete examples, with the goal of developing our intuition about Nash and optimal flows. We first return to the familiar examples of Section 1.2—Pigou's example and Braess's Paradox—and then present three more examples that demonstrate further differences between Nash and optimal flows, as well as a multicommodity extension of Braess's Paradox.

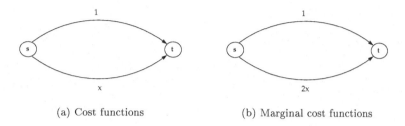

(a) Cost functions   (b) Marginal cost functions

Figure 2.2
Pigou's example revisited (Example 2.5.1).

Example 2.5.1 (Pigou's Example) Recall that, in Pigou's example of Section 1.2.1, we have a network with two nodes s and t, two parallel edges with cost functions $c(x) = 1$ and $c(x) = x$, and a traffic rate of 1 (see Figure 2.2(a)). Note that these cost functions are semiconvex in the sense of Definition 2.4.2(d).

Routing all flow on the bottom link equalizes the costs of the two available s-t paths at 1, and thus by Proposition 2.2.2 provides a flow f at Nash equilibrium. By Proposition 2.2.4, or directly by equations (2.2) or (2.3), the cost $C(f)$ of f is 1.

Next, the marginal cost functions of the network are $c^*(x) = 1$ and $c^*(x) = 2x$ (see Figure 2.2(b)). Routing half of the traffic on each link thus equalizes the marginal costs of the two s-t paths at 1, and so by Corollary 2.4.6 furnishes an optimal flow f^*. By (2.2) or (2.3), the cost of f^* is

$$C(f^*) = \frac{1}{2} \cdot \frac{1}{2} + \frac{1}{2} \cdot 1 = \frac{3}{4}.$$

The price of anarchy in Pigou's example is therefore 4/3.

Example 2.5.2 (Braess's Paradox) Next we consider the network of Braess's Paradox after the addition of the zero-cost edge (see Figure 2.3(a)). Setting the traffic rate r to 1, we see that the flow f that routes all traffic on the path $s \to v \to w \to t$ equalizes the cost of the three s-t paths at 2, and thus, by Proposition 2.2.2, f is at Nash equilibrium with cost $C(f) = 2$. Switching to marginal cost functions, shown in Figure 2.3(b), we find that the flow f^* that routes half the traffic on each of the paths $s \to v \to t$ and $s \to w \to t$ equalizes the marginal costs of the three s-t paths at 2, and is therefore, by Corollary 2.4.6, optimal. The cost $C(f^*)$ of f^* is 3/2, and the price of anarchy is again 4/3.

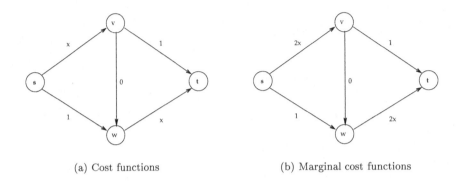

(a) Cost functions   (b) Marginal cost functions

Figure 2.3
Braess's Paradox revisited (Example 2.5.2).

Section 1.2.2 noted that Braess's Paradox demonstrates two different principles. First, all traffic may strictly prefer a coordinated outcome to the flow at Nash equilibrium. In economic language, we would say that the Nash flow is *strictly Pareto-dominated* by the optimal flow. Second, if network users route selfishly, then augmenting a network with an additional link may strictly increase everyone's cost. The second phenomenon implies the first in the augmented network, since by coordinating additional links can always be ignored. The converse, however, is not true. In the next example, the flow at Nash equilibrium is strictly Pareto-dominated by another flow and yet cannot be improved by the deletion of any number of network links.

Example 2.5.3 (Strict Pareto Suboptimality) We will consider the network shown in Figure 2.4, which is two copies of the network of Pigou's example glued together in series. Setting the traffic rate r to be 1, the flow f that routes all traffic along the two bottom links equalizes the cost of all four s-t paths at 2 and is thus at Nash equilibrium. There is an optimal flow f^* that routes half of the traffic on the path comprising the top link of the first subnetwork and the bottom link of second subnetwork, and the rest of the traffic on the path comprising the other two links. In the flow f^*, all traffic experiences only $3/2$ units of cost. All traffic is thus better off in the flow f^* than in the Nash flow f. Moreover, it is easy to check that there is no subset of the links whose removal improves the Nash flow.

Example 2.5.3 plays an important role in Section 4.7.

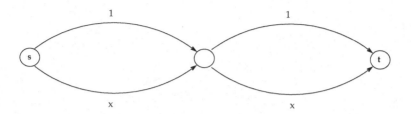

Figure 2.4
The Nash flow can be strictly Pareto-dominated by the optimal flow in the absence of Braess's Paradox (Example 2.5.3).

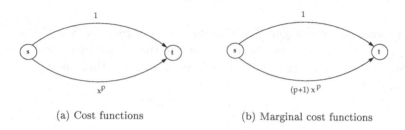

(a) Cost functions   (b) Marginal cost functions

Figure 2.5
A nonlinear version of Pigou's example (Example 2.5.4).

The price of anarchy in Examples 2.5.1–2.5.3 is 4/3. This is not entirely a coincidence, as in the next chapter we will see that the price of anarchy is at most 4/3 in every multicommodity flow network in which the cost of every edge increases linearly with the edge congestion, like in the previous three examples. We now show that this strong hypothesis on the network cost functions is necessary for such a strong upper bound on the inefficiency of Nash flows, as such flows can be arbitrarily more costly than optimal flows in networks with nonlinear edge cost functions.

Example 2.5.4 (Nonlinear Pigou's Example) Consider modifying Pigou's example by replacing the linear cost function $c(x) = x$ by the highly nonlinear one $c(x) = x^p$, with p large (see Figure 2.5(a)). With the usual traffic rate of 1, the Nash flow f is the same as in Pigou's example: for every choice of p, all flow is routed on the bottom link and incurs one unit of cost. On the other hand, the discrepancy between the cost functions, shown in Figure 2.5(a), and the marginal

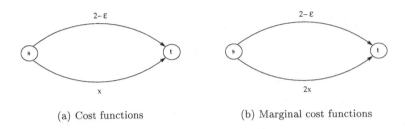

(a) Cost functions   (b) Marginal cost functions

Figure 2.6
The optimal flow may sacrifice some traffic to a path with large cost to minimize the total cost (Example 2.5.5).

cost functions, shown in Figure 2.5(b), is now much larger. The flow f^* that routes $(p+1)^{-1/p}$ units of traffic on the lower link and the remainder on the upper link equalizes the marginal costs of the two links at 1 and is thus optimal. The cost $C(f^*)$ of f^* is

$$1 - p \cdot (p+1)^{-(p+1)/p},$$

which tends to 0 as $p \to \infty$. Thus, if arbitrary cost functions are allowed, the price of anarchy of selfish routing can be arbitrarily large. This negative result motivates restricting the allowable edge cost functions (Sections 3.2–3.5), seeking different types of bounds (Sections 3.6 and 4.6), and ways of using modest centralized control to improve the prince of anarchy (Part III).

In Examples 2.5.1–2.5.4, the optimal flow has been superior to the Nash flow in a strong sense. The optimal flows in these examples, rather than merely achieving a smaller cost than a Nash flow, have the property that *all* traffic is at least as well off as in the flow at Nash equilibrium. We can attribute this run of luck only to our good fortune, and not to anything deeper at work. In particular, the next example shows that an optimal flow can sacrifice some traffic to paths with large cost in order to minimize the overall cost experienced by traffic.

Example 2.5.5 (Unfairness of Optimal Flows) Consider the minor variation on Pigou's example shown in Figure 2.6(a), where the cost function $c(x) = 1$ is replaced with the cost function $c(x) = 2 - \epsilon$ for a small positive constant $\epsilon > 0$. As usual, we set the traffic rate r to 1. In the flow at Nash equilibrium, all traffic is routed on the bottom link and experiences one unit of cost. In the optimal flow,

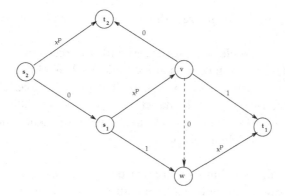

Figure 2.7
In a multicommodity network, adding a new edge can increase the cost of some traffic by an
arbitrarily large amount (Example 2.5.6).

however, only $1 - \epsilon/2$ units of flow are routed on the bottom link—routing the
other $\epsilon/2$ units of traffic on the upper link equalizes the marginal costs of the two
edges at $2 - \epsilon$. Intuitively, a small fraction of the traffic is sacrificed to the slow edge
in order to (slightly) reduce the cost experienced by the overwhelming majority of
network users.

We will briefly study Example 2.5.5 in Section 4.7.

Examples 2.5.1–2.5.5 are all single-commodity instances, in which all traffic
shares the same source and destination. We will also be concerned with multicommodity networks. For the most part, our bounds on the price of anarchy in Part II of
this book will not depend on the number of commodities of an instance. In Part III,
by contrast, we will see that reducing the price of anarchy with limited centralized control is usually a fundamentally more difficult problem in multicommodity
networks than in single-commodity networks. The final example of this section, a
multicommodity variant of Braess's Paradox, foreshadows this dichotomy.

Example 2.5.6 (Multicommodity Braess's Paradox) Consider the two-commodity network shown in Figure 2.7. Set both traffic rates to 1 and let the cost
functions be as shown. Consider first the network with the edge (v, w) absent.
In the Nash flow, the first commodity routes one third of its traffic on the path
$s_1 \to v \to t_1$ and the rest on the path $s_1 \to w \to t_1$. The second commodity routes
one third of its traffic on the path $s_2 \to s_1 \to v \to t_2$ and the rest on the direct
(s_2, t_2) link. Traffic of the first and second commodity experience cost $1 + (2/3)^p$

and $(2/3)^p$, respectively. For p large, these two costs are arbitrarily close to 1 and 0, respectively.

Now suppose we include the edge (v, w) with the cost function $c(x) = 0$ into the network. In the new Nash flow, as in Example 2.5.2, all of the first commodity's traffic travels on the path $s_1 \to v \to w \to t_1$. This in turn forces all of the second commodity's traffic to resort to the direct (s_2, t_2) link. All traffic incurs cost 1 in this Nash flow. In particular, traffic of the second commodity incurs arbitrarily more cost than in the original network as $p \to \infty$.

Chapter 5 studies Braess's Paradox in great detail. Among other things, it proves that in a fixed network with only one commodity, adding edges cannot increase the cost of traffic by an unbounded amount.

2.6   Existence and Uniqueness of Nash Flows

In this section, we exploit the similarity between the characterizations of Nash and optimal flows—Propositions 2.2.2 and 2.4.4(b)—to establish the existence and essential uniqueness of flows at Nash equilibrium.

We begin with a proposition that will enable us to harness the full power of Section 2.4 to study flows at Nash equilibrium.

Proposition 2.6.1 *Let (G, r, c) be an instance. Then, the nonlinear program*

$$Min \quad \sum_{e \in E} h_e(f_e)$$

subject to:

(CP)

$$\sum_{P \in \mathcal{P}_i} f_P = r_i \qquad\qquad \forall i \in \{1, \ldots, k\}$$

$$f_e = \sum_{P \in \mathcal{P}: e \in P} f_P \qquad\qquad \forall e \in E$$

$$f_P \geq 0 \qquad\qquad \forall P \in \mathcal{P},$$

where $h_e(x) = \int_0^x c_e(t)dt$, is convex. Moreover, the Nash flows of (G, r, c) are precisely the optima of (CP).

As in Section 2.4, we are not distinguishing a flow from the point in $(|\mathcal{P}| + |E|)$-dimensional Euclidean space that it naturally induces.

Proof: By definition, the derivative of h_e is the continuous, nondecreasing function c_e. Therefore, each h_e is a convex function, and (CP) is a convex program. Propositions 2.2.2 and 2.4.4(b) then imply that a feasible solution to (CP) is optimal if and only if it is a Nash flow for (G, r, c). ∎

Existence of Nash flows now follows immediately.

Proof of Proposition 2.2.5: The convex program (CP) has a continuous objective function and a closed, bounded feasible region, and therefore admits an optimal solution. The proposition then follows from Proposition 2.6.1. ∎

We next consider the uniqueness of Nash flows.

Corollary 2.6.2 *If f and $\tilde{f}$ are Nash flows for (G, r, c), then $c_e(f_e) = c_e(\tilde{f}_e)$ for every edge e.*

Proof: Suppose that f and $\tilde{f}$ are flows at Nash equilibrium for (G, r, c), and thus global optima for the convex program (CP). Since the objective function of (CP) is convex, inequality (2.5) must hold for all convex combinations of f and $\tilde{f}$. Since f and $\tilde{f}$ are global optima for (CP) and all of their convex combinations are feasible for (CP), (2.5) must hold with equality for all of these convex combinations. Since every function h_e in (CP) is convex, this can occur only if every function h_e is linear between f_e and $\tilde{f}_e$. By the definition of h_e and continuity of the cost function c_e, it follows that every function c_e is constant between f_e and $\tilde{f}_e$. ∎

Proposition 2.2.6, which states that all Nash flows have equal cost, now follows easily.

Proof of Proposition 2.2.6: The proposition follows directly from Proposition 2.2.4 and Corollary 2.6.2. ∎

Further corollaries of Proposition 2.6.1 follow. The first states that the property of being at Nash equilibrium is a property only of the induced flow on edges, and not of the particular path decomposition.

Corollary 2.6.3 *If f is a Nash flow for (G, r, c) and $\tilde{f}$ is a feasible flow for (G, r, c) that induces the same flow on edges as f, then $\tilde{f}$ is at Nash equilibrium for (G, r, c).*

Proof: The objective function of the convex program (CP) in Proposition 2.6.1 depends only on the induced flow on edges. ∎

The next corollary sharpens the uniqueness statement of Corollary 2.6.2 for strictly increasing cost functions.

Corollary 2.6.4 *If f and $\tilde{f}$ are Nash flows for (G, r, c), then $f_e = \tilde{f}_e$ whenever c_e is strictly increasing.*

Proof: Immediate from Corollary 2.6.2. ∎

Remark 2.6.5 Corollaries 2.6.2 and 2.6.4 are in some sense the best uniqueness results possible. By considering a two-node, two-link network in which both edges have cost function $c(x) = 1$, it is easy to see that in networks with constant cost functions, different Nash flows can route differing amounts of flow on an edge. Even when all cost functions are strictly increasing, Corollary 2.6.3 shows that there can be many Nash flows (on paths). Of course, Corollary 2.6.4 proves that all such Nash flows must induce the same flow on edges.

Proposition 2.4.4 gives another alternative characterization of Nash flows, which will be useful in Sections 3.3 and 4.3.

Corollary 2.6.6 *A flow f feasible for (G, r, c) is at Nash equilibrium if and only if*

$$\sum_{e \in E} c_e(f_e) f_e \leq \sum_{e \in E} c_e(f_e) f_e^*$$

for every flow f^* feasible for (G, r, c).

Proof: Immediate from Propositions 2.4.4 and 2.6.1. ∎

Corollary 2.6.6 can also be proved directly using Proposition 2.2.2.

The final corollary of this section notes that Nash flows can be computed efficiently.

Corollary 2.6.7 *If (G, r, c) is an instance, then a Nash flow for (G, r, c) can be computed, up to an arbitrarily small error term, in time polynomial in the size of the instance and the number of bits of precision required.*

Proof: The corollary follows from Proposition 2.6.1 and the fact that the convex program (CP) can be solved in polynomial time (see Fact 2.4.9). ∎

2.7 Nash Flows in Single-Commodity Networks

In Sections 4.7 and 5.2, we will focus on the special case of single-commodity networks, where all traffic shares the same source and destination. This section proves that Nash flows in these simpler networks possess more structure than Nash flows in general networks.

Section 2.7.1 begins with a review of some classical results about network flow, and Section 2.7.2 applies these to Nash flows in single-commodity networks.

2.7.1 Classical Network Flow Theory

This section reviews several basic facts of network flow theory. While all of the results described here have analogues in multicommodity networks, this book requires them only in single-commodity networks.

Recall from Section 2.1 that a flow in a single-commodity network is by definition a nonnegative vector indexed by the s-t paths $\mathcal{P}$, and a flow f is feasible for an instance (G, r, c) if $\sum_{P \in \mathcal{P}} f_P = r$. Call a flow on edges $\{f_e\}_{e \in E}$ *feasible* for an instance (G, r, c) if it is induced by some flow (on paths) feasible for (G, r, c). The next proposition gives a partial characterization of the feasible flows on edges.

Proposition 2.7.1 *Let (G, r, c) be a single-commodity instance.*

(a) If a flow on edges $\{f_e\}_{e \in E}$ is feasible for (G, r, c), then it is a feasible solution to the following linear system:

$$\sum_{e \in \delta^+(s)} x_e - \sum_{e \in \delta^-(s)} x_e = r \tag{2.9}$$

$$\sum_{e \in \delta^+(t)} x_e - \sum_{e \in \delta^-(t)} x_e = -r \tag{2.10}$$

$$\sum_{e \in \delta^+(v)} x_e - \sum_{e \in \delta^-(v)} x_e = 0 \qquad \text{for all } v \in V \setminus \{s, t\} \tag{2.11}$$

$$x_e \geq 0 \qquad \text{for all } e \in E, \tag{2.12}$$

where $\delta^+(v)$ is the set of edges with tail v and $\delta^-(v)$ is the set of edges with head v.

(b) If $\{f_e\}_{e \in E}$ is a feasible solution to (2.9)–(2.12), then there is a feasible flow on edges $\{\tilde{f}_e\}_{e \in E}$ with $\tilde{f}_e \leq f_e$ for all edges e.

Proposition 2.7.1(a) asserts that a feasible flow on edges must be a nonnegative

vector that satisfies the *conservation constraints* (2.9)–(2.11): except at the source
and the sink, the amount of flow entering a vertex should equal the amount of
flow exiting the vertex; at the source, r more units of flow should exit than
enter; and at the sink, r more units of flow should enter than exit. This follows
from the fact that every s-t path exits but does not enter s, enters but does not
exit t, and enters and exits each vertex other than s or t the same number of
times (once or not at all). While the converse of this statement does not hold,
Proposition 2.7.1(b) gives a partial converse: every nonnegative vector satisfying
the conservation constraints is (componentwise) greater than or equal to a feasible
flow on edges. Proposition 2.7.1(b) is proved by iteratively assigning flow to s-t
paths until a feasible flow (on paths) $\tilde{f}$ is obtained. This argument is somewhat
similar to the proof of Proposition 2.7.3 below, and further details are omitted.

Next, for a single-commodity network G, an s-t *cut* of G is a subset of vertices
that includes s but excludes t. The following classical result states that, with respect
to a feasible flow, the net amount of flow crossing every s-t cut equals the traffic
rate.

Proposition 2.7.2 *If f is feasible for the single-commodity instance (G, r, c) and
S is an s-t cut of G, then*

$$\sum_{e \in \delta^+(S)} f_e - \sum_{e \in \delta^-(S)} f_e = r,$$

*where $\delta^+(S)$ is the set of edges with tail in S and head outside S, and $\delta^-(S)$ is the
set of edges with head in S and tail outside S.*

Proof: Apply Proposition 2.7.1 to the flow on edges induced by f and sum the
conservation constraints (2.9) and (2.11) for all vertices in S. ∎

A flow f in a network G is *directed acyclic* if there is no (directed) cycle of
edges in G with $f_e > 0$ for every edge e in the cycle. The next section shows that
single-commodity instances admit directed acyclic Nash flows. The proof of this
requires the following proposition.

Proposition 2.7.3 *Let f be a flow feasible for the single-commodity instance
(G, r, c). Then, there is a directed acyclic flow $\tilde{f}$ with $\tilde{f}_e \leq f_e$ for all edges e that is
feasible for (G, r, c).*

Proof: Let f be feasible for the single-commodity instance (G, r, c), and suppose

$f_e > 0$ for every edge e in the cycle H. Let $\delta = \min_{e \in H} f_e$ and define the vector $\{\hat{f}_e\}_{e \in E}$ by $\hat{f}_e = f_e - \delta$ for $e \in H$ and $\hat{f}_e = f_e$ otherwise. Note that $\hat{f}$ is a nonnegative vector and that for at least one edge e, $\hat{f}_e = 0$ while $f_e > 0$.

By Proposition 2.7.1(a), $\{f_e\}_{e \in E}$ is feasible for (2.9)–(2.12). Since subtracting δ from the amount of flow on each edge of H decreases both of the sums in a conservation constraint (2.9)–(2.11) by either δ (if the corresponding vertex lies in H) or by zero (otherwise), the vector $\hat{f}$ is also a feasible solution to (2.9)–(2.12). Proposition 2.7.1(b) then implies that there is a feasible flow $\tilde{f}$ with $\tilde{f}_e \leq \hat{f}_e \leq f_e$ for every edge e. We have therefore defined a procedure that maintains feasibility, only decreases the amount of flow on each edge, and strictly decreases the number of edges that carry flow. Iterating this procedure must therefore terminate with the desired directed acyclic flow. ∎

2.7.2   Monotone Orderings

This section identifies useful mathematical structure possessed by Nash flows in single-commodity instances. The first result is that every single-commodity instance admits a directed acyclic Nash flow.

Proposition 2.7.4 *Every single-commodity instance admits a directed acyclic Nash flow.*

Proof: Let (G, r, c) be a single-commodity instance. By Proposition 2.2.5, there is a Nash flow f feasible for (G, r, c). By Proposition 2.7.3, there is a directed acyclic flow $\tilde{f}$ feasible for (G, r, c) with $\tilde{f}_e \leq f_e$ for all edges e. Proposition 2.6.1 shows that the Nash flows of (G, r, c) are the minima of a convex program with an objective function that is nondecreasing in the amount of flow on each edge. Since f is a Nash flow and $\tilde{f}_e \leq f_e$ for all edges e, $\tilde{f}$ must also be a Nash flow. ∎

Simple examples demonstrate that Proposition 2.7.4 does not carry over to multicommodity networks.

Next, we show that a certain type of vertex ordering exists relative to a directed acyclic Nash flow in a single-commodity instance.

Definition 2.7.5 Let f be a Nash flow for the single-commodity instance (G, r, c). Let $d(v)$ denote the length of a shortest s-v path with respect to edge lengths $c_e(f_e)$. An ordering of the vertices of G is *f-monotone* if it satisfies the following three properties.

(P1) The source s is the first vertex in the ordering.

(P2) All f-flow travels forward in the ordering.

(P3) The d-values of vertices are nondecreasing in the ordering.

Example 2.7.6 Consider Braess's Paradox, after the zero-cost edge has been added (Example 2.5.2). For the unique Nash flow f, the unique f-monotone ordering is s, v, w, t. Properties (P1) and (P2) are clearly satisfied by this ordering; property (P3) holds because $d(s) = 0$, $d(v) = d(w) = 1$, and $d(t) = 2$.

Property (P2) implies that an f-monotone ordering can only exist if f is a directed acyclic flow. We next show that there are no other obstructions, in the sense that an f-monotone ordering exists relative to every directed acyclic Nash flow f. To prove this, we require the following alternative definition of Nash flows, which will also be useful in Section 5.2.

Proposition 2.7.7 *Let f be a flow feasible for (G, r, c). For a vertex v in G, let $d(v)$ denote the length, with respect to edge lengths $c_e(f_e)$, of a shortest s-v path in G. Then*

$$d(w) - d(v) \leq c_e(f_e) \tag{2.13}$$

for all edges $e = (v, w)$, and f is at Nash equilibrium if and only if equality holds whenever $f_e > 0$.

Proof: Inequality (2.13)—the "triangle inequality"—holds for every flow f by the definition of the shortest path labels d. In more detail, by the definition of $d(v)$ there is an s-v path with length $d(v)$. Appending the edge $e = (v, w)$ to this path yields an s-w path with length $d(v) + c_e(f_e)$, which is an upper bound on the length $d(w)$ of a shortest s-w path.

Since $d(s) = 0$, for an s-t path $P \in \mathcal{P}$ we can write

$$
\begin{aligned}
c_P(f) &= \sum_{e \in P} c_e(f_e) \\
&\geq \sum_{e=(v,w) \in P} d(w) - d(v) \tag{2.14} \\
&= d(t) - d(s) = d(t).
\end{aligned}
$$

By the definition of $d(t)$, an s-t path P is minimum-cost with respect to f if and only if $c_P(f) = d(t)$. This occurs if and only if equality holds in (2.14), which in turn is true if and only if $d(w) - d(v) = c_e(f_e)$ for all edges e of P. The proposition now follows from Proposition 2.2.2. ∎

We can now prove that an f-monotone ordering exists relative to a directed acyclic Nash flow f.

Proposition 2.7.8 *If f is a directed acyclic Nash flow for the single-commodity instance (G, r, c), then there is an f-monotone ordering of the vertices of G.*

Proof: Since f is a directed acyclic flow, the vertices of G can be topologically sorted to ensure properties (P1) and (P2) of Definition 2.7.5; see Section 2.8 for more details. We will maintain these two properties throughout the following procedure, which will achieve property (P3).

Define distance labels d as in Definition 2.7.5. An ordered pair (v, w) of vertices is *bad* if $d(w) < d(v)$ in spite of w following v in the ordering. Property (P3) of Definition 2.7.5 is equivalent to the absence of bad vertex pairs.

If there is a bad vertex pair, there is one such pair (v, w) with v and w adjacent in the ordering. We would like to transpose v and w. Since $d(s) = 0$ and all d-values are nonnegative, $s \neq v$, and so this transposition does not violate property (P1). By Proposition 2.7.7 and the nonnegativity of cost functions, d-values cannot decrease across an edge e with $f_e > 0$. Hence, there is no flow-carrying edge from v to w. Transposing v and w therefore does not violate property (P2) of Definition 2.7.5 and strictly decreases the number of bad vertex pairs. Finitely many such transpositions therefore yields an f-monotone ordering. ∎

2.8 Notes

Section 2.1

Most of the terminology and definitions from Section 2.1 are standard in graph theory and combinatorial optimization. An introduction to the jargon of graph theory can be found on the first few pages of any good text on the subject, such as [54, 123, 397]. In some texts, a path is allowed to contain cycles and a path with no cycles is called *simple*. Also, graph theory often concentrates on *undirected* graphs, where an edge is an unordered pair of vertices and traffic is permitted to traverse it in either direction. Nearly all of the results of this book can be reworked for undirected graphs with little difficulty.

Network flow theory has been a very active area of research since the 1962 book of Ford and Fulkerson [157], if not earlier. Recent textbooks that give a thorough treatment of network flow include [5, 45, 90, 237, 355]. The emphasis of these texts, and more generally of traditional network flow theory, tends to differ from that of this book in several respects. Most importantly, edge cost functions are usually assumed to be constant, as in the classical *min-cost flow* problem. Selfish routing only becomes interesting when cost functions are nonconstant. Ahuja, Magnanti, and Orlin [5] and Bertsekas [45], however, also discuss flow problems with nonconstant cost functions. Also, traditional network flow theory usually associates a *capacity* on each edge that restricts the amount of flow that can be routed on it. Except in Section 4.3, this book does not consider edge capacities. One reason to exclude edge capacities from the model is that they can be modeled implicitly with cost functions that take on extremely large values once the (implicit) capacity has been exceeded. Finally, in traditional network flow theory, flows on edges are the primary object of study while flows on paths play a secondary role. While most of this book could be rewritten to avoid any mention of flows on paths, this would discard the primary game-theoretic interpretation of flows as routes chosen by noncooperative agents. On the other hand, working with flows (on paths) does introduce some additional awkwardness in the treatment of traditional network flow results in Section 2.7.

The interpretation of flow as the aggregated routes chosen by a large population of individuals of infinitesimal size is common in combinatorial optimization. Classical game theory, on the other hand, typically assumes a discrete population of agents. See below and Section 4.4 for further discussion of this distinction.

Throughout this book, cost functions are assumed nonnegative, continuous, and nondecreasing. While all of the preliminary results in this chapter hold with cost functions that are not nonnegative, simple examples show that no interesting upper bounds on the price of anarchy of selfish routing are possible with such functions (cf., Chapter 3). Indeed, Definition 2.3.1 is not even meaningful when the cost of a flow can be negative, and some alternative definition of the price of anarchy would be required in this case. Continuity of cost functions is required for the existence of Nash flows; see the notes on Section 2.6 below. This assumption should not pose a serious problem in applications, since a discontinuous cost function can typically be closely approximated with a continuous one. Finally, cost functions arising in applications are usually but not always nondecreasing. For example, Blonski [53] points out that people typically have nonmonotone preferences about the congestion in a restaurant or at a concert, preferring a moderate crowd to total isolation or to being packed in like a sardine. Unfortunately, many of the results of this book are not true for networks with nonmonotone cost functions—for example, the price of anarchy can be unbounded in networks with linear cost functions that can be either increasing or decreasing (cf., Section 3.2).

Our objective function, the cost, is the most popular objective function in both the transportation science and computer science literatures. For example, this objective function is implicit in Pigou [320] and explicit in Wardrop [394]. We will, however, study an alternative objective function in Section 4.7. Similarly, while (2.1) is arguably the most natural way to define the cost of a path, other definitions make sense in certain applications. See Cole, Dodis, and Roughgarden [89] for examples and further discussion. See also [50, 60, 67, 359] for examples of specific cost functions used in practical applications. Finally, in some of the theoretical computer science literature, cost functions are called *latency functions* [347].

At the end of Section 2.1, we used the fact that a real-valued continuous function defined on a closed and bounded subset of Euclidean space attains its minimum. This is a standard result in introductory analysis, and can be found in the references listed in Section 1.5.

Section 2.2

As discussed in Section 1.5, Nash flows were first described qualitatively by Pigou [320] and Knight [227]. Several decades later, Wardrop [394] wrote a seminal paper that put the model on more secure mathematical footing. Because of this paper's importance, several of the concepts from Section 2.2 traditionally carry Wardrop's name, as described below. Beckmann, McGuire, and Winsten [40] studied Wardrop's model in great detail, proved several of its basic properties, and proposed many extensions. Several other fundamental papers on traffic modeling appeared during the 1950s; see the discussion and references in Beckmann [39], Florian and Hearn [154], and Boyce, Mahmassani, and Nagurney [61]. A final classic paper that must be singled out is Dafermos and Sparrow [108], the paper on which this chapter's presentation is most closely based.

Our definition of flows at Nash equilibrium, Definition 2.2.1, is from Dafermos and Sparrow [108]. Many authors, including Wardrop [394] and Beckmann, McGuire, and Winsten [40], use Proposition 2.2.2 as the definition of a Nash flow. Proposition 2.2.2, which states that all traffic travels on minimum-cost paths, is often called *Wardrop's first principle* or simply *Wardrop's principle*. This book uses Definition 2.2.1 because it is slightly more flexible in extensions of the basic selfish routing model.

In much of the transportation science literature, Nash flows are called *Wardrop equilibria* or *user equilibria*. This book uses the phrase "flow at Nash equilibrium" to emphasize that this notion of equilibrium fits squarely into the realm of noncooperative game theory. Selfish routing differs from classical games in some respects, however; see the end of this section for details.

Proposition 2.2.4 is implicit in Beckmann, McGuire, and Winsten [40]. Propositions 2.2.5 and 2.2.6 are discussed in the notes to Section 2.6, below.

Since the early papers of Pigou, Knight, and Wardrop, the basic selfish routing model described in Sections 2.1 and 2.2 has been generalized in countless different directions. We will study some of these extensions in Chapter 4 but will only scratch the surface of the vast literature in this area. For example, generalizations not considered in Chapter 4 include models in which different types of individuals can cause and experience different amounts of congestion [3, 53, 151, 230], the cost of an edge can depend on the amount of flow on other edges [1, 66, 75, 100, 101, 103, 153, 189, 249, 260, 286, 297, 315], the amount of traffic can vary with the network congestion [89, 105, 135, 155, 173, 174, 289], there is an explicit notion of time [73, 114, 175, 204, 274, 275, 369, 400], or individuals have incomplete information about the network [113, 118, 165, 199]. The references above are far from an exhaustive list of the papers written on these topics. Further references, along with overviews of some of these papers, can be found in Florian and Hearn [154] and the books by Nagurney [288] and Sheffi [359]. Finally, a substantially different model of selfish routing was recently proposed by Nesterov [294] and Nesterov and De Palma [295].

Section 2.3

As mentioned in Section 1.5, the price of anarchy was first defined by Koutsoupias and Papadimitriou [239], who initially called it the coordination ratio, and the phrase "price of anarchy" is from Papadimitriou [303]. In [239], the price of anarchy was defined for general noncooperative games, where, in contrast to Proposition 2.2.6, different Nash equilibria can have different objective function values. In this case, the price of anarchy is the ratio of objective function values of the worst Nash equilibrium and an optimal outcome. The price of anarchy of selfish routing was first studied by Roughgarden and Tardos [347].

The ratio of objective function values of the *best* Nash equilibrium and an optimal solution—which has been called the *optimistic price of anarchy* [15] and the *price of stability* [14]—has also be studied. See Sections 4.3 and 4.4 for examples of this concept. See also Tennenholtz [381, 382] and Mirrokni and Vetta [282] for recent variants on the price of anarchy that do not assume that noncooperative agents reach a Nash equilibrium.

Several researchers anticipated the definition of the price of anarchy. As early as 1950, Spengler [370] effectively established an upper bound on the price of anarchy in what would now be called a "decentralized supply chain." For selfish routing, P. Marcotte (personal communication, November 2002) obtained some preliminary, unpublished results measuring the difference in total travel time of Nash and optimal flows in 1979. A few years later Mason [271], who considered the distributed version of selfish routing discussed in Section 1.3.2, explicitly identified quantifying the price of anarchy of selfish routing as an interesting research problem.

The price of anarchy is also similar to several well-established concepts in theoretical computer science. For example, the *approximation ratio* of an algorithm for an optimization problem with a positive objective function is typically defined as the worst-case ratio, over all instances of the optimization problem, between the objective function value of a solution produced by the algorithm and that of an optimal solution. See also Definition 5.1.1. Approximation ratios of algorithms—typically for polynomial-time algorithms that approximately solve NP-hard optimization problems—have been extensively studied in theoretical computer science ever since NP-completeness was first discovered. See Johnson [209] for an early reference; textbook introductions to the field include [25, 195, 387].

Similarly, for an "online algorithm"—one that attempts to solve an optimization problem over time and must commit to irrevocable decisions before encountering all of the input—its *competitive ratio* is defined as the worst-case ratio between the objective function value of a solution output by the algorithm and that of an optimal solution. See Sleator and Tarjan [363] for a seminal reference from the 1980s and Borodin and El-Yaniv [56] for thorough coverage of the area.

The best approximation ratio achievable by a polynomial-time algorithm for an NP-hard optimization problem can be viewed as quantifying the cost of a lack of sufficient computational power to solve the problem exactly. Similarly, the best competitive ratio achievable by an online algorithm for an online optimization problem is a measure of the cost of a lack of foreknowledge about the input. These concepts are thus very similar in spirit to the price of anarchy, which quantifies the cost of a lack of coordination among the participants of a noncooperative game. Koutsoupias and Papadimitriou [239] explicitly stated that their definition of the price of anarchy was motivated by these parallels.

Section 2.4

Section 2.4 is primarily based on the classical work of Beckmann, McGuire, and Winsten [40] and Dafermos and Sparrow [108]. The nonlinear program (NLP) is explicit in both [40] and [108]. For the compact formulation mentioned in Remark 2.4.1 see, for example, Ahuja, Magnanti, and Orlin [5, Chapter 17]. Definition 2.4.2(a)–(c) is classical; see Rockafellar [333], for example, for a good reference on convexity. Definition 2.4.2(d) is already present in Beckmann, McGuire, and Winsten [40], but no standard terminology for this condition has emerged in the literature.

The equivalence of conditions (a)–(c) in Proposition 2.4.4 dates to Beckmann, McGuire, and Winsten [40]. The equivalence of condition (d) with the first three is implicit in Smith [366]. In the proof of Proposition 2.4.4, the estimate in (2.6) follows from Taylor's Theorem; details can be found in the calculus references mentioned in Section 1.5. The linear approximation in (2.7) follows from the same argument, together with the definition of convexity.

Definition 2.4.5 and Corollary 2.4.6 are implicit in Pigou [320] and explicit in Beckmann, McGuire, and Winsten [40]. The discussion in Remark 2.4.7 is also essentially due to Pigou [320].

Fact 2.4.9 follows from known results in convex programming. For example, the ellipsoid method of Khachiyan [225] can be used to solve (NLP) in polynomial time when all cost functions are semiconvex. See Schrijver [354] and Grötschel, Lovász, and Schrijver [180] for more details on this approach. More practical interior-point methods can also be used, provided the cost functions are sufficiently smooth. Karmarkar [217] gave the first provably polynomial-time interior-point algorithm, and Renegar [328] is an accessible survey of more recent work in the area. In single-commodity networks, computing an optimal flow in a network with semiconvex cost functions is the same as the well-studied *convex cost flow* problem. For fast algorithms for the convex cost flow problem, see the books by Ahuja, Magnanti, and Orlin [5] and Bertsekas [45], and the paper by Hochbaum and Shanthikumar [196]. There has also been enormous effort to develop special-purpose—though not necessarily polynomial-time—algorithms for computing optimal (or, by Corollary 2.4.6, Nash) flows in multicommodity networks. A detailed discussion of this work is outside the scope of this book, but a selection of papers on the topic includes [1, 23, 46, 47, 48, 49, 100, 101, 151, 152, 153, 154, 170, 175, 190, 191, 253, 260, 297, 384, 385, 395, 403].

Remark 2.4.10 discussed the need to specify an encoding of an instance in order to speak about polynomial-time algorithms. A simple way to encode a reasonably large class of cost functions is to assume that cost functions are piecewise polynomial, and to explicitly give the coefficients of all of the polynomials. More sophisticated approaches are also possible, but the details are not included here. More on this topic can be found in, for example, the books of Aho, Hopcroft, and Ullman [4], Ahuja, Magnanti, and Orlin [5], Grötschel, Lovász, and Schrijver [180], and Papadimitriou and Steiglitz [306].

Finally, Fact 2.4.12 is due to Cole, Dodis, and Roughgarden [87].

Section 2.5

As mentioned in Section 1.5, Examples 2.5.1 and 2.5.2 are due to Pigou [320] and Braess [64], respectively, with the specific cost functions taken from Roughgarden and Tardos [347, 348] and Schulman (personal communication, October 1999). Example 2.5.3 is from Milchtaich [279]. Much more on Pareto suboptimality can be found in any good textbook on economics, such as Mas-Colell, Whinston, and Green [270]. Example 2.5.4 is due to Roughgarden and Tardos [347, 348], and Example 2.5.5 was discussed by Roughgarden [340]. Example 2.5.6 is based on a family of networks described by Lin et al. [257].

Section 2.6

Proposition 2.6.1 and the proof of Proposition 2.2.5 are explicit in Beckmann, McGuire, and Winsten [40]. The uniqueness results—Proposition 2.2.6 and Corollaries 2.6.2–2.6.4— are also explicit or implicit in [40]. For single-commodity networks, existence and uniqueness of Nash flows were established earlier by Duffin [129]. Nash flows need not exist if cost functions are not continuous and need not be unique if cost functions are not continuous or are not nondecreasing; see [342], for example, for more details.

Corollary 2.6.6 was first proved by Smith [366]. Dafermos [103] related it to the classical theory of variational inequalities; see Nagurney [287], for example, for further background. The connection between equilibria and variational inequalities continues to prove useful in transportation science (see [120, 287], for example), and it is also exploited in Chapter 3 to upper bound the price of anarchy of selfish routing.

As in Fact 2.4.9, Corollary 2.6.7 notes that a Nash flow can be found in polynomial time via algorithms for general convex programming. See the notes on Section 2.4 above for further details on this and on special-purpose algorithms for the problem.

Section 2.7

Everything in Section 2.7.1 is part of classical network flow theory and is treated thoroughly in the references on the topic listed in Section 1.5. A formal proof of Proposition 2.7.1 can also be found in these textbooks. The more classical version of Proposition 2.7.1(b) states that every flow on edges admits a decomposition into paths and flow cycles. Similarly, Proposition 2.7.3 is normally summarized as "removing flow cycles." The multicommodity analogue of Proposition 2.7.3 only asserts the existence of a flow in which, for each i, the flow belonging to commodity i is directed acyclic. Note that this condition does not preclude a flow cycle in which the flow belongs to two or more different commodities.

Proposition 2.7.4 is implicit in many papers, including Beckmann, McGuire, and Winsten [40] and Braess [64]. It is explicitly discussed in Roughgarden [338]. Definition 2.7.5, Proposition 2.7.7, and Proposition 2.7.8 are also from [338]. The first step of the proof of Proposition 2.7.8 is to sort the vertices of the network according to a directed acyclic flow. This "topological sort" is, by definition, an ordering of the vertices in which all flow-carrying edges travel forward—that is, property (P2) of Definition 2.7.5. Such an ordering can always be found by the following "greedy algorithm": place the source s first, then iteratively assign the next position in the ordering to a vertex that receives flow only from vertices already placed in the ordering. More details on this procedure can be found in any good algorithms textbook, such as Cormen et al. [91]. Note that the algorithm above also ensures property (P1) of Definition 2.7.5—the source s is first in the produced ordering.

Classical Noncooperative Game Theory

An extremely brief review of classical noncooperative games follows, with the goal of comparing and contrasting them to selfish routing. More details can be found in any of the game theory texts listed in Section 1.5.

A *finite normal form game*, or simply a *game*, consists of the following ingredients. There are n *players*, where player i has a finite set S_i of available *pure strategies*. An element of the product space $S = S_1 \times \cdots \times S_n$ is a *strategy profile* or an *outcome* of the game. Each player i has a *utility function* $u_i : S \to \mathcal{R}$ that assigns a real number (a *payoff*) to each outcome of the game. Payoffs are assumed to summarize all preferences of a player, with higher payoffs of course preferred to lower ones. A *mixed strategy* of player i is a probability distribution over the set S_i of pure strategies. A collection $s_1, \ldots, s_n$ of mixed strategies, one for each player, naturally defines a probability distribution over the outcomes of the game in which each player randomizes independently. Players are assumed risk-neutral and are interested only in their expected payoffs under such a distribution. Such a collection of mixed strategies is a *Nash equilibrium* if, for each player i, s_i maximizes the expected payoff of player i, assuming other players' mixed strategies are held fixed. For example, the Prisoner's Dilemma game of Section 1.5 has two players, each with two strategies. The payoff to a player could be defined as the amount of its reward minus the length of its jail sentence, and in the unique Nash equilibrium both prisoners confess with probability 1. For another example, see the notes on the "KP model" in Section 3.7.

While similar, selfish routing and classical noncooperative games differ in a few important respects. First, standard noncooperative games have a finite set of players, while selfish routing assumes an infinite set of infinitesimally small players. In game theory parlance, selfish routing is a *nonatomic* game. Nonatomic games are also well-studied in the game theory literature, and are usually described in a way analogous to finite games: a closed real interval represents the set of players, with each point of the interval representing a player; an outcome of the game is a function mapping each point of the interval to a strategy; and a payoff function maps game outcomes to payoffs to all of the players.

Selfish routing is a significantly simpler model than is a general nonatomic game. Since all players with a given source and destination are interchangeable, all of the salient features of a game outcome can be summarized with a relatively simple mathematical object—a finite-dimensional flow vector. Similarly, payoffs (or costs) to the players are by definition summarized by a single univariate cost function on each edge. Section 4.1 and the corresponding notes in Section 4.8 discuss in detail both general nonatomic games and nonatomic games with mathematical structure similar to that inherent in selfish routing.

Possessing an infinite player set may appear to elevate selfish routing to a level of greater complexity than finite games. When it comes to equilibria, however, the opposite is true. For finite noncooperative games, even such games with only two players that each have two strategies, there need not be a collection of pure strategies that is at Nash equilibrium. On the other hand, Nash's Theorem [292, 293] states that every finite normal form game admits a Nash equilibrium in mixed strategies. Indeed, this existence theorem is arguably the primary motivation for allowing players to choose mixed strategies in noncooperative games.

By contrast, the distinction between pure and mixed strategies is not important in selfish routing. For example, if f is a flow at Nash equilibrium in the instance (G, r, c)—and such a flow must exist by Proposition 2.2.5—then it is easily interpreted as a pure-strategy outcome, with an (arbitrary) f_P/r_i fraction of the players traveling from s_i to t_i selecting the s_i-t_i path P for each i and $P \in \mathcal{P}_i$. Similar reasoning shows that allowing mixed strategies adds nothing to the basic selfish routing model, at least from the flow-centric perspective of this book. A rigorous formulation of this assertion is left to the reader, but the idea is that for every mixed-strategy outcome of a selfish routing game, there is a pure-strategy outcome that induces an identical flow. For these reasons, this book never considers mixed strategies, despite the concept's fundamental role in classical noncooperative game theory.

Proving the existence of an equilibrium is also more difficult in finite games than in selfish routing. While all known proofs of Nash's Theorem rely on so-called fixed point theorems (see e.g. Border [55]), the proof of Proposition 2.2.5 only requires calculus and the fact that a continuous real-valued function defined on a closed and bounded subset of Euclidean space attains its minimum. Moreover, as mentioned above, no uniqueness result analogous to Proposition 2.2.6 holds in general noncooperative games.

Finally, Nash [292, 293] only studied finite games, and the use of the term "Nash equilibrium" in this book for a nonatomic game is somewhat unconventional; see also the notes on Section 2.2 above. On the other hand, the connection between flows at Nash equilibrium and Nash equilibria in finite normal form games is not merely conceptual. Indeed, flows at Nash equilibrium can be rigorously characterized as the limit, as the number of players goes to infinity, of Nash equilibria in a natural atomic version of selfish routing. See Devarajan [117], Haurie and Marcotte [187, 188], and Milchtaich [278] for details. See also Section 4.4 for results on the price of anarchy in atomic variants of selfish routing.

II BOUNDING THE PRICE OF ANARCHY

3 How Bad Is Selfish Routing?

This chapter is a cornerstone of this book. Examples 2.5.1–2.5.6 demonstrate the suboptimality of selfish routing and motivate the study of *how much* centralized optimization can improve upon selfish routing. Specifically, what is the *price of anarchy*, the worst-possible ratio between the cost of a flow at Nash equilibrium and that of a socially optimal outcome?

This chapter describes the most basic results on the price of anarchy of selfish routing. Chapter 4 extends this work in many different directions.

3.1 Overview

As suggested by Example 2.5.4, the price of anarchy of selfish routing depends crucially on the "steepness" of the network cost functions. This chapter presents techniques for computing the price of anarchy in an incremental fashion, with each section considering successively more general sets of allowable edge cost functions.

Section 3.2 begins by studying the price of anarchy of selfish routing in networks with cost functions of the form $c(x) = ax + b$, for $a, b \geq 0$. We will call such cost functions *linear*. Linear cost functions are interesting in their own right—for example, they suffice to model the strings and springs example of Section 1.3.3—and the analysis of this section also paves the way for more general results. Section 3.2 proves that in every multicommodity flow network with linear cost functions, the cost of a flow at Nash equilibrium is at most 4/3 times that of an optimal flow. Examples 2.5.1–2.5.3 show that this bound is the best possible.

Section 3.3 focuses on networks with more general edge cost functions and proves a general upper bound on the price of anarchy for a fixed but arbitrary set of allowable edge cost functions. Example 2.5.4 mandates that this bound be $+\infty$ for sufficiently general sets of cost functions, but the bound is finite and small for a vast collection of sets of cost functions. For example, all of the upper bounds shown in Table 3.1 are direct consequences of this general result. The M/M/1 delay functions mentioned in Table 3.1 are common in queueing theory and networking, as Section 3.5 discusses.

Section 3.4 proves that the upper bound of Section 3.3 is optimal for (almost) all sets of allowable edge cost functions. For example, it shows that all of the upper bounds in Table 3.1 are the best possible. Moreover, the simplest of networks suffice to achieve the upper bound proved in Section 3.3. For example, under weak hypotheses on the set of allowable cost functions, the price of anarchy is achieved

Table 3.1
The price of anarchy for several sets of edge cost functions.

Description	Typical Representative	Price of Anarchy
Linear	$ax + b$	$4/3 \approx 1.333$
Quadratic	$ax^2 + bx + c$	$\frac{3\sqrt{3}}{3\sqrt{3}-2} \approx 1.626$
Cubic	$ax^3 + bx^2 + cx + d$	$\frac{4\sqrt[3]{4}}{4\sqrt[3]{4}-3} \approx 1.896$
Polynomials of degree $\leq p$	$\sum_{i=0}^{p} a_i x^i$	$\frac{(p+1)\sqrt[p]{p+1}}{(p+1)\sqrt[p]{p+1}-p} = \Theta(p/\ln p)$
M/M/1 Delay Functions	$(u - x)^{-1}$	$\frac{1}{2}\left(1 + \sqrt{\frac{u_{min}}{u_{min}-R_{max}}}\right)$

Polynomial coefficients are assumed nonnegative. The parameter u is the expectation of the associated queue service rate distribution, or an edge capacity. The parameters R_{max} and u_{min} denote the maximum allowable amount of network traffic and the minimum allowable edge capacity, respectively.

by a single-commodity instance on a set of parallel links. In the special case of a set of cost functions that includes all of the constant functions, a network with only two parallel links suffices to achieve the price of anarchy. This implies that the set of allowable edge cost functions completely dictates the price of anarchy, in that no nontrivial restriction on the network topology or on the number of commodities can excise all worst-case instances.

Section 3.5 gives closed-form formulas for the price of anarchy in several examples, including all of the expressions listed in Table 3.1.

Section 3.6 studies networks with arbitrary continuous, nondecreasing cost functions. Example 2.5.4 implies that the price of anarchy is $+\infty$ for these networks. A bound on the inefficiency of Nash flows in general networks is nonetheless possible, via a so-called bicriteria approach. Specifically, Section 3.6 shows that in every network, the cost of a Nash flow is at most that of an optimal flow that is forced to route twice as much traffic between each source-destination pair. This result has the following alternative interpretation: in lieu of centralized control, the inefficiency of routing selfishly can be offset by a moderate increase in link speed. For popular queueing delay functions, this increase can be effected by a modest increase in the network capacity.

Finally, while Sections 3.2–3.5 should be read in order, Section 3.6 does not depend on earlier results of the chapter and can be read immediately following Section 2.2.

3.2 The Price of Anarchy with Linear Cost Functions

This section considers the scenario in which the cost of each edge e is linear in the edge congestion—where each edge has a cost function $c_e(x) = a_e x + b_e$ for some $a_e, b_e \geq 0$. We have already seen, in Examples 2.5.1–2.5.3, three networks with linear cost functions in which the price of anarchy (Definition 2.3.1) is 4/3. The main result in this section, Theorem 3.2.6, is a matching upper bound for networks with linear cost functions. Some of the techniques used to prove this theorem also form the basis of the analysis in the next section, which considers the price of anarchy in networks with nonlinear cost functions.

3.2.1 Preliminaries

The first step of the analysis is to observe that the characterizations of Nash and optimal flows given in Chapter 2 have particularly simple and useful forms in networks with linear cost functions. First, the total cost $C(f)$ of a flow f is

$$C(f) = \sum_{e \in E} a_e f_e^2 + b_e f_e.$$

Since $a_e \geq 0$, this is a convex quadratic function and the nonlinear program (NLP) of Section 2.4 is a convex program. We can therefore use Proposition 2.4.4 to characterize its optimal solutions. Moreover, in the notation of Definition 2.4.5, if the cost function c_e of edge e is $c_e(x) = a_e x + b_e$, then the marginal cost function c_e^* of e is simply $c_e^*(x) = 2a_e x + b_e$. The following lemma summarizes this discussion, together with specialized versions of Propositions 2.2.2 and 2.4.4.

Lemma 3.2.1 *Let (G, r, c) be an instance with a linear cost function $c_e(x) = a_e x + b_e$ for each edge $e \in E$. Then,*

(a) a feasible flow f is at Nash equilibrium for (G, r, c) if and only if for each commodity i and s_i-t_i paths $P_1, P_2 \in \mathcal{P}_i$ with $f_{P_1} > 0$,

$$\sum_{e \in P_1} a_e f_e + b_e \leq \sum_{e \in P_2} a_e f_e + b_e; \tag{3.1}$$

(b) a feasible flow f^* is optimal for (G, r, c) if and only if for each commodity i and s_i-t_i paths $P_1, P_2 \in \mathcal{P}_i$ with $f_{P_1}^* > 0$,

$$\sum_{e \in P_1} 2a_e f_e^* + b_e \leq \sum_{e \in P_2} 2a_e f_e^* + b_e. \tag{3.2}$$

As an aside, note that Lemma 3.2.1 immediately implies that in networks in which the cost of each edge is proportional to its congestion, Nash and optimal flows coincide.

Corollary 3.2.2 *If (G, r, c) is an instance in which each edge cost function c_e is of the form $c_e(x) = a_e x$, then a flow feasible for (G, r, c) is optimal if and only if it is at Nash equilibrium.*

Proof: When $b_e = 0$ for every edge e, inequality (3.1) holds if and only if inequality (3.2) holds. ∎

Lemma 3.2.1 also implies the next lemma, which plays a crucial role in the proof of the main theorem of this section. The lemma establishes a surprisingly strong connection between Nash and optimal flows in networks with linear cost functions.

Lemma 3.2.3 *Suppose (G, r, c) has linear cost functions and f is a flow at Nash equilibrium. Then,*

(a) $c_e^*(f_e/2) = c_e(f_e)$ for each edge e;
(b) the flow $f/2$ is optimal for $(G, r/2, c)$.

Proof: Part (a) follows from the fact that all cost functions are linear. For part (b), simply note that if f satisfies the conditions of Lemma 3.2.1(a) for (G, r, c), then $f/2$ satisfies the conditions of Lemma 3.2.1(b) for $(G, r/2, c)$. ∎

3.2.2 Proof Approach

The outline of the proof of the main theorem of this section is as follows. We will create an optimal flow for an instance (G, r, c) via a two-step process. In the first step, we route a flow optimal for the instance $(G, r/2, c)$—by Lemma 3.2.3(b), half of a Nash flow for (G, r, c)—and in the second step we augment this flow to one optimal for (G, r, c). Note that this augmentation may increase *or decrease* the amount of flow on any given edge. For example, in Example 2.5.2 (Braess's Paradox), the Nash flow f, and hence the flow $f/2$, make use of the zero-cost edge (v, w), while the optimal flow eschews it.

We will show separate lower bounds on the cost of the two steps: if f is a Nash flow, then the scaled-down Nash flow costs at least $C(f)/4$; and augmenting the scaled-down flow to the original traffic rates costs at least $C(f)/2$. The first lower bound is a simple calculation, but the second requires some work.

3.2.3 Proof of Upper Bound

We begin with the simpler of the two lower bounds.

Lemma 3.2.4 *Let f be a flow for an instance (G, r, c) with linear cost functions. Then,*

$$C(f/2) \geq \frac{1}{4} \cdot C(f).$$

Proof: Write $c_e(x) = a_e x + b_e$ for each edge e. Then,

$$
\begin{aligned}
C(f/2) &= \sum_{e \in E} \left(\frac{1}{2} a_e f_e + b_e \right) \frac{f_e}{2} \\
&\geq \frac{1}{4} \sum_{e \in E} (a_e f_e + b_e) f_e \\
&= \frac{1}{4} \cdot C(f).
\end{aligned}
$$

∎

Next, we lower bound the cost of augmenting a scaled-down Nash flow $f/2$ to a flow feasible for the full traffic rates in terms of the marginal costs c^* of edges with respect to $f/2$.

Lemma 3.2.5 *Let (G, r, c) be an instance with linear cost functions and f^* an optimal flow. Then for every $\delta > 0$, a feasible flow for the instance $(G, (1 + \delta)r, c)$ has cost at least*

$$C(f^*) + \delta \sum_{e \in E} c_e^*(f_e^*) f_e^*.$$

Proof: Fix an instance (G, r, c) with linear cost functions, an optimal flow f^*, and a value for the parameter $\delta > 0$. Suppose f is a feasible flow for $(G, (1 + \delta)r, c)$. The amount of flow f_e on edge e may be larger or smaller than f_e^*. For every edge $e \in E$, convexity of the function $x \cdot c_e(x) = a_e x^2 + b_e x$ implies that we can obtain a lower bound on the function via a linear approximation at the point f_e^* (see Figure 2.1 on page 26):

$$c_e(f_e) f_e \geq c_e(f_e^*) f_e^* + (f_e - f_e^*) c_e^*(f_e^*). \tag{3.3}$$

Inequality (3.3) states that estimating the cost of changing the flow value on edge e from f_e^* to f_e by $(f_e - f_e^*) c_e^*(f_e^*)$—by the marginal cost of flow increase at f_e^* times the size of the perturbation—can only underestimate the cost of an increase (when $f_e > f_e^*$) and overestimate the benefit of a decrease (when $f_e < f_e^*$). We may thus derive

$$
\begin{aligned}
C(f) &= \sum_{e \in E} c_e(f_e) f_e \\
&\geq C(f^*) + \sum_{e \in E} (f_e - f_e^*) c_e^*(f_e^*).
\end{aligned}
\tag{3.4}
$$

Since f^* is optimal for (G, r, c) and linear cost functions are semiconvex (Definition 2.4.2(d)), applying Proposition 2.4.4(d) to the flow $f/(1 + \delta)$ gives

$$
\frac{1}{1 + \delta} \sum_{e \in E} c_e^*(f_e^*) f_e \geq \sum_{e \in E} c_e^*(f_e^*) f_e^*,
$$

which together with (3.4) implies the lemma. ∎

The main theorem of this section now follows easily from Lemmas 3.2.4 and 3.2.5. Recall that $\rho(G, r, c)$ denotes the price of anarchy of the instance (G, r, c) (Definition 2.3.1).

Theorem 3.2.6 *If (G, r, c) has linear cost functions, then*

$$
\rho(G, r, c) \leq \frac{4}{3}.
$$

Proof: Let f be a flow at Nash equilibrium for (G, r, c). By Lemma 3.2.3, $f/2$ is an optimal flow for the instance $(G, r/2, c)$ with $c_e^*(f_e/2) = c_e(f_e)$ for each edge e. Applying Lemma 3.2.5 with $\delta = 1$ and then Lemma 3.2.4, we find that if f^* is feasible for (G, r, c), then

$$
\begin{aligned}
C(f^*) &\geq C(f/2) + \sum_{e \in E} c_e^*(f_e/2) \frac{f_e}{2} \\
&\geq \frac{1}{4} \cdot C(f) + \frac{1}{2} \sum_{e \in E} c_e(f_e) f_e \\
&= \frac{3}{4} \cdot C(f),
\end{aligned}
$$

which proves the theorem. ∎

3.2.4 Discussion

As already noted, Pigou's example (Example 2.5.1) shows that the upper bound of 4/3 in Theorem 3.2.6 cannot be improved. The fact that this upper bound is achieved in such a simple example is worthy of additional discussion.

Given the inefficiency of Nash flows, a natural goal is to seek out the causes of this inefficiency. In Pigou's example, the cause is easy to find: the Nash flow is inefficient because selfish users cannot resist overcongesting an edge that is beneficial when used in moderation. Put differently, the singular obstruction preventing Nash flows from optimizing the cost in Pigou's example is the inability (or unwillingness) of selfish users to discern which of two competing routes is superior from a global perspective.

In general multicommodity flow networks, even with linear cost functions, we might expect additional problems to arise with unregulated traffic. For example, it is plausible that centralized control could be used to prevent different commodities from interfering with one another, thereby radically improving upon the network performance achieved by selfish routing. Such problems would in turn complicate any explanation for the worst-case losses caused by selfish routing. Theorem 3.2.6 and Pigou's example imply that, at least for networks with linear cost functions, more severe obstructions to selfish users optimizing the cost *do not arise* in multicommodity flow networks. In turn, the worst-case inefficiency due to selfish routing can always be explained with the simplest of networks, with Pigou's example providing a "succinct certificate."

Section 3.3 extends these ideas far beyond the domain of networks with linear cost functions.

3.2.5 Consequences for Strings and Springs

We now return to the mechanical networks of strings and springs discussed in Section 1.3.3 and exemplified in Figure 1.3. Viewing the support as a source, the suspended weight as a destination, and each string and spring as an edge, the equilibrium position of the mechanical device can be modeled as a flow at Nash equilibrium in an instance (G, r, c), with force corresponding to flow and support-weight distance corresponding to the common cost of every source-destination flow path. Strings, as perfectly inelastic objects, are modeled as links with constant cost functions, and (perfectly elastic) springs correspond to links with cost functions that include a term of the form ax. The instance (G, r, c) thus has linear cost functions. Severing a string or spring corresponds to deleting an edge from (G, r, c). Every realizable equilibrium of the mechanical network, possibly after destroying some of its constituent parts, corresponds to a Nash equilibrium in a subgraph of G—a network obtained from G by discarding some of its edges.

Although Theorem 3.2.6 addresses the cost of flows—a concept with no obvious analogue in these mechanical networks—we can still apply it in the following way. By Theorem 3.2.6, every flow feasible for (G, r, c)—in particular, every flow at Nash equilibrium in a subgraph of G—has cost at least 3/4 times that of a Nash flow f for (G, r, c). By Proposition 2.2.4, if the common cost of every flow path of f is D and f^* is a flow at Nash equilibrium in a subgraph of G, then the common cost of every flow path of f^* must be at least $3D/4$. Reinterpreting this result for networks of strings and springs yields the following corollary of Theorem 3.2.6.

Corollary 3.2.7 *In every network of strings and springs carrying a single weight with support-weight distance D, the support-weight distance after severing an arbitrary collection of strings and springs is at least $3D/4$.*

Remark 3.2.8 A construction similar to the one described in Section 1.3.3 shows that removing a diode from a two-terminal electrical network of resistors and diodes can decrease the voltage drop from source to ground. Thus, removing a conducting link can increase the network conductivity. As in Corollary 3.2.7, Theorem 3.2.6 implies that the voltage drop from source to ground after removing any number of resistors and diodes from such an electrical network is at least 3/4 times the voltage drop in the original network.

3.3   A General Upper Bound on the Price of Anarchy

The goal of this section is to provide an upper bound on the price of anarchy, given a fixed but arbitrary (nonempty) set of allowable cost functions. Example 2.5.4 demonstrates that the price of anarchy depends crucially on this set. This observation motivates a bound that is parameterized by the set of allowable cost functions.

Toward this end, we will associate a real number $\alpha(\mathcal{C}) \geq 1$ to every set $\mathcal{C}$ of allowable edge cost functions. Intuitively, the value $\alpha(\mathcal{C})$ will quantify the steepness of the cost functions in $\mathcal{C}$. We will then prove that for every instance (G, r, c) with cost functions in the set $\mathcal{C}$, the price of anarchy $\rho(G, r, c)$ is at most $\alpha(\mathcal{C})$. In Section 3.4, we will provide a matching lower bound by exhibiting, for every set $\mathcal{C}$, instances with cost functions in $\mathcal{C}$ and ρ-value arbitrarily close to $\alpha(\mathcal{C})$.

Despite the fact that this result has far greater reach than Theorem 3.2.6, the proof is actually shorter. On the other hand, it is difficult to imagine how the crucial definitions of Section 3.3.1 would come about without the foreknowledge provided by Pigou's example and Theorem 3.2.6:

the simplest of networks determine the price of anarchy.

3.3.1   The Anarchy Value

The first task is to find a definition for a real number $\alpha(\mathcal{C})$ that captures how ill-behaved a set $\mathcal{C}$ of allowable cost functions is. Motivated by Theorem 3.2.6 and the discussion in Section 3.2.4, we will define $\alpha(\mathcal{C})$ to be the worst-case ratio between the cost of a Nash flow and of an optimal flow in a Pigou-like example with cost functions in $\mathcal{C}$. Here a "Pigou-like example" means instances in the spirit of Examples 2.5.1 and 2.5.4.

To make this precise, consider a motivating example. Suppose we are given a set $\mathcal{C}$ of allowable cost functions and wish to construct an example in which the price of anarchy is large. A natural idea is to mimic Example 2.5.4 as best we can, given that $\mathcal{C}$ is the set of cost functions that we are permitted to employ. For simplicity, assume that $\mathcal{C}$ contains all of the constant functions and let c_1 denote the function $c_1(x) = 1$. Then, consider the usual two-node, two-link network of Pigou's example and assign the first link the cost function c_1 and the second link the most pernicious cost function in $\mathcal{C}$. More formally, suppose that $c_2 \in \mathcal{C}$ is assigned to the second link where c_2 satisfies $c_2(0) < 1$ and $c_2(x) > 1$ for x sufficiently large. Choosing $r > 0$ so that $c_2(r) = 1$, a Nash flow at the traffic rate r routes all of its flow on the second edge for a total cost of r. The cost of an optimal flow for this instance is, by definition,

$$\min_{x \le r} \left[(r - x) + x \cdot c_2(x) \right].$$

Since c_2 is nondecreasing and $c_2(r) = 1$, we can let x range over the nonnegative line without changing this minimum. Since this argument can be used with c_1 replaced by any constant function, we arrive at the following definition.

Definition 3.3.1 Let c be a cost function. The *anarchy value* $\alpha(c)$ of c is

$$\alpha(c) = \sup_{x, r \ge 0} \frac{r \cdot c(r)}{x \cdot c(x) + (r - x)c(r)}, \tag{3.5}$$

with the understanding that $0/0 = 1$.

The definition of the anarchy value of a cost function c looks rather opaque from a mathematical perspective, but it is nothing more than the worst-case inefficiency of selfish routing in Pigou-like examples that make use of the cost function c.

Equation (3.5) is not necessarily very useful for evaluating the anarchy value of a function. Fortunately, under the mild assumptions that a cost function is continuously differentiable and semiconvex, Definition 3.3.1 simplifies considerably. In the statement of this simplification, we require the notion of a marginal cost function, first defined in Definition 2.4.5.

Proposition 3.3.2 *If c is a continuously differentiable and semiconvex cost function, then*

$$\alpha(c) = \sup_{r \geq 0}[\lambda\mu + (1-\lambda)]^{-1}, \tag{3.6}$$

where $\lambda \in [0,1]$ solves $c^*(\lambda r) = c(r)$, $\mu = c(\lambda r)/c(r) \in [0,1]$, and $0/0$ is defined to be 1.

Proof: Let c be a continuously differentiable, semiconvex cost function. We need to evaluate equation (3.5). For a fixed value of $r \geq 0$, equation (3.5) is the ratio between the cost of a Nash flow and of an optimal flow in a two-node, two-link network with traffic rate r and cost functions $c_1(x) = c(r)$ and c. Every Nash flow in this network has cost $r \cdot c(r)$. Since c is continuously differentiable and nondecreasing, the marginal cost function c^* is continuous with $c^*(x) = c(x) + x \cdot c'(x) \geq c(x)$ for all $x \geq 0$. By the Intermediate Value Theorem, there is then a value of $\lambda \in [0,1]$ solving $c^*(\lambda r) = c(r)$. By Proposition 2.4.4, routing λr units of flow on the second link and the rest on the first link provides an optimal flow. The ratio of the cost of a Nash flow and that of an optimal flow is then

$$\frac{r \cdot c(r)}{\lambda r \cdot c(\lambda r) + (r - \lambda r)c(r)} = [\lambda\mu + (1-\lambda)]^{-1}, \tag{3.7}$$

where $\mu = c(\lambda r)/c(r)$. Since all optimal flows trivially have the same cost, the right-hand side of (3.7) is independent of the choice of λ that solves $c^*(\lambda r) = c(r)$. ∎

Since we are interested only in the most ill-behaved cost functions of a set, the next definition should be unsurprising.

Definition 3.3.3 The *anarchy value* $\alpha(\mathcal{C})$ of a set $\mathcal{C}$ of cost functions is

$$\alpha(\mathcal{C}) = \sup_{0 \neq c \in \mathcal{C}} \alpha(c).$$

Remark 3.3.4 The anarchy value of a set lies in $[1, \infty]$ and need not be finite.

Remark 3.3.5 The anarchy value of a set may appear a fearsome expression to compute analytically, even when Proposition 3.3.2 applies, but Section 3.5 shows that it can be determined in several interesting cases.

As argued informally earlier, if $\mathcal{C}$ contains the constant functions, then $\alpha(\mathcal{C})$ lower bounds the price of anarchy for instances with cost functions in $\mathcal{C}$. This lower bound is based only on single-commodity instances in a two-node, two-link network. The next result shows that the anarchy value $\alpha(\mathcal{C})$ *upper* bounds the price of anarchy of *every* instance with cost functions in $\mathcal{C}$, irrespective of the complexity of the network G and the number of commodities.

3.3.2 Proof of the Upper Bound

We begin with a lemma that follows trivially from Definitions 3.3.1 and 3.3.3.

Lemma 3.3.6 *Let $\mathcal{C}$ be a set of cost functions with anarchy value $\alpha(\mathcal{C})$. For $c \in \mathcal{C}$ and $x, r \geq 0$,*

$$x \cdot c(x) \geq \frac{r \cdot c(r)}{\alpha(\mathcal{C})} + (x - r)c(r).$$

We now prove the main result of this section: the anarchy value of a set $\mathcal{C}$ of cost functions upper bounds the price of anarchy in every instance with cost functions in $\mathcal{C}$.

Theorem 3.3.7 *Let $\mathcal{C}$ be a set of cost functions with anarchy value $\alpha(\mathcal{C})$, and (G, r, c) an instance with cost functions in $\mathcal{C}$. Then*

$$\rho(G, r, c) \leq \alpha(\mathcal{C}).$$

Proof: Let f^* and f be optimal and Nash flows, respectively, for an instance (G, r, c) with cost functions in the set $\mathcal{C}$. We can now write

$$
\begin{aligned}
C(f^*) &= \sum_{e \in E} c_e(f_e^*) f_e^* \\
&\geq \frac{1}{\alpha(\mathcal{C})} \sum_{e \in E} c_e(f_e) f_e + \sum_{e \in E} (f_e^* - f_e) c_e(f_e) \\
&\geq \frac{C(f)}{\alpha(\mathcal{C})},
\end{aligned}
$$

where for the first inequality we have applied Lemma 3.3.6 to each edge e with $x = f_e^*$ and $r = f_e$, and the second inequality follows from Corollary 2.6.6. ∎

3.4 Matching Lower Bounds in Simple Networks

We now prove that the upper bound on the price of anarchy of selfish routing in Theorem 3.3.7 is tight for nearly all sets of allowable edge cost functions. Moreover, we show that this upper bound is achieved in the simplest of networks.

Section 3.4.1 proves that, for a set $\mathcal{C}$ of cost functions that contains the constant functions, the worst possible value of $\rho(G, r, c)$ for a multicommodity instance (G, r, c) with cost functions in $\mathcal{C}$ is realized, up to an arbitrarily small additive factor, by a single-commodity instance on a two-node, two-link network. Section 3.4.2 proves that under significantly weaker conditions on the set of allowable cost functions, the worst-case ρ-value is achieved, up to an arbitrarily small factor, by a single-commodity instance on a network of parallel links. Section 3.4.3 shows that worst-case examples are simple for still broader sets of cost functions, including the queueing delay functions mentioned in Section 3.1. Finally, Section 3.4.4 demonstrates how these results imply that no nontrivial restriction on the allowable network topologies reduces the price of anarchy.

3.4.1 Lower Bounds in Two-Link Networks

We begin by formalizing an argument of the previous section. The following lemma is essentially a restatement of Definitions 3.3.1 and 3.3.3.

Lemma 3.4.1 *Let G_2 denote the graph with one source vertex, one sink vertex, and two edges directed from source to sink. Let $\mathcal{C}$ denote a set of cost functions that contains the constant functions, with anarchy value $\alpha(\mathcal{C})$. If $\mathcal{I}_2$ denotes the set of*

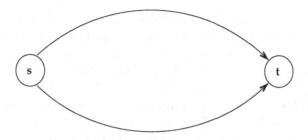

Figure 3.1
Worst-case networks for sets of cost functions that include the constant functions.

all single-commodity instances with underlying network G_2 and cost functions in $\mathcal{C}$, then

$$\sup_{(G_2,r,c)\in\mathcal{I}_2} \rho(G_2,r,c) \geq \alpha(\mathcal{C}).$$

Combining Theorem 3.3.7 and Lemma 3.4.1, we find that the price of anarchy with respect to a set of cost functions that contains the constant functions is achieved, up to an arbitrarily small factor, in instances defined on two-node, two-link networks (see Figure 3.1).

Theorem 3.4.2 *Let G_2 denote the graph with one source vertex, one sink vertex, and two edges directed from source to sink. Let $\mathcal{C}$ be a set of cost functions that contains the constant functions. If $\mathcal{I}$ denotes the set of all instances with cost functions in $\mathcal{C}$ and $\mathcal{I}_2 \subseteq \mathcal{I}$ the single-commodity instances with underlying network G_2, then*

$$\sup_{(G_2,r,c)\in\mathcal{I}_2} \rho(G_2,r,c) = \alpha(\mathcal{C}) = \sup_{(G,r,c)\in\mathcal{I}} \rho(G,r,c).$$

3.4.2 Lower Bounds in Networks of Parallel Links

We now relax the assumption that the set of allowable cost functions contains all of the constant functions and assume instead a much weaker condition that we call *diversity*.

Definition 3.4.3 A set $\mathcal{C}$ of cost functions is *diverse* if for each positive scalar $\gamma > 0$ there is a cost function $c \in \mathcal{C}$ satisfying $c(0) = \gamma$.

For a set of cost functions that is closed under multiplication by positive scalars, diversity merely asserts that some cost function is positive when evaluated at 0.

We next show that networks of parallel links always furnish worst-case examples with respect to a diverse set of allowable cost functions.

Lemma 3.4.4 *Let G_m denote the graph with one source vertex, one sink vertex, and m edges directed from source to sink. Let $\mathcal{C}$ be a diverse set of cost functions with anarchy value $\alpha(\mathcal{C})$. If $\mathcal{I}_m$ denotes the set of all single-commodity instances with underlying network G_m and cost functions in $\mathcal{C}$, then*

$$\sup_{(G,r,c)\in\cup_m \mathcal{I}_m} \rho(G,r,c) \geq \alpha(\mathcal{C}).$$

Proof: Assume that $\alpha(\mathcal{C})$ is finite; the straightforward modifications necessary for the $\alpha(\mathcal{C}) = +\infty$ case are left to the interested reader.

We will reduce the lemma to the previous case of a set of cost functions that contains the constant functions. We will compensate for the absence of a constant function $c(x) = \gamma$—which need not lie in $\mathcal{C}$—by simulating it with many parallel links endowed with cost functions satisfying $c(0) = \gamma$.

For any $\epsilon > 0$, choose a nonzero cost function $c_2 \in \mathcal{C}$ and nonnegative numbers r and $x \leq r$ so that the right-hand side of (3.5) is at least $\alpha(\mathcal{C}) - \epsilon/2$. By the definition of the anarchy value, these parameter choices correspond to an instance $\mathcal{I}$ in a two-node, two-link network with traffic rate r, cost functions $c_1(x) = c_2(r)$ and c_2, and ρ-value at least $\alpha(\mathcal{C}) - \epsilon/2$. This instance has a large price of anarchy but is not immediately useful to us, as the constant cost function $c_1(x) = c_2(r)$ need not lie in $\mathcal{C}$.

The set $\mathcal{C}$ is diverse, so there is a function $c \in \mathcal{C}$ with $c(0) = c_2(r)$. Suppose there is an optimal flow f^* for the instance $\mathcal{I}$ that routes λr units of flow on the second link and the rest on the first link. Let m be so large that

$$c\left(\frac{(1-\lambda)r}{m-1}\right) \leq c_2(r) + \delta, \tag{3.8}$$

where δ is a sufficiently small positive number, depending on ϵ, to be chosen later. For all $\delta > 0$, such an integer m exists because the cost function c is continuous at 0. Define an instance on the network G_m of m parallel links with traffic rate r, cost function c_2 on the last link, and cost function c on the first $m - 1$ links. As in the original instance $\mathcal{I}$, routing all flow on the last link yields a Nash flow with cost $c_2(r)r$. By our choice of m, the inequality (3.8) holds and hence the flow routing λr units of flow on the last link and $(1 - \lambda)r/(m - 1)$ units of flow on each of the

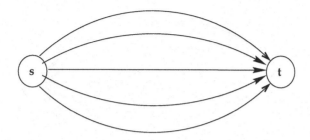

Figure 3.2
Worst-case networks for diverse sets of cost functions. The number of parallel links can be arbitrarily large.

first $m - 1$ links has cost at most

$$c(\lambda r)\lambda r + (c_2(r) + \delta)(1 - \lambda)r.$$

This cost approaches the cost of the optimal flow f^* in the original instance $\mathcal{I}$ as $\delta \to 0$. Choosing δ sufficiently small gives an instance with cost functions in $\mathcal{C}$ and ρ-value at least $\alpha(\mathcal{C}) - \epsilon$. Since $\epsilon > 0$ was arbitrary, the lemma follows. ∎

Theorem 3.3.7 and Lemma 3.4.4 together imply that the worst-case inefficiency of Nash flows with respect to a diverse set of allowable cost functions occurs in networks of parallel links (Figure 3.2).

Theorem 3.4.5 *Let G_m denote the graph with one source vertex, one sink vertex, and m edges directed from source to sink. Let $\mathcal{C}$ be a diverse set of cost functions. If $\mathcal{I}$ denotes the set of all instances with cost functions in $\mathcal{C}$ and $\mathcal{I}_m \subseteq \mathcal{I}$ the single-commodity instances with underlying network G_m, then*

$$\sup_{(G,r,c) \in \cup_m \mathcal{I}_m} \rho(G,r,c) = \alpha(\mathcal{C}) = \sup_{(G,r,c) \in \mathcal{I}} \rho(G,r,c).$$

Remark 3.4.6 The set $\mathcal{C} = \{c(x) = a + x : a \geq 0\}$ shows that the conclusion of the theorem is false with $\cup_m \mathcal{I}_m$ replaced by $\mathcal{I}_2$. The set $\mathcal{C} = \{c(x) = 1 + x\}$ shows that the conclusion of the theorem is also false when the set of allowable cost functions need not be diverse.

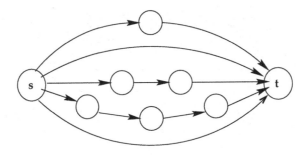

Figure 3.3
Worst-case networks for inhomogeneous sets of cost functions. The number of paths and the
number of edges in each path can be arbitrarily large.

3.4.3   Lower Bounds in Networks of Disjoint Paths

This section gives us our third and final result stating that worst-case examples for
selfish routing always occur in simple networks. We will replace the hypothesis of
diversity (Definition 3.4.3) with the still weaker condition that some available cost
function is positive when evaluated with zero congestion. The motivation is not
generalization for its own sake; as Section 3.5 shows, sets of cost functions common
in networking applications need not be diverse. In addition to characterizing worst-
possible network topologies for such function classes, the results of this section
are essential for computing the price of anarchy with respect to these sets, as in
Section 3.5.

As in the previous section, we begin with a definition.

Definition 3.4.7 A set $\mathcal{C}$ of cost functions is *homogeneous* if $c(0) = 0$ for all $c \in \mathcal{C}$
and *inhomogeneous* otherwise.

It is clear that a diverse set of cost functions is inhomogeneous but that the converse
need not hold.

Call a network a *union of paths* if it can be obtained from a network of parallel
links by repeated edge subdivisions (see Figure 3.3). The main result of this section
states that unions of paths provide worst-case examples for the inefficiency of Nash
flows with respect to an inhomogeneous set of cost functions.

Lemma 3.4.8 *Let $\mathcal{C}$ be an inhomogeneous set of cost functions with anarchy value*
$\alpha(\mathcal{C})$. *If $\mathcal{I}_u$ denotes the set of all single-commodity instances with an underlying*

network that is a union of paths and cost functions in $\mathcal{C}$, then

$$\sup_{(G,r,c)\in\mathcal{I}_u} \rho(G,r,c) \geq \alpha(\mathcal{C}).$$

Proof: Let $\mathcal{C}$ be an inhomogeneous set of allowable cost functions. We again assume for simplicity that $\alpha(\mathcal{C})$ is finite. As in the proof of Lemma 3.4.4, the idea is to work with a richer set of cost functions and then argue that any cost function in the set can be simulated with a collection of edges all possessing cost functions in $\mathcal{C}$.

Let $\overline{\mathcal{C}}$ denote the closure of $\mathcal{C}$ under multiplication by positive scalars, so that $\overline{\mathcal{C}} = \{\beta c : c \in \mathcal{C}, \beta > 0\}$. Since $\mathcal{C}$ is inhomogeneous, $\overline{\mathcal{C}}$ is diverse. Examination of Definition 3.3.1 shows that the functions c and βc have equal anarchy value for every $\beta > 0$, so we also have $\alpha(\overline{\mathcal{C}}) = \alpha(\mathcal{C})$. For every $\epsilon > 0$, Lemma 3.4.4 then assures us of a single-commodity instance $(\overline{G}, \overline{r}, \overline{c})$ on a network $\overline{G}$ of parallel links with cost functions in $\overline{\mathcal{C}}$ and ρ-value at least $\alpha(\mathcal{C}) - \epsilon/2$. We next transform this instance into one on a union of paths with cost functions in $\mathcal{C}$ and ρ-value at least $\alpha(\mathcal{C}) - \epsilon$.

For each edge e of $\overline{G}$, write $\overline{c}_e = \beta_e c_e$ for $\beta_e > 0$ and $c_e \in \mathcal{C}$. The ratio ρ is a continuous function of each scalar β_e (see Section 3.7 for details), so we may replace each β_e by a sufficiently close positive rational number γ_e to obtain a new instance with ρ-value at least $\alpha(\mathcal{C}) - \epsilon$. Since multiplying all of the cost functions of an instance by a common positive number does not affect its ρ-value, we can clear denominators and assume that each scalar γ_e is a positive integer.

The rest of the proof consists of observing that integral multiples of cost functions can be simulated with a path of edges, all possessing the original cost function. More precisely, define G by replacing each edge e of $\overline{G}$ by a directed path of γ_e new edges, each endowed with the cost function $c_e \in \mathcal{C}$. Since $\overline{G}$ is a network of parallel links, G is a union of paths. As is straightforward to check, the natural bijective correspondence between flows feasible for $(\overline{G}, \overline{r}, \gamma c)$ and flows feasible for $(G, \overline{r}, c)$ preserves both the cost of a flow and the property of being at Nash equilibrium. Hence, $\rho(G, \overline{r}, c) \geq \alpha(\mathcal{C}) - \epsilon$. Since $\epsilon > 0$ is arbitrary, we have proved the lemma. ∎

By Theorem 3.3.7 and Lemma 3.4.8, worst-case examples for an inhomogeneous set of allowable cost functions can occur in networks that are unions of paths.

Theorem 3.4.9 *Let $\mathcal{C}$ be an inhomogeneous set of cost functions, $\mathcal{I}$ the set of instances with cost functions in $\mathcal{C}$, and $\mathcal{I}_u \subseteq \mathcal{I}$ the single-commodity instances in* *which the underlying network is a union of paths. Then*

$$\sup_{(G,r,c)\in\mathcal{I}_u} \rho(G,r,c) = \alpha(\mathcal{C}) = \sup_{(G,r,c)\in\mathcal{I}} \rho(G,r,c).$$

Remark 3.4.10 The conclusion of Theorem 3.4.9 fails if the set $\mathcal{I}_u$ of instances in which the underlying network is a union of paths is replaced by the smaller set of instances defined on networks of parallel links. Corollary 3.2.2 implies that it also fails if the hypothesis of inhomogeneity is omitted, since every instance (G,r,c) with cost functions in the homogeneous set $\mathcal{C} = \{ax : a > 0\}$ satisfies $\rho(G,r,c) = 1$, while $\alpha(\mathcal{C}) = 4/3$.

3.4.4   The Price of Anarchy Is Independent of the Allowable Network Topologies

Sections 3.2 and 3.3 show that restricting the set of allowable cost functions can reduce the price of anarchy. The results of Section 3.4 imply that, for any fixed restriction on the allowable cost functions, no nontrivial restriction on the allowable network topologies or on the number of commodities can reduce the price of anarchy further. To make this precise, call a nonempty set $\mathcal{G}$ of networks *nontrivial* if there is a network $G \in \mathcal{G}$ and a source-destination pair (s_i, t_i) of G such that G contains two distinct s_i-t_i paths, and *trivial* otherwise. If $\mathcal{G}$ is trivial, then $\rho(G,r,c) = 1$ whenever $G \in \mathcal{G}$, since for every vector r of traffic rates and set c of cost functions, (G,r,c) admits only one feasible flow. If $\mathcal{G}$ is nontrivial, on the other hand, then the following proposition holds.

Proposition 3.4.11 *Let $\mathcal{G}$ be a nontrivial set of networks and $\mathcal{C}$ a set of cost functions containing all of the constant functions. Let $\mathcal{I}$ denote the set of instances with an underlying network in $\mathcal{G}$ and cost functions in $\mathcal{C}$. Then,*

$$\sup_{(G,r,c)\in\mathcal{I}} \rho(G,r,c) = \alpha(\mathcal{C}),$$

where $\alpha(\mathcal{C})$ is the anarchy value of $\mathcal{C}$.

The proof of Proposition 3.4.11 in similar to that of Theorem 3.4.2 and only an informal sketch is given here. Suppose $\mathcal{G}$ is nontrivial and $\mathcal{C}$ contains all of the constant cost functions. There is then a network $G \in \mathcal{G}$, a source-destination pair (s_i, t_i) of G, and distinct s_i-t_i paths P_1 and P_2. Define the traffic rate of all commodities other than i to be zero (or sufficiently small). Give every edge outside

P_1 and P_2 a cost function everywhere equal to a sufficiently large constant. Let the common prefix of P_1 and P_2 terminate at the vertex u (possibly s_i), and let (u, v) and (u, w) be the subsequent (distinct) edges on P_1 and P_2, respectively. Give edge (u, v) a cost function c with anarchy value arbitrarily close to $\alpha(\mathcal{C})$ and set the traffic rate r_i so that the right-side of (3.5) is arbitrarily close to $\alpha(c)$ (for the appropriate choice of $x \geq 0$). Give the edge (u, w) the constant cost function c_2 that is everywhere equal to $c(r_i)$. All other edges in P_1 and P_2 receive the zero cost function. This defines an instance on G with cost functions in $\mathcal{C}$ that has the same price of anarchy as a two-node, two-link instance with traffic rate r_i and cost functions c and c_2. The cost function c and the traffic rate r_i can be chosen so that this instance has a price of anarchy that is arbitrarily close to $\alpha(\mathcal{C})$.

More general versions of Proposition 3.4.11, for sets of cost functions that need not contain all of the constant functions, are also possible. Details are left to the interested reader.

3.5 Computing the Price of Anarchy

The past two sections showed that simple examples exhibit worst-possible losses due to selfish routing. One consequence of this work, Theorem 3.4.9, is that the price of anarchy with respect to an inhomogeneous set $\mathcal{C}$ of allowable cost functions is nothing more than the anarchy value $\alpha(\mathcal{C})$ of Definition 3.3.3. This provides a general reduction from a combinatorial problem—finding a worst-case example among all possible multicommodity flow instances—to the much simpler analytical one of finding the worst cost function in a given set. This reduction permits the computation of the price of anarchy for many different function classes. This section illustrates such computations by determining the price of anarchy for two different function classes: degree-bounded polynomials with nonnegative coefficients, and the delay functions of M/M/1 queues. Other sets of functions can be treated in a similar way.

3.5.1 The Price of Anarchy with Polynomial Cost Functions

For a positive integer p, let $\mathcal{C}_p$ denote the set of polynomials with nonnegative coefficients and degree at most p. As the first showcase for our machinery, we next compute the price of anarchy with respect to the cost functions $\mathcal{C}_p$, thereby discovering that the networks of Example 2.5.4 are the worst possible.

Proposition 3.5.1 *If $\mathcal{I}_p$ is the set of instances with cost functions in $\mathcal{C}_p$, then*

$$\sup_{(G,r,c)\in\mathcal{I}_p} \rho(G,r,c) = [1 - p \cdot (p+1)^{-(p+1)/p}]^{-1} = \Theta\left(\frac{p}{\ln p}\right).$$

Proof: Since $\mathcal{C}_p$ contains the constant functions, Theorem 3.4.2 implies that the price of anarchy is simply the anarchy value of $\mathcal{C}_p$. Since the cost functions in $\mathcal{C}_p$ are continuously differentiable and convex, we can compute the anarchy value using the equation (3.6) of Proposition 3.3.2. We further assert that we need only compute the anarchy value of the functions of $\mathcal{C}_p$ that comprise only one term—$\{ax^i : a \geq 0, i \in \{0,1,2,\ldots,p\}\}$, a set we denote by $\widetilde{\mathcal{C}}_p$—in that $\alpha(\mathcal{C}_p) = \alpha(\widetilde{\mathcal{C}}_p)$. This assertion holds because an instance (G,r,c) with cost functions in $\mathcal{C}_p$ can be transformed into an equivalent instance with cost functions in $\widetilde{\mathcal{C}}_p$, by replacing an edge e of G with the cost function $c_e(x) = \sum_{i=0}^{p} a_i x^i$ by a directed path of $p+1$ edges, with the ith edge of the path possessing the cost function $\widetilde{c}_{e,i}(x) = a_i x^i$.

We next use Proposition 3.3.2 to compute the anarchy value $\alpha(c)$ of an arbitrary nonzero function $c(x) = ax^i$ of $\widetilde{\mathcal{C}}_p$. If $i = 0$ then $\alpha(c) = 1$. For $i > 0$, the corresponding marginal cost function c^* is strictly increasing and the scalar λ in (3.6) is then uniquely determined by the choice of r. Solving for λ, we obtain $\lambda = (i+1)^{-1/i}$ and hence $\mu = \lambda^i = (i+1)^{-1}$. It follows that

$$[\lambda\mu + (1-\lambda)]^{-1} = [(i+1)^{-(i+1)/i} + (1 - (i+1)^{-1/i})]^{-1} = [1 - i \cdot (i+1)^{-(i+1)/i}]^{-1}.$$

Since this expression is independent of $r > 0$,

$$\alpha(c) = [1 - i \cdot (i+1)^{-(i+1)/i}]^{-1}. \tag{3.9}$$

The right-hand side of (3.9) is independent of a, and a simple derivative test shows that it is increasing in i. The functions of $\widetilde{\mathcal{C}}_p$ with largest anarchy value are therefore those of the form ax^p for $a > 0$. Theorem 3.4.2 then gives

$$\sup_{(G,r,c)\in\mathcal{I}_p} \rho(G,r,c) = \alpha(\widetilde{\mathcal{C}}_p) = [1 - p \cdot (p+1)^{-(p+1)/p}]^{-1}. \tag{3.10}$$

Elementary calculations, omitted here, show that the right-hand side of (3.10) is asymptotically $\Theta(p/\ln p)$ as $p \to \infty$. $\blacksquare$

In particular, Proposition 3.5.1 shows that when cost functions are low-degree polynomials, the price of anarchy is a small constant. For example, for quartic polynomials—common in transportation applications, see Section 3.7—the price of anarchy is roughly 2. More generally, Proposition 3.5.1 can be viewed as confirming the following moral:

the price of anarchy is small unless cost functions are extremely steep.

Remark 3.5.2 Proposition 3.5.1 is stated for polynomials with nonnegative coefficients, but not all nondecreasing polynomials have only nonnegative coefficients. The price of anarchy with respect to arbitrary (nondecreasing) polynomials of degree at most p obviously lies in the interval $[(1 - p \cdot (p+1)^{-(p+1)/p})^{-1}, \infty]$. Despite the fact that this price of anarchy is simply the anarchy value of the corresponding set of cost functions, no other upper or lower bounds have yet been established.

3.5.2 The Price of Anarchy with M/M/1 Delay Functions

Cost functions of the form $c(x) = (u - x)^{-1}$ for $x < u$ arise as the (expected) delay function of an M/M/1 queue—a single queue with Poisson arrivals and exponentially distributed service times. Readers unfamiliar with this queueing theory terminology can think of such a function as a natural way to model an edge capacity u, with the delay of the link approaching infinity as the amount of traffic approaches the capacity. In any case, these M/M/1 delay functions are ubiquitous in networking (see Section 3.7).

M/M/1 delay functions do not directly fit into our model, since they are defined only on the set $[0, u)$, rather than on the entire nonnegative line. However, this is not an important distinction, as this section shows.

Now we fix two parameters, the largest allowable sum of all traffic rates R_{max} and the smallest allowable edge capacity u_{min}. For the moment, make the strong assumption that $R_{max} < u_{min}$. The following analysis shows that in the absence of this or similar assumptions, the price of anarchy is $+\infty$. Under this assumption, the restricted domains of the cost functions pose no difficulty, as every feasible flow routes at most R_{max} units of flow on every edge and hence has a well-defined cost.

Let $\mathcal{C}$ denote the set of cost functions $\{c(x) = (u - x)^{-1} : u \geq u_{min}\}$. For this example, we redefine the anarchy value $\alpha(c)$ of Definition 3.3.1 and Proposition 3.3.2 so that the variable r can only range over $[0, R_{max}]$, rather than the entire nonnegative line.

Next, it is straightforward to check that Theorem 3.4.9 remains valid with our new definition of anarchy value, provided we are only concerned with the worst-possible value of ρ achieved by instances with sum of all traffic rates at most R_{max}. Since the set $\mathcal{C}$ is inhomogeneous, Theorem 3.4.9 implies that the price of anarchy for instances with cost functions in $\mathcal{C}$ and sum of all traffic rates at most R_{max} is precisely the anarchy value of $\mathcal{C}$. The next proposition computes this anarchy value.

Proposition 3.5.3 *If $\mathcal{I}$ is the set of instances with cost functions in $\mathcal{C}$ and sum of all traffic rates at most $R_{max} < u_{min}$, then*

$$\sup_{(G,r,c)\in\mathcal{I}} \rho(G,r,c) = \frac{1}{2}\left(1 + \sqrt{\frac{u_{min}}{u_{min} - R_{max}}}\right). \tag{3.11}$$

Proof: The previous discussion implies that we need only check that $\alpha(\mathcal{C})$ is equal to the right-hand size of (3.11). Since every function in $\mathcal{C}$ is continuously differentiable and convex, we can compute anarchy values using equation (3.6) of Proposition 3.3.2.

We begin by computing the anarchy value of an arbitrary function in $\mathcal{C}$, $c(x) = (u - x)^{-1}$ for $u \geq u_{min}$. The marginal cost function c^* is given by $\frac{d}{dx}(x(u - x)^{-1})$ and hence $c^*(x) = u/(u - x)^2$. Now fix $r \in (0, R_{max}]$; solving for λ in $c^*(\lambda r) = c(r)$ we obtain $\lambda = (u - \sqrt{u(u - r)})/r$. Next,

$$\mu = \frac{c(\lambda r)}{c(r)} = \frac{u - r}{u - \lambda r} = \frac{u - r}{u - (u - \sqrt{u}\sqrt{u - r})} = \frac{\sqrt{u - r}}{\sqrt{u}}.$$

It remains to compute $[\lambda\mu + (1 - \lambda)]^{-1}$:

$$\begin{aligned}
[\lambda\mu + (1 - \lambda)]^{-1} &= \left[\frac{u - \sqrt{u}\sqrt{u - r}}{r}\frac{\sqrt{u - r}}{\sqrt{u}} + 1 - \frac{u - \sqrt{u}\sqrt{u - r}}{r}\right]^{-1} \\
&= \left[\frac{2u\sqrt{u - r} - 2u\sqrt{u} + 2r\sqrt{u}}{r\sqrt{u}}\right]^{-1} \\
&= \frac{1}{2}\frac{r}{\sqrt{u}\sqrt{u - r} - (u - r)} \cdot \frac{\sqrt{u}\sqrt{u - r} + (u - r)}{\sqrt{u}\sqrt{u - r} + (u - r)} \\
&= \frac{1}{2}\left(1 + \sqrt{\frac{u}{u - r}}\right).
\end{aligned}$$

Since this expression is increasing in r, it follows that

$$\alpha(c) = \frac{1}{2}\left(1 + \sqrt{\frac{u}{u - R_{max}}}\right).$$

Since the anarchy value is decreasing in the edge capacity, $\alpha(\mathcal{C})$ equals the right-hand side of (3.11), as claimed. ∎

Remark 3.5.4 The set $\mathcal{C} = \{c(x) = (u - x)^{-1} : u \geq u_{min}\}$ is not diverse, since $c(0) \leq 1/u_{min}$ for all $c \in \mathcal{C}$. Therefore, Theorems 3.4.2 and 3.4.5 are not sufficient to compute the price of anarchy in this application.

As mentioned earlier, the anarchy value of $\mathcal{C}$, and hence the price of anarchy, goes to $+\infty$ as $R_{max} \uparrow u_{min}$. We can therefore conclude that selfish routing is, in the worst case, quite costly in networks with M/M/1 delay functions.

On the bright side, Proposition 3.5.3 confirms the intuition that selfish routing should not be costly in a lightly loaded network. Proposition 3.5.3 also easily extends to other classes of networks in which our draconian assumption that $R_{max} < u_{min}$ fails. Roughly speaking, the price of anarchy remains finite provided Nash flows are guaranteed to leave some bounded fraction of capacity unused on all edges of the network:

> selfish routing is benign when there is excess capacity.

The next section develops this moral further with a simple design strategy for combating the inefficiency of selfish routing in congested networks with M/M/1 delay functions: doubling the capacity of every edge in the network reduces the cost at least as much as routing traffic optimally.

3.6 A Bicriteria Bound in General Networks

Example 2.5.4 shows that if no restrictions are placed on the cost functions of a network, then the price of anarchy is unbounded, even in two-node, two-link networks. On the other hand, this example does not rule out interesting bounds that avoid directly comparing the costs of Nash and optimal flows. Toward this end, we study a so-called bicriteria comparison, which compares the cost of a flow at Nash equilibrium to that of an optimal flow that must route additional traffic.

Example 3.6.1 In Example 2.5.4, an optimal flow feasible for a rate $r > 1$ assigns the additional flow to the upper link, now incurring a cost that tends to $r - 1$ as $p \to \infty$. In particular, for every p an optimal flow feasible for twice the rate ($r = 2$) has cost at least 1, which equals the cost of the flow at Nash equilibrium at the original traffic rate.

The main result of this section is that the bound stated in Example 3.6.1 holds for *all* instances.

Theorem 3.6.2 *If f is a flow at Nash equilibrium for (G, r, c) and f^* is feasible*

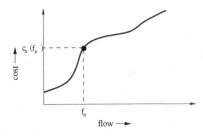

(a) Graph of cost function c_e and its value at flow value f_e

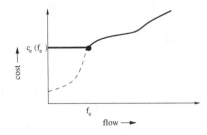

(b) Graph of cost function $\bar{c}_e$

Figure 3.4
Construction in the proof of Theorem 3.6.2 of modified cost function $\bar{c}_e$ given original cost function c_e and Nash flow value f_e. Solid lines denote graphs of functions.

for $(G, 2r, c)$, *then*

$$C(f) \leq C(f^*).$$

Proof: Suppose f and f^* satisfy the hypotheses of the theorem. By Corollary 2.2.3, for each commodity $i = 1, \ldots, k$, all s_i-t_i flow paths of f have a common cost $c_i(f)$. By Proposition 2.2.4,

$$C(f) = \sum_i c_i(f) r_i.$$

We next define a set of cost functions $\bar{c}$ that satisfies two convenient properties. First, the new cost functions approximate the original ones, in the sense that the cost of a flow with respect to cost functions $\bar{c}$ will be close to its original cost. Second, the cost functions $\bar{c}$ are constructed so that a strong lower bound on the cost of f^* is easy to obtain. For each edge e, the cost function $\bar{c}_e$ is defined as follows:

$$\bar{c}_e(x) = \begin{cases} c_e(f_e) & \text{if } x \leq f_e \\ c_e(x) & \text{if } x \geq f_e. \end{cases}$$

Figure 3.4 illustrates this construction. The cost $C(f)$ of the Nash flow f is left unchanged by this construction.

We first compare the cost of the flow f^* under the new cost functions $\bar{c}$ to its original cost $C(f^*)$. For every edge e, $\bar{c}_e(x) - c_e(x)$ is zero for $x \geq f_e$ and bounded above by $c_e(f_e)$ for $x < f_e$, so

$$x(\bar{c}_e(x) - c_e(x)) \leq c_e(f_e)f_e \tag{3.12}$$

for all $x \geq 0$. The left-hand side of (3.12)—the discrepancy between $x\bar{c}_e(x)$ and $xc_e(x)$—is maximized when x is slightly smaller than f_e and when $c_e(x) = 0$. In this case, the value of the left-hand side of (3.12) is essentially the area of the rectangle enclosed by dashed lines in Figure 3.4(a), which in turn is the cost incurred by the Nash flow f on the edge e. The difference between the new cost (with respect to $\bar{c}$) and the old cost (with respect to c) can now be bounded above as follows:

$$\begin{aligned}
\sum_e \bar{c}_e(f_e^*)f_e^* - C(f^*) &= \sum_{e \in E} f_e^*(\bar{c}_e(f_e^*) - c_e(f_e^*)) \\
&\leq \sum_{e \in E} c_e(f_e)f_e \\
&= C(f). \tag{3.13}
\end{aligned}$$

In other words, evaluating f^* with cost functions $\bar{c}$, rather than c, increases its cost by at most an additive $C(f)$ factor.

On the other hand, if f_0 denotes the zero flow in G, then by construction $\bar{c}_P(f_0) \geq c_i(f)$ for every path $P \in \mathcal{P}_i$. Since $\bar{c}_e$ is nondecreasing for each edge e, it follows that $\bar{c}_P(f^*) \geq c_i(f)$ for every path $P \in \mathcal{P}_i$. Thus, the cost of f^* with respect to $\bar{c}$ can be bounded from below:

$$\begin{aligned}
\sum_{P \in \mathcal{P}} \bar{c}_P(f^*)f_P^* &\geq \sum_i \sum_{P \in \mathcal{P}_i} c_i(f)f_P^* \\
&= \sum_i 2c_i(f)r_i \\
&= 2C(f). \tag{3.14}
\end{aligned}$$

Combining inequalities (3.13) and (3.14), we obtain the theorem:

$$\begin{aligned}
C(f^*) &\geq \sum_P \bar{c}_P(f^*)f_P^* - C(f) \\
&\geq 2C(f) - C(f) \\
&= C(f).
\end{aligned}$$

∎

The same proof also shows the following more general result.

Theorem 3.6.3 *If f is a flow at Nash equilibrium for (G, r, c) and f^* is feasible for $(G, (1 + \xi)r, c)$ with $\xi > 0$, then*

$$C(f) \leq \frac{1}{\xi} \cdot C(f^*).$$

Remark 3.6.4 Example 2.5.4 shows that Theorem 3.6.3 is tight for all values of $\xi > 0$.

The following corollary notes that comparing a Nash flow to an optimal flow forced to route more traffic is equivalent to comparing a Nash flow in a better network to an optimal flow in the original network.

Corollary 3.6.5 *Let (G, r, c) be an instance and define the modified cost function $\tilde{c}_e$ by $\tilde{c}_e(x) = c_e(x/2)/2$ for each edge e. Let $\tilde{f}$ and f^* be Nash and feasible flows for $(G, r, \tilde{c})$ and (G, r, c), respectively. Let $\tilde{C}(\tilde{f})$ and $C(f^*)$ denote their respective costs. Then,*

$$\tilde{C}(\tilde{f}) \leq C(f^*).$$

Proof: Let f be a Nash flow for $(G, r/2, c)$ and f^* a flow feasible for (G, r, c). By Theorem 3.6.2,

$$\sum_{e \in E} c_e(f_e) f_e \leq \sum_{e \in E} c_e(f_e^*) f_e^*. \tag{3.15}$$

Now consider the flow $\tilde{f} = 2f$, viewed as a feasible flow for $(G, r, \tilde{c})$. Since $\tilde{c}_e(\tilde{f}_e) = c_e(f_e)/2$ for each edge e and f is a Nash flow for (G, r, c), $\tilde{f}$ is a Nash flow for $(G, r, \tilde{c})$. Moreover, f and $\tilde{f}$ have the same costs in their respective instances:

$$\sum_{e \in E} \tilde{c}_e(\tilde{f}_e) \tilde{f}_e = \sum_{e \in E} \left(\frac{1}{2} c_e(f_e) \right)(2f_e) = \sum_{e \in E} c_e(f_e) f_e. \tag{3.16}$$

Since $\tilde{f}$ is a Nash flow for $(G, r, \tilde{c})$, combining (3.15) and (3.16) proves the corollary. ∎

As the chapter introduction and the end of Section 3.5 promise, Corollary 3.6.5 suggests the following moral: the benefit of centralized control is equaled or exceeded by the benefit of a sufficient improvement in link technology. This moral takes on a particularly nice form in instances in which all cost functions are the M/M/1 delay functions of Section 3.5.2. In this case, if the cost function c_e of edge e is $c_e(x) = (u_e - x)^{-1}$, then the modified function $\tilde{c}_e$ is

$$\tilde{c}_e(x) = 1/2(u_e - x/2) = 1/(2u_e - x).$$

Corollary 3.6.5 thus offers the following advice for networks with M/M/1 delay functions:

to beat optimal routing, double the capacity of every edge.

3.7 Notes

Section 3.2

Section 3.2 is based on Roughgarden and Tardos [347, 348].

Networks with linear cost functions have been studied as a special case of selfish routing for a long time. For example, Dafermos and Sparrow [108] singled out linear cost functions as an interesting special case, and Braess's Paradox [64, 285] was first described in a network with linear cost functions. Since these early works, many other authors have given special attention to this type of cost function [9, 8, 161, 162, 310, 313, 373, 374]. Some authors use the word *affine* instead of linear to describe these cost functions.

As discussed at the end of Section 3.2, linear cost functions naturally describe mechanical and electrical networks, like those in Section 1.3.3 and in Cohen and Horowitz [82]. Another interesting motivation for linear cost functions was discovered by Friedman [164], who showed how linear cost functions arise in a simple model of selfish users transferring files over a network employing a congestion control protocol, such as the popular Internet protocol TCP.

Lemma 3.2.1 first appeared in Dafermos and Sparrow [108]. Corollary 3.2.2 is implicit in [108], and is explicit in Barro and Romer [32] and Altman et al. [9, 8]. Other properties of cost functions of the form $c(x) = ax$ have been investigated in the context of electrical networks [57, 85]. Lemmas 3.2.3–3.2.5 and Theorem 3.2.6 are from Roughgarden and Tardos [347, 348]. In [347, 348] the proof of Lemma 3.2.5 did not explicitly use Proposition 2.4.4 and for this reason was somewhat longer than the proof included here. The discussion in Section 3.2.4 is based on Roughgarden [341, 343]. The phrase "succinct certificate" in this discussion is meant to parallel the definition of the computational complexity class NP; see Papadimitriou [302], for example, for further details. Corollary 3.2.7 was first observed by L. A. Goldberg (personal communication, November 2000) and appeared in Roughgarden and Tardos [348].

Finally, the proof of Theorem 3.2.6 given in Section 3.2 is not the shortest possible, though it is arguably the easiest to motivate. Specializing the proof of Theorem 3.3.7 to linear cost functions gives a shorter proof, and Correa, Schulz, and Stier Moses [93] give a direct short proof of Theorem 3.2.6.

Section 3.3

Section 3.3 is based on Roughgarden [341, 343] and Correa, Schulz, and Stier Moses [93, 356]. Theorem 3.3.7 has undergone several iterations in just a few short years. Roughgarden [339] first proved Theorem 3.3.7 for the special case of bounded-degree polynomials with nonnegative coefficients. Compared to the techniques used in Section 3.3, the proof in [339] was more closely based on the linear cost function analysis of Section 3.2. The proof in [339] was fairly complex, relied on the semiconvexity of polynomials with nonnegative coefficients in several different ways, and did not explicitly take advantage of the variational inequality given in Corollary 2.6.6. Roughgarden [341] extended this proof to arbitrary sets of semiconvex cost functions, using (3.6) as the definition of the anarchy value. A. Ronen (personal communication, March 2002) pointed out that Corollary 2.6.6 could be used to vastly simplify the proof of Theorem 3.3.7 for sets of semiconvex cost functions. This revised analysis appears in Roughgarden [343]. Correa, Schulz, and Stier Moses [93] then showed that, once the proof is based on Corollary 2.6.6, it can be modified so that the semiconvexity of the cost functions no longer plays any role. The more general definition of the anarchy value in Definition 3.3.1 and the proof of Theorem 3.3.7 given in Section 3.3 are both taken from [93].

Section 3.4

The results of Sections 3.4.1–3.4.3 are all from Roughgarden [341, 343]. Proposition 3.4.11 is also implicit in [343]. In [341], inhomogeneous sets of cost functions were called "nondegenerate."

The proof of Lemma 3.4.8 assumed that the price of anarchy of a certain instance is continuous under a restricted type of perturbation of its cost functions. This assumption can be established rigorously in several different ways. For example, it follows from the quite general results of Rockafellar [332] on the continuity of minima of convex programs.

Section 3.5

This section is also based on Roughgarden [341, 343]. As noted above, Proposition 3.5.1 was first proved in [339]. The calculations showing that $[1 - p \cdot (p+1)^{-(p+1)/p}]^{-1}$ grows like $\Theta(p/\ln p)$ as $p \to \infty$ are standard Taylor expansions and estimates using the exponential function. In fact, these calculations show that

$$\frac{p/\ln p}{[1 - p \cdot (p+1)^{-(p+1)/p}]^{-1}} \xrightarrow{p \to \infty} 1;$$

in other words, the leading constant is 1 (B. von Stengel, personal communication, July 2004). As noted in the main text, quartic polynomials are one of the most popular types of cost functions in transportation applications. See Sheffi [359], for example, for details.

The trick used in the proof of Proposition 3.5.1—reducing the computation of the anarchy value of a polynomial to that of a monomial—illustrates the following more general principle. If $\mathcal{C}$ is the *cone*—the set of all finite nonnegative linear combinations—generated by a (possibly infinite) set of cost functions S, then the price of anarchy of instances with cost functions in S equals the price of anarchy of instances with cost functions in $\mathcal{C}$.

For background on queueing theory and M/M/1 delay functions, see, for example, Grimmett and Stirzaker [178], Gross and Harris [179], Hillier and Lieberman [193], or Karlin and Taylor [216]. Because routing switches are essentially networks of queues and because M/M/1 queues are the simplest ones to analyze, M/M/1 delay functions are among the most popular cost functions in computer networking research. For examples of this, see the textbooks of Bertsekas and Tsitsiklis [51] and Bertsekas and Gallagher [50], and many of the references therein.

Proposition 3.5.3 is from Roughgarden [341, 343]. The fact that the price of anarchy of instances with M/M/1 delay functions and unrestricted traffic rates is infinite was noted earlier by Friedman [164].

For applications of Theorem 3.4.9 to still more sets of cost functions, see Roughgarden [343] and Correa, Schulz, and Stier Moses [93]. M/G/1 queueing delay functions are treated in the former paper, and several other sets, including concave cost functions, are considered in the latter.

Section 3.6

The results of Section 3.6 are due to Roughgarden and Tardos [347, 348]. The term "bicriteria" is commonly used in the theoretical computer science community to indicate that two objective functions are being simultaneously optimized. In Section 3.6, the two objective functions are the cost of a Nash flow relative to an optimal flow, and the amount of extra traffic that the optimal flow is forced to route. Theorem 3.6.3 quantifies the trade-off between these two objective functions. Theorem 3.6.2, and especially its reformulation as Corollary 3.6.5, are inspired by *resource augmentation*. The idea of resource augmentation is to give a protagonist—traditionally an algorithm, but in Section 3.6 a Nash flow—extra resources before comparing its performance to the best-achievable performance. Corollary 3.6.5, which gives faster links to the Nash flow than to the optimal flow, is clearly an example of this approach. The idea of resource augmentation dates back at least to Sleator and Tarjan [363], who studied algorithms for managing computer caches. A decade later, Kalyanasundaram and Pruhs [211] spearheaded a resurgence of the resource augmentation philosophy, with applications to machine scheduling problems. See [44, 131, 273, 319] for more recent papers in this line of research.

As in Section 3.5, M/M/1 delay functions require a technical aside because they are finite-valued only on a strict subset of the nonnegative real line. Indeed, some of the groundwork laid in Chapter 2 does not carry over to cost functions that can be infinite-valued. For example, there are networks with M/M/1 delay functions in which some Nash flows have finite cost and others have infinite cost (cf., Proposition 2.2.6). In Section 3.5 these difficulties were eluded by restricting the sum of all traffic rates of a network to be strictly less than its minimum edge capacity. A successful application of Corollary 3.6.5 to networks with M/M/1 delay functions requires a far weaker assumption—merely that all Nash flows in the double-capacity network have finite cost. See [342] for further details.

The Price of Anarchy in the KP Model

The price of anarchy is a very general concept, applicable to every noncooperative game with a natural objective function. Indeed, there have been many successful analyses of the price of anarchy for games that do not involve selfish routing. Since this book aims for depth more than breadth, most of these results are only briefly mentioned. However, one such game-theoretic model has been highly influential and warrants more detailed discussion. The following review of that model assumes comfort with discrete probability at the level of, say, Stirzaker [376].

Koutsoupias and Papadimitriou [239] invented a load-balancing model that we will call the *KP model*. As noted earlier, the price of anarchy was first defined in the KP model, where it was called the *coordination ratio* [239]. In the KP model, there are n network users, each of which wants to route its traffic on one of m parallel links. Unlike the selfish routing model studied in most of this book, network users control a nonnegligible fraction of the overall traffic. User j is assumed to have a *size* w^j indicating the amount of traffic that it controls. Each user j is allowed to choose a probability distribution $\{p_1^j, \ldots, p_m^j\}$ over the links—in the terminology of Section 2.8, a *mixed strategy*—where p_i^j is the probability that user j routes all of its traffic on the link i. Users are not permitted to split traffic over multiple links.

In the most basic version of the model, each link i has a cost function defined by one parameter, its *speed* s_i. If a total of W units of traffic are routed on link i, then its cost is defined to be W/s_i. Given a collection of probability distributions $\{p^j\}$, one for each user, the *expected load* of link i is simply $(\sum_{j=1}^{n} p_i^j w^j)/s_i$. User j's cost is defined as the expected load on the link on which its traffic is routed:

$$\sum_{i=1}^{m} \frac{p_i^j}{s_i} \left(w^j + \sum_{j' \neq j} p_i^{j'} w^{j'} \right).$$

The KP model is thus a finite normal form game in the sense of Section 2.8. Accordingly, a *Nash equilibrium* is a collection of probability distributions, one for each user, so that no user can decrease its cost by changing its probability distribution, assuming that all other users' distributions remain fixed. Nash's theorem [292, 293] guarantees the existence of a Nash equilibrium.

The social objective function is defined as the expected load of the most loaded link:

$$\mathbf{E}\left[\max_{i=1}^{m} \left(\sum_{j=1}^{n} I_i^j w^j \right) \right], \tag{3.17}$$

where I_i^j is the indicator random variable for the event that user j routes its traffic on link i, and the expectation is over the product distribution $p^1 \times \cdots \times p^n$. This objective function differs from the one used in most of this book, as (3.17) is determined by the maximum, rather than the average, cost incurred by traffic. This book studies this type of objective function only in Section 4.7.

The price of anarchy is defined, as in Definition 2.3.1, as the worst-case ratio between the objective function value of a Nash equilibrium and of an optimal solution. In contrast to

Proposition 2.2.6, different Nash equilibria can possess different objective function values in the KP model. As discussed following Definition 2.3.1, the price of anarchy is then determined by the Nash equilibrium with the worst objective function value.

Koutsoupias and Papadimitriou [239] proved several upper and lower bounds on the price of anarchy in the KP model. In particular, Koutsoupias and Papadimitriou [239] noticed a fundamental connection between the KP model and classical analyses of "balls and bins," based on the following example. Suppose there are m users and m links, with all sizes and speeds equal to 1. An optimal solution, with each user deterministically selecting a unique link, has social objective function value 1. This is also a Nash equilibrium. On the other hand, suppose all users select the uniform distribution. By symmetry, this defines another Nash equilibrium. The problem of computing the social objective function value of this Nash equilibrium is isomorphic to throwing m balls into m bins uniformly at random and determining the expected number of balls in the most densely populated bin. The latter problem has been extensively studied, and this expectation is asymptotically equal to $\Theta(\ln m / \ln \ln m)$ as $m \to \infty$. This fact can be proved via, for example, the Chernoff-Hoeffding bounds [77, 197], which are described in the textbooks of Motwani and Raghavan [284] and Alon and Spencer [7]. As a result, the price of anarchy in the KP model, even for uniform user sizes and uniform link speeds, is $\Omega(\ln m / \ln \ln m)$.

Koutsoupias and Papadimitriou [239] were able to prove an upper bound of roughly $O(\sqrt{m})$ on the price of anarchy, which left a significant gap between their upper and lower bounds. Mavronicolas and Spirakis [272] were the first to make progress toward closing this gap, by showing that when all link speeds are equal, all *fully mixed* Nash equilibria—all equilibria for which $p_i^j > 0$ for all links i and users j—have a social objective function value that is $O(\ln m / \ln \ln m)$ times that of an optimal solution. They also showed a bound of $O(\ln n / \ln \ln n)$ for fully mixed Nash equilibria and for links with different speeds, under the two assumptions that $m \leq n$ and that all users have equal size. The proofs in [272] were quite complicated. Subsequently, three separate groups of researchers, whose work is described here in increasing order of generality, independently made further progress on the problem. Bradford [63] showed that the price of anarchy is $O(\ln m / \ln \ln m)$ when all links have the same speed and $n/m = O(1)$. Koutsoupias, Mavronicolas, and Spirakis [238] showed that the price of anarchy is $O(\ln m / \ln \ln m)$ with uniform link speeds and no additional assumptions. The third paper, Czumaj and Vöcking [99], completely settled the problem. First, they also showed an $O(\ln m / \ln \ln m)$ upper bound on the price of anarchy for uniform link speeds, and proved that the leading constant term equals 1. Moreover, Czumaj and Vöcking [99] showed that this upper bound follows readily from standard Hoeffding bounds [197]. Most importantly, Czumaj and Vöcking [99] also settled the general problem where both link speeds and user sizes are arbitrary. By establishing matching upper and lower bounds, they proved that the price of anarchy for general speeds and sizes is asymptotically equal to the rather startling expression $\Theta(\ln m / \ln \ln \ln m)$.

Even with its price of anarchy resolved, work on the KP model has continued at a rapid pace. Recent research includes studies of the complexity of computing Nash equilibria with various properties [136, 142, 159, 169], further study of fully mixed equilibria [169, 259], and bounds on the price on anarchy for variants of the KP model [28, 42, 98, 160, 167, 168]. For more details, see the surveys of Czumaj [97] and Feldmann et al. [143].

The Price of Anarchy in Other Games

These notes conclude with brief descriptions of several successful analyses of the price of anarchy in games other than selfish routing, extensions thereof, and the KP model. For several more very recent analyses of the price of anarchy in applications not described below, see [24, 145, 183, 206]. For work on the many extensions of the basic selfish routing model, see Chapter 4

First, Vetta [388] analyzed the price of anarchy in a fairly broad class of profit-maximization games. A facility location example illustrates his results. Suppose there are k players, each of whom can locate a factory at one of n locations. At each location there is a market that is willing to pay an amount p_j to receive a good. The cost to a player of providing this good to a location is assumed equal to the distance c_{ij} between the player's factory i and the location j. Players offer goods at whatever price they desire, and a market j will purchase the good at the lowest available price, or not at all if all of the offered prices exceed p_j. Competition is assumed to dictate the result as follows: each location j is served by the closest factory i, at a price equal to $\min\{c_{kj}, p_j\}$, where k is the second-closest factory. The justification for this price is that any higher price will either allow profitable undercutting by the player owning factory k or cause market j to refuse the good, while any lower price will simply decrease the profits of the player owning i. The objective function of a player is simply its profit—the revenue it receives minus its shipping costs. The social objective function is assumed to be the total consumer surplus, where the consumer surplus of location j is its willingness to pay p_j minus the price it is actually charged for receiving the good, or is 0 if it does not receive the good at all. Vetta [388] showed that this price of anarchy is exactly 2, in the sense that every Nash equilibrium of this game has a consumer surplus that is at least half of the maximum achievable. He also gave an example showing that no better bound is possible. In addition, Vetta [388] described similar results for more general facility location problems, auctions, and a profit-maximization version of selfish routing. Mirrokni and Vetta [282] recently proved that many of these bounds on the price of anarchy hold even if players only "partially converge" to a Nash equilibrium. For an analysis of the price of anarchy of noncooperative facility location with a cost-minimization objective, see Devanur et al. [116].

Anshelevich et al. [15] and Fabrikant et al. [137] studied the price of anarchy in network design games, with the goal of understanding how the decentralized formation of a network like the Internet compares to what could have been achieved with hindsight. Such network design games have a rich history; see the survey by Jackson [202], for example, for more details.

The basic game in Anshelevich et al. [15] is the following. There is a graph $G = (V, E)$, directed or undirected, where edge e has a constant cost c_e. There are k players, each of which wants to connect its source vertex s_i to a common destination vertex t. Each player decides on a vector of payments, one for each edge. If the sum of payments for an edge is at least its cost, then the edge is bought. A set of payment vectors is feasible if the subset of bought edges includes an s_i-t path for each player i. The goal of each player is to minimize its total payments, while the social objective is to minimize the cost of the bought edges. Anshelevich et al. [15] showed that the worst-case price of anarchy in these games is precisely k, and instead focused on the price of stability—the ratio between the objective function values of a best Nash equilibrium and an optimal solution—a concept that was mentioned in Section 2.8.

Although the price of stability does not give the strong worst-case guarantee of the price of anarchy, it is still an interesting quantity to bound; see Sections 4.3 and 4.4 and in particular Remark 4.3.5 for more on this point. Anshelevich et al. [15] showed, among other things, that the price of stability for this game is 1—some optimal solution also arises as a Nash equilibrium. See also Anshelevich et al. [14] for further work on the price of stability in this and related network design games.

Fabrikant et al. [137] considered a somewhat different network design game, as follows. There are n vertices, which are the players, and each decides on a set of undirected edges to pay for. The result is a graph $G = (V, E)$ where V is the set of players, and E is the union of the bought edges. Each player is assumed to have two opposing goals: each wants to buy few edges, yet wants to be well connected to the rest of the vertices in the final graph. To model this, the authors assumed that each vertex wants to minimize the sum of its distances to the other $n - 1$ vertices plus α times the number of edges that it pays for, where distances are with respect to the full graph of bought edges and α is a nonnegative parameter. If two vertices are not connected by a path then their distance is interpreted as infinite, so every Nash equilibrium results in a connected graph. When α is small, connectivity is the main objective, while as α grows large, buying as few edges as possible accrues paramount importance. The price of anarchy in this game turns out to depend fundamentally on the value of α. Fabrikant et al. [137] proved that the price of anarchy when $\alpha < 2$ is at most 4/3, but is at least 3 for sufficiently large α. For large α, they proved an upper bound of $O(\sqrt{\alpha})$ on the price of anarchy, and an upper bound of 5 for Nash equilibria in which the resulting graph is a tree. A significant gap remains between the upper and lower bounds on the price of anarchy for general Nash equilibria for large values of α.

Finally, Johari and Tsitsiklis [208] studied the price of anarchy in a bandwidth allocation game. In the simplest version of the game, n players seek a share of the capacity of a single link. Each player i is assumed to have a smooth, strictly increasing, nonnegative, and concave utility function, and submits a bid to a third party. The third party then uses the bids to allocate the capacity of the shared link to the players. The goal of each player i is to maximize the utility of its share of capacity, minus the payment promised by its bid w_i. Kelly [222] showed that sharing the capacity proportionally—giving a w_i/W fraction of the capacity to user i, where W is the sum of the bids—has the property that the unique equilibrium maximizes the sum of the player utilities over all feasible capacity allocations. Two details of this guarantee require elaboration. First, note that bids factor into individual objective functions but not into the social objective function. While this is a standard assumption in much of economics, it is rather different from the games that we have seen so far. Second, we must be precise about what an "equilibrium" is. Kelly [222] assumed that users are *price-takers*; for proportional capacity sharing, this means that a set of bids is defined to be an equilibrium if for each player i the derivative

of $[U_i(w_i/W) - w_i]$ is equal to 0, where W is the sum of the bids and is assumed constant
in the calculation of the derivative. The concavity of the utility functions ensures that
a zero derivative is a sufficient condition for a global maximum. Price-taking models are
often justified by assuming a large population of small users, so that the actions of a
single individual have negligible impact on the overall system. Johari and Tsitsiklis [208]
were interested in discarding the price-taking assumption, and instead assuming that users
are *price anticipating*. Under proportional sharing, this means that user i seeks a bid w_i
where the derivative of $[U(w_i/\sum_j w_j) - w_i]$ is zero. In other words, a price-anticipating
user takes into account the fact that increasing its bid also increases the sum of the
bids, and it therefore does not result in as large an increase in awarded capacity as
a price-taking user would expect. Since price-anticipating users behave differently than
price-taking ones, we cannot expect Kelly's result [222] to hold for them. Indeed, Johari
and Tsitsiklis [208] showed that there are examples in which the equilibrium for price-
anticipating users recovers only a 3/4 fraction of the maximum-possible sum of utilities.
On the other hand, they also showed that no worse example is possible: the price of anarchy
is precisely 4/3. Some of the ideas in the proof are similar to those discussed earlier in this
book. In particular, Johari and Tsitsiklis [208] prove a fact analogous to Proposition 2.6.1,
that equilibria for price-anticipating users maximize an objective function that is closely
related to the sum of utilities. In a much more technical result, they showed that the
price of anarchy remains 4/3 in a natural generalization of the capacity sharing game to
networks with arbitrary topologies. The fact that the price of anarchy does not increase
in general networks provides a parallel to the moral of Section 3.4, that the simplest of
examples can also be the worst ones. Recent extensions of these results can be found
in [205, 207].

4 Extensions

This chapter gives several extensions of and variations on the results in the previous chapter. The first four sections generalize the traffic routing model of Chapter 2 in four ways and ask if the bounds in Chapter 3 continue to apply; the answer usually, but not always, is affirmative. Section 4.1 generalizes selfish routing beyond the confines of a network, Section 4.2 considers approximate equilibria, Section 4.3 adds explicit edge capacities, and Section 4.4 allows network users to control a nonnegligible fraction of the overall traffic.

The next three sections leave the traffic routing model unchanged but consider different types of bounds on the consequences of selfish routing. Section 4.5 begins with the usual price of anarchy but gives different bounds than in Chapter 3. These bounds need not be optimal but can be easier to compute than the anarchy value of Section 3.3. Section 4.6 shows that the price of anarchy of every instance is much better for many traffic rates than it is for a worst-case traffic rate. Section 4.7 considers a new objective function that differs from the cost by attempting to account for the fairness of a solution.

The sections of this chapter can be read in any order, and the rest of the book does not depend on them. Each section considers only a single extension to the basic model and bounds of the previous two chapters. However, many of these extensions can be successfully combined. A detailed study of the harmonious combinations is left to the interested reader.

4.1 Nonatomic Congestion Games

Both the traffic model of Chapter 2 and the theorems of Chapter 3 can be recast in a more general and abstract setting, which also enjoys many connections with current research in game theory. This section pursues this generalization. Section 4.1.1 gives the basic definitions and Section 4.1.2 describes the extensions of the bounds on the price of anarchy from Chapter 3. Connections to research in game theory are discussed in Section 4.8. Because of the similarity to the definitions and results of Chapters 2 and 3, this section proceeds at a fairly rapid pace.

4.1.1 Definitions

This section defines nonatomic congestion games, which are a natural generalization of the traffic routing games that we have already studied. The perspective is more abstract than in the rest of the book.

Consider a finite ground set E of *elements*, with each element e possessing a *cost function* c_e. As in Chapter 2, we assume that each cost function is nonnegative, continuous, and nondecreasing. There are k *player types* $1, 2, \ldots, k$, and for each player type i there is a finite multiset $\mathcal{S}_i$ of subsets of E, called the *strategy set* of players of type i. Elements of $\mathcal{S}_i$ are called *strategies*. The continuum of players of type i is represented by the interval $[0, n_i]$, endowed with Lebesgue measure. Readers unfamiliar with measure theory, which for our purposes is just a way to formalize the size of a subset of the real line, will lose little by ignoring all statements that refer to it.

To a player type i, a strategy $S \in \mathcal{S}_i$, and an element $e \in S$, we associate a positive *rate of consumption* $a_{S,e}$ that defines the amount of congestion contributed to element e by players of type i selecting strategy S. A *nonatomic congestion game (NCG)* is defined by a 5-tuple $(E, c, \mathcal{S}, n, a)$. See Sections 2.8 and 4.8 for background on the terms "nonatomic" and "congestion".

The traffic routing model of Chapter 2 is clearly a nonatomic congestion game, with network edges as resources, commodities defining player types, strategy sets equal to collections of source-destination paths, and unit rates of consumption. On the other hand, nonatomic congestion games are more general than the traffic routing model in several respects. For example, one strategy in a strategy set can strictly contain another, and strategy sets for different player types need not be disjoint. Even in games that take place in a network, strategy sets could be cuts, spanning trees, or cycles, and could be different types of objects for different player types. Finally, the rates of consumption can vary wildly between players types, strategies, and the elements in the strategies. For example, if strategies represent tasks that can be accomplished by players of a given type, then the rates of consumption can model the fact that different tasks require different amounts of the available resources.

A (feasible) *action distribution* is a vector x of nonnegative real numbers with components indexed by the disjoint union of $\mathcal{S}_1, \ldots, \mathcal{S}_k$, with the property that $\sum_{S \in \mathcal{S}_i} x_S = n_i$ for each player type i. We interpret x_S as the measure of the set of players of type i selecting strategy S. Write x_e for the total amount of congestion induced on element e by the action distribution x:

$$x_e = \sum_{i=1}^{k} \sum_{S \in \mathcal{S}_i : e \in S} a_{S,e} x_S.$$

With respect to an action distribution x, players of type i selecting strategy $S \in \mathcal{S}_i$

incur a *cost* $c_S(x)$ defined by

$$c_S(x) = \sum_{e \in S} a_{S,e} c_e(x_e),$$

reflecting the idea that the sensitivity of a player to the cost of an element should be equal to the rate at which the player requires it. The cost incurred by a player depends only on its type, its chosen strategy, and on the congestion experienced by the elements in its strategy—the identities of the players that induce the congestion are of no importance.

The *cost* $C(x)$ of an action distribution x is the total disutility experienced by the players, so

$$C(x) = \sum_{i=1}^{k} \sum_{S \in \mathcal{S}_i} c_S(x) x_S.$$

An *optimal* action distribution minimizes the cost over all feasible action distributions.

Our final definition is the obvious extension of Definition 2.2.1 to NCGs.

Definition 4.1.1 An action distribution x of an NCG $(E, c, \mathcal{S}, n, a)$ is an *equilibrium* if for all player types i, all strategies $S_1, S_2 \in \mathcal{S}_i$ with $x_{S_1} > 0$, and all $\delta \in (0, x_{S_1}]$,

$$c_{S_1}(x) \le c_{S_2}(\tilde{x}),$$

where

$$\tilde{x}_S = \begin{cases} x_S - \delta & \text{if } S = S_1 \\ x_S + \delta & \text{if } S = S_2 \\ x_S & \text{otherwise.} \end{cases}$$

4.1.2   Bounding the Price of Anarchy in NCGs

All of the results of Chapter 3 carry over, with the same proofs, to the more general setting of NCGs. To see this, first note that the two definitions of cost, (2.2) and (2.3), continue to coincide when extended to NCGs. The optimization problem of computing an optimal action distribution can thus be modeled as a nonlinear program like the program (NLP) of Section 2.4. Because of this, all of the key propositions of Sections 2.2, 2.4, and 2.6 extend to NCGs without difficulty. The price of anarchy of an NCG is defined as in Definition 2.3.1.

Careful scrutiny of the proofs of Chapter 3 reveals that the combinatorial structure of the underlying network and the uniformity of rates of consumption were never used. Because of this, these proofs extend, *mutatis mutandis*, to the more general setting of NCGs. A summary of the main consequences follows.

Extension of Theorem 3.3.7: Let $\mathcal{C}$ be a set of cost functions with anarchy value $\alpha(\mathcal{C})$, as defined in Definitions 3.3.1 and 3.3.3. Then the price of anarchy in an NCG with cost functions in $\mathcal{C}$ is at most $\alpha(\mathcal{C})$.

Extension of Theorem 3.4.2: Let $\mathcal{C}$ be a set of cost functions containing the constant functions. Then the price of anarchy of NCGs with cost functions in $\mathcal{C}$ is achieved, up to an arbitrarily small additive factor, by NCGs with two resources, one player type, singleton strategies, and unit rates of consumption.

Extension of Theorem 3.4.9: Let $\mathcal{C}$ be a set of cost functions that is inhomogeneous in the sense of Definition 3.4.7. Then the price of anarchy of NCGs with cost functions in $\mathcal{C}$ is achieved, up to an arbitrarily small additive factor, by NCGs with one player type, disjoint strategies, and unit rates of consumption.

Extension of Theorem 3.6.2: The cost of an equilibrium in an arbitrary NCG is at most the cost of an optimal action distribution for the same NCG with twice as many players of each type.

Remark 4.1.2 It is reasonable to wonder at this point whether *any* conceivable statement that holds for the network model of Chapter 2 fails to carry over to NCGs. One argument that does not immediately generalize from networks to NCGs is provided by the forthcoming proof of Theorem 4.7.6, which bounds the price of anarchy of selfish routing in single-commodity networks with arbitrary cost functions with respect to the maximum cost incurred by the network traffic. The proof of this theorem makes use of the graph-theoretic notions of acyclicity and cuts, notions without obvious analogues in NCGs. Indeed, even the (best-possible) guarantee of Theorem 4.7.6 is a function of the number of network vertices. Since NCGs possess an analogue of an edge set (resources) but not of a vertex set, it is not even clear what sort of generalization of Theorem 4.7.6 to NCGs would be possible.

4.2 Approximate Nash Flows

This section asks if the bounds on the inefficiency of selfish routing in Chapter 3 carry over to flows that are in some sense only *approximately* at Nash equilibrium. Such extensions weaken the standing assumption that traffic is capable of settling into an exact equilibrium.

Our notion of approximate equilibrium will be the following: the path chosen by an agent need not have minimum cost, but its cost cannot exceed the minimum by more than a $(1 + \epsilon)$ multiplicative factor, where $\epsilon > 0$ is a fixed constant. The following definition formalizes this idea as a flow at ϵ-*approximate Nash equilibrium*, and it is an obvious modification of Definition 2.2.1.

Definition 4.2.1 A flow f feasible for the instance (G, r, c) is at ϵ-*approximate Nash equilibrium* if for all $i \in \{1, \ldots, k\}$, $P_1, P_2 \in \mathcal{P}_i$ with $f_{P_1} > 0$, and $\delta \in (0, f_{P_1}]$,

$$c_{P_1}(f) \leq (1 + \epsilon)c_{P_2}(\tilde{f}),$$

where

$$\tilde{f}_P = \begin{cases} f_P - \delta & \text{if } P = P_1 \\ f_P + \delta & \text{if } P = P_2 \\ f_P & \text{if } P \notin \{P_1, P_2\}. \end{cases}$$

We then have the following analogue of Proposition 2.2.2.

Proposition 4.2.2 *A flow f is at ϵ-approximate Nash equilibrium if and only if for every $i \in \{1, \ldots, k\}$ and $P_1, P_2 \in \mathcal{P}_i$ with $f_{P_1} > 0$,*

$$c_{P_1}(f) \leq (1 + \epsilon)c_{P_2}(f).$$

Of course, we cannot prove bounds on the cost of flows at ϵ-approximate Nash equilibrium for ϵ arbitrarily large. Our goal, therefore, is to prove bounds that degrade gracefully as a function of ϵ. Our bounds will include the $\epsilon = 0$ results of Chapter 3 as a special case.

This section extends two of the theorems of Chapter 3: the bicriteria bound of Section 3.6 (Theorem 3.6.2) and the upper bound on the price of anarchy for networks with linear cost functions (Theorem 3.2.6). Other extensions of this sort are left to the interested reader.

First is an analogue of Theorem 3.6.2 for flows at ϵ-approximate Nash equilibrium.

Theorem 4.2.3 *If* $\epsilon \in [0,1)$, f *is at* ϵ-*approximate Nash equilibrium for* (G,r,c), *and* f^* *is feasible for* $(G,2r,c)$, *then*

$$C(f) \leq \frac{1+\epsilon}{1-\epsilon} \cdot C(f^*).$$

Proof: Suppose ϵ, f, and f^* satisfy the hypotheses of the theorem. For $i = 1, \ldots, k$, let $c_i(f)$ be the minimum cost of an s_i-t_i path with respect to f. Since f is at ϵ-approximate Nash equilibrium, Proposition 4.2.2 implies that every s_i-t_i flow path must have cost at most $(1+\epsilon)c_i(f)$. We therefore have

$$C(f) \leq (1+\epsilon) \sum_{i=1}^{k} c_i(f)r_i. \tag{4.1}$$

Following the proof of Theorem 3.6.2, we define a new set of cost functions $\bar{c}$ by

$$\bar{c}_e(x) = \begin{cases} c_e(f_e) & \text{if } x \leq f_e \\[2mm] c_e(x) & \text{if } x \geq f_e \end{cases}$$

(recall Figure 3.4). As in the proof of Theorem 3.6.2, the cost of a flow with respect to $\bar{c}$ exceeds its cost with respect to c by at most an additive factor of $C(f)$.

If f_0 denotes the zero flow in G, then by construction $\bar{c}_P(f_0) \geq c_i(f)$ for every i and every path $P \in \mathcal{P}_i$. Since $\bar{c}_e$ is nondecreasing for every edge e, $\bar{c}_P(f^*) \geq c_i(f)$ for every i and every path $P \in \mathcal{P}_i$. This allows us to bound the cost of f^* with respect to $\bar{c}$ from below:

$$\sum_{P} \bar{c}_P(f^*)f_P^* \geq \sum_{i} \sum_{P \in \mathcal{P}_i} c_i(f)f_P^*$$

$$= \sum_{i} 2c_i(f)r_i$$

$$\geq \frac{2}{1+\epsilon} \cdot C(f),$$

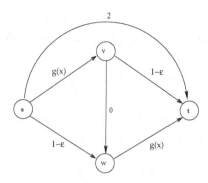

Figure 4.1
Theorem 4.2.3 is optimal (Example 4.2.4). Edges are labeled with their cost functions.

where the last inequality follows from (4.1). To conclude, we derive

$$C(f^*) \geq \sum_P \bar{c}_P(f^*)f_P^* - C(f)$$

$$\geq \frac{2}{1+\epsilon} \cdot C(f) - C(f)$$

$$= \frac{1-\epsilon}{1+\epsilon} \cdot C(f).$$

∎

Example 4.2.4 The factor of $(1+\epsilon)/(1-\epsilon)$ in Theorem 4.2.3 cannot be improved. To see this, fix $\epsilon \in [0,1)$ and consider the network G shown in Figure 4.1. This is the graph from Braess's Paradox (Figure 2.3), with an additional direct s-t edge. Four of the edges have constant cost functions, as shown. By $g(x)$ we mean a nondecreasing, continuous function equal to 0 on $[0, 1-\delta]$ and to $1+\epsilon$ on $[1, \infty)$, where $\delta > 0$ is a small positive number. Routing 1 unit of flow on the three-hop path $s \to v \to w \to t$ defines an ϵ-approximate Nash equilibrium for $(G, 1, c)$ with cost $2(1+\epsilon)$. On the other hand, the flow that routes $1 - \delta$ units of flow on each of the two-hop paths and 2δ units of flow on the s-t edge is feasible and has a cost approaching $2(1 - \epsilon)$ as $\delta \to 0$.

Next is a version of Theorem 3.2.6 for ϵ-approximate Nash flows in networks with linear cost functions. Because the proof of the following theorem is similar to that of Theorem 3.2.6, some details are omitted.

Theorem 4.2.5 *If $\epsilon \in [0,3)$, f is at ϵ-approximate Nash equilibrium for an instance (G, r, c) with linear cost functions, and f^* is feasible for (G, r, c), then*

$$C(f) \leq \frac{4 + 4\epsilon}{3 - \epsilon} \cdot C(f^*).$$

Proof: As in Section 3.2, the proof starts with a flow f at ϵ-approximate Nash equilibrium for (G, r, c) and considers the scaled-down flow $f/2$. Lemma 3.2.4, which states that $C(f/2) \geq C(f)/4$, holds as in Section 3.2. Unfortunately, Lemma 3.2.3, which states that $f/2$ is optimal for $(G, r/2, c)$, is now only *approximately* correct.

To make sense of this statement, let $c_i(f)$ denote the minimum cost of an s_i-t_i path with respect to f. As in the proof of Theorem 4.2.3, inequality (4.1) holds. By Lemma 3.2.3(a), the marginal cost of every s_i-t_i path with respect to $f/2$ is at least $c_i(f)$, and the marginal cost of every flow path of $f/2$ is at most $(1 + \epsilon)c_i(f)$.

Now consider augmenting $f/2$ to a flow f^* feasible for (G, r, c). By (3.3) on page 55, the cost of this augmentation can be lower bounded on each edge by the change in flow value times the marginal cost with respect to $f/2$. At worst, this augmentation will remove $r_i/2$ units of flow between each commodity i at a marginal benefit of $(1 + \epsilon)c_i(f)$ per flow unit and will add r_i units of flow at a marginal cost of $c_i(f)$ per flow unit. This argument proves that

$$
\begin{aligned}
C(f^*) &\geq \frac{1}{4}C(f) - (1 + \epsilon)\sum_{i=1}^{k} c_i(f)\frac{r_i}{2} + \sum_{i=1}^{k} c_i(f)r_i \\
&= \frac{1}{4}C(f) + \left(\frac{1 - \epsilon}{2}\right)\sum_{i=1}^{k} c_i(f)r_i \\
&\geq C(f)\left(\frac{1}{4} + \frac{1 - \epsilon}{2(1 + \epsilon)}\right) \\
&= \frac{3 - \epsilon}{4 + 4\epsilon} \cdot C(f).
\end{aligned}
$$

∎

Remark 4.2.6 A straightforward modification of Example 4.2.4 shows that the factor of $(4 + 4\epsilon)/(3 - \epsilon)$ in Theorem 4.2.5 cannot be improved.

4.3   Edge Capacities

Section 2.8 noted that in classical network flow theory, every network edge is typically given an explicit *capacity* that restricts the maximum amount of flow that can feasibly travel across the edge. It also noted that edge capacities can be modeled implicitly with cost functions that become extremely large when the flow on the edge exceeds the (implicit) capacity. Nevertheless, adding explicit capacities to the basic selfish routing model leads to an interesting theory, which is described in this section.

We denote a capacitated network by (G, r, c, u), where edge e has capacity u_e. A flow f is feasible only if the flow f_e is no more than the capacity u_e on every edge e of G. Capacitated instances will always be assumed to admit at least one feasible flow.

The definition of flows at Nash equilibrium in networks with explicit edge capacities is the obvious extension of Definition 2.2.1.

Definition 4.3.1 A flow f feasible for the capacitated instance (G, r, c, u) is at *Nash equilibrium*, or is a *Nash flow*, if for all $i \in \{1, \ldots, k\}$, $P_1, P_2 \in \mathcal{P}_i$ with $f_{P_1} > 0$, and $\delta \in (0, f_{P_1}]$, either

$$c_{P_1}(f) \leq c_{P_2}(\tilde{f}),$$

where

$$
\tilde{f}_P = \begin{cases}
f_P - \delta & \text{if } P = P_1 \\
f_P + \delta & \text{if } P = P_2 \\
f_P & \text{if } P \notin \{P_1, P_2\},
\end{cases}
$$

or $\tilde{f}$ is infeasible.

The only difference between Definitions 2.2.1 and 4.3.1 is that in a capacitated network, an agent may not be able to switch to a path with smaller cost because of a capacity constraint. Other definitions of flows at Nash equilibrium in a capacitated network have also been considered; see Section 4.8 for details.

Next is the analogue of Proposition 2.2.2.

Proposition 4.3.2 *A flow f feasible for the instance (G, r, c, u) is at Nash equilibrium if and only if for every $i \in \{1, \ldots, k\}$ and $P_1, P_2 \in \mathcal{P}_i$ with $f_{P_1} > 0$, one of*

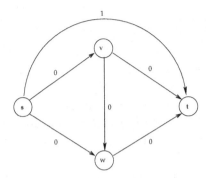

Figure 4.2
In capacitated networks with constant cost functions, Nash flows can cost arbitrarily more than optimal flows (Example 4.3.3). Edges are labeled with their (constant) cost functions.

the following conditions holds:

(i) $c_{P_1}(f) \le c_{P_2}(f)$; or

(ii) there is an edge $e \in P_2 \setminus P_1$ with $f_e = u_e$.

By now, we might believe that capacitated networks will not present any surprises. The next example is a rude awakening.

Example 4.3.3 Consider the network G shown in Figure 4.2. The network is identical to that of Example 4.2.4 (Figure 4.1), which in turn is the same network as in Braess's Paradox (Figure 2.3), except that a direct s-t link has been added. All edges have cost 0, except for the direct s-t link, which has cost 1. The culprits of this example are the capacities on the edges of the network: $1/2$ on edges (s,v) and (w,t), and $+\infty$ on the other four edges.

As in Braess's Paradox, routing half of the flow on each of the paths $s \to v \to t$ and $s \to w \to t$ defines a flow f^* feasible for $(G,1,c,u)$. The flow f^* has cost 0. Now define another feasible flow f by routing half a unit of flow on the $s \to v \to w \to t$ path and the rest on the direct s-t link. The flow f is at Nash equilibrium, as the traffic stuck on the direct s-t link cannot switch paths without violating some capacity constraint. The cost of f is $1/2$.

Example 4.3.3 shows that Theorem 3.3.7 fails spectacularly in capacitated networks. Even when the cost functions are *constant,* Nash flows can be *infinitely* more costly than optimal flows.

Example 4.3.3 is less shocking after a little reflection. After all, the cost functions in the example are not *really* constant; they are only constant on the domain $[0, u_e]$, where u_e is the edge capacity, and are essentially equal to $+\infty$ on (u_e, ∞). Given how effectively steep such a cost function is at its capacity, we might have even predicted an unbounded price of anarchy based on the lessons of Chapter 3.

The forthcoming positive results are, therefore, all the more surprising. To motivate them, return to Example 4.3.3. In it, we defined a Nash flow f and another flow f^* and observed that the cost of f can be arbitrarily larger than that of f^*. On the other hand, the flow f^* is obviously also a flow at Nash equilibrium. Thus Proposition 2.2.6 also fails spectacularly: different Nash flows for the same capacitated instance can have very different costs.

Example 4.3.3 ensures the futility of any effort to prove bounds on the cost of arbitrary Nash flows in capacitated networks. Our only hope is that every network is like the one in Example 4.3.3, admitting *some* exemplary flow at Nash equilibrium that has small cost. In fact, in every capacitated network, the general upper bound given in Theorem 3.3.7 applies to some Nash flow. We will state the bound in terms of the anarchy value, a quantity introduced in Definitions 3.3.1 and 3.3.3.

Theorem 4.3.4 *Let (G, r, c, u) be a capacitated network with cost functions in the set C, and let C have anarchy value $\alpha(C)$. Let f^* denote an optimal flow for (G, r, c, u). Then, there is a flow f at Nash equilibrium for (G, r, c, u) with*

$$C(f) \leq \alpha(C) \cdot C(f^*).$$

Remark 4.3.5 The guarantee of Theorem 4.3.4 is questionable. What use is a guarantee that applies to some Nash flows and not to others? Most obviously, Example 4.3.3 shows that there is no nontrivial guarantee that applies to all Nash flows in capacitated networks. But also, the appealing stability of a Nash flow still makes Theorem 4.3.4 interesting in the following sense. An optimal flow resists implementation with selfish routers because if given the slightest chance, some agents would deviate and switch paths. Thus, some kind of incessant babysitting is in general needed for an optimal flow to persist with selfish routing. Similarly, when there are many Nash flows, it is not clear how to agree on a particular one; some kind of coordination or intervention by a centralized authority is typically required. Once a Nash flow is reached, however, it is self-enforcing and requires no further supervision. Comparing the best-case Nash flow to the optimal flow therefore measures the inefficiency of an isolated opportunity for centralized control, relative to what is achievable with permanent centralized control.

An overview of the proof of Theorem 4.3.4 follows. The proof of the uncapacitated version of this theorem, Theorem 3.3.7, followed easily from Corollary 2.6.6 and Lemma 3.3.6. The reduction from the theorem to these two results, as well as Lemma 3.3.6, carry over to capacitated networks without any modifications. To prove Theorem 4.3.4, we therefore need only prove a weaker analogue of Corollary 2.6.6. This requires salvaging whatever we can from Proposition 2.4.4 and its proof, which gave several equivalent characterizations of optimal flows in uncapacitated networks and in turn implied Corollary 2.6.6.

Lemma 4.3.6 *Let* (G, r, c, u) *be a capacitated instance. Then there is a flow* f *at Nash equilibrium for* (G, r, c, u) *with the property that*

$$\sum_{e \in E} c_e(f_e) f_e \leq \sum_{e \in E} c_e(f_e) f_e^* \tag{4.2}$$

for every flow f^* *feasible for* (G, r, c, u).

Proof: Consider the obvious extension of the convex program (CP) from Proposition 2.6.1 to capacitated networks:

$$\text{Min} \quad \sum_{e \in E} \int_0^{f_e} c(x)\, dx$$

subject to:

(CAP)
$$\sum_{P \in \mathcal{P}_i} f_P = r_i \qquad \forall i \in \{1, \ldots, k\}$$
$$f_e = \sum_{P \in \mathcal{P}: e \in P} f_P \qquad \forall e \in E$$
$$f_e \leq u_e \qquad \forall e \in E$$
$$f_P \geq 0 \qquad \forall P \in \mathcal{P}.$$

As in Sections 2.4 and 2.6, we identify flows feasible for (G, r, c, u) with their corresponding points in $(|\mathcal{P}| + |E|)$-dimensional Euclidean space.

The key claim is that if f is an optimal solution to (CAP), then f is a Nash flow for (G, r, c, u), and in addition (4.2) holds for every feasible flow f^*. This claim implies the lemma, since (CAP) has a continuous objective function and a closed and bounded feasible region, and therefore admits an optimal solution.

The proof that f is a Nash flow for (G, r, c, u) is similar to the second paragraph of the proof of Proposition 2.4.4, and the details are left to the reader. To prove that f satisfies (4.2) for all feasible flows f^*, we argue the contrapositive. Suppose

f is a feasible flow for (G, r, c, u), but there is also a feasible flow f^* with

$$\sum_{e \in E} c_e(f_e) f_e^* < \sum_{e \in E} c_e(f_e) f_e. \tag{4.3}$$

Since f and f^* are feasible flows for (G, r, c, u), so are all of their convex combinations. Consider a convex combination of the form $(1 - \lambda)f + \lambda f^*$ for small λ. At the point f, the objective function of (CAP) is continuously differentiable with the partial derivative corresponding to edge e equal to $c_e(f_e)$. The objective function value of $(1 - \lambda)f + \lambda f^*$ is therefore equal to

$$\int_0^{f_e} c_e(x) + \lambda \left[\sum_{e \in E} c_e(f_e) f_e^* - \sum_{e \in E} c_e(f_e) f_e \right]$$

plus an error term that vanishes quickly as $\lambda \downarrow 0$. Inequality (4.3) now implies that, for sufficiently small λ, the objective function value of $(1 - \lambda)f + \lambda f^*$ is smaller than that of f, and hence f is not an optimal solution of (CAP). ■

The main bicriteria bound (Theorem 3.6.2) also fails for arbitrary Nash flows in capacitated networks, even when all edge cost functions are constant.

Example 4.3.7 Consider the network shown in Figure 4.3, which is a natural outgrowth of the network in Example 4.3.3. As in the previous example, all edges have cost 0 except for the direct s-t link, which has cost 1. All edges have infinite capacity except for the edges (s, u), (v, w), and (x, t), each of which has capacity $2/3$. Routing $2/3$ units of flow on the path $s \to u \to v \to w \to x \to t$ and $1/3$ units of flow on the direct s-t link yields a Nash flow with cost $1/3$. On the other hand, splitting two units of flow equally between the paths $s \to u \to t$, $s \to v \to w \to t$, and $s \to x \to t$ sends twice as much traffic at zero cost.

The pattern in Examples 4.3.3 and 4.3.7 and in Figures 4.2 and 4.3 can be generalized to show that in capacitated networks, it is possible to send arbitrarily more flow than a Nash flow, at arbitrarily lower cost. Details are left to the reader, though Section 5.2.2 includes a similar infinite family of instances.

Fortunately, as in Theorem 4.3.4, we can extend Theorem 3.6.2 to some Nash flow of every instance.

Theorem 4.3.8 *If (G, r, c, u) is a capacitated instance, then there is a Nash flow f for (G, r, c, u) such that*

$$C(f) \le C(f^*)$$

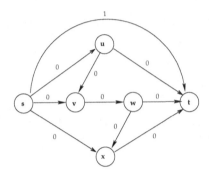

Figure 4.3
In capacitated networks with constant cost functions, Nash flows can cost arbitrarily more than flows that send twice as much traffic (Example 4.3.7). Edges are labeled with their (constant) cost functions.

for every flow f^* feasible for $(G, 2r, c, u)$.

Proof: We require only small modifications to the proof of Theorem 3.6.2. Because most of that proof carries over without change to capacitated networks, we need only prove inequality (3.14). This inequality states that if we replace the original cost functions c with the more severe cost functions $\bar{c}$ defined by

$$\bar{c}_e(x) = \max\{c_e(f_e), c_e(x)\},$$

where f is a Nash flow, then the new cost of the flow f^* must be at least $2C(f)$.

Example 4.3.7 implies that this property will not hold with respect to an arbitrary Nash flow of (G, r, c, u). On the other hand, let f be a Nash flow satisfying (4.2) in Lemma 4.3.6. Then,

$$\sum_{e \in E} \bar{c}_e(f_e^*) f_e^* \geq \sum_{e \in E} c_e(f_e) f_e^*$$

$$= 2 \sum_{e \in E} c_e(f_e) \frac{f_e^*}{2}$$

$$\geq 2 \sum_{e \in E} c_e(f_e) f_e$$

$$= 2C(f),$$

where the final inequality follows from (4.2), since $f^*/2$ is a feasible flow for (G, r, c, u). We have proved the theorem. ∎

We have in fact proved a stronger theorem, which applies when the optimal flow that must send twice as much traffic as the Nash flow is allowed to use twice as much capacity.

Theorem 4.3.9 *If (G, r, c, u) is a capacitated instance, then there is a Nash flow f for (G, r, c, u) such that*

$$C(f) \leq C(f^*)$$

for every flow f^* feasible for $(G, 2r, c, 2u)$.

Remark 4.3.10 In Theorem 4.3.8, there may be no feasible flows for $(G, 2r, c, u)$, in which case the theorem is vacuous. In Theorem 4.3.9, the assumption that (G, r, c, u) admits a feasible flow implies that $(G, 2r, c, 2u)$ also admits a feasible flow, so the theorem always asserts a nontrivial bound.

4.4 Atomic Selfish Routing

So far, we have assumed that all network users control a negligible fraction of the overall traffic. This section discards that assumption. We instead study networks in which there are a finite number of agents, each of which controls a nonnegligible amount of flow. Adopting standard game theory jargon as in Sections 2.8 and 4.1, agents are now called *atomic*. In networks with atomic agents, an additional modeling decision must be made: can an agent use only one path, or can it split its flow over many paths? Section 4.4.1 shows that all of the positive results of Chapter 3 carry over to the splittable model, while Section 4.4.2 notes that only weaker versions of these bounds hold in the unsplittable model. The positive results of Chapter 3 are thus driven by the fractional nature of flow, rather than by the assumption of a large population of network users.

4.4.1 Splittable Flow

As usual, consider a network G with continuous, nondecreasing cost functions c. In addition, there are k *users*, where user i intends to send r_i units of flow from the source s_i to the destination t_i. Distinct users are allowed to have identical source-destination pairs. We continue to denote an instance by (G, r, c), and the instance is called *atomic splittable*. A *flow* f now consists of k nonnegative real vectors, one for each user, with the vector $f^{(i)}$ indexed by the set $\mathcal{P}_i$ of s_i-t_i paths.

The feasible flows in an atomic splittable instance are isomorphic to those in the corresponding nonatomic instance, but the two models differ in a game-theoretic sense. For a flow f feasible for an atomic splittable instance (G, r, c), we denote the total cost experienced by user i by $C_i(f)$. Thus,

$$C_i(f) = \sum_{P \in \mathcal{P}_i} c_P(f) f_P^{(i)}. \tag{4.4}$$

As usual, a flow will be at *Nash equilibrium* if no user can decrease the cost it experiences by rerouting its flow. For atomic splittable instances, this translates to the following definition.

Definition 4.4.1 A flow f feasible for the atomic splittable instance (G, r, c) is at *Nash equilibrium* or is a *Nash flow* if for each agent i, $f^{(i)}$ minimizes $C_i(f)$ while holding $f^{(j)}$ fixed for every $j \neq i$.

The difference between Nash flows for atomic instances (Definition 4.4.1) and nonatomic ones (Definition 2.2.1 and Proposition 2.2.2) is that in the former, the definition (4.4) of an agent's cost ensures that an agent looks out for its own, in the sense that it will take into account the congestion it causes for its own traffic. The agent will not, of course, care about the consequences of its decisions for the costs of other agents. Agents therefore partially internalize the social loss caused by their traffic. In the extreme case of a single agent, the flows at Nash equilibrium are precisely the optimal flows. At the other extreme, in the nonatomic case, agents are so small that they can completely ignore congestion effects. See also Remark 2.4.7 for related discussion.

In this section, we only study networks with semiconvex cost functions. Under this assumption, we have the following fact.

Fact 4.4.2 *Every atomic splittable instance admits a flow at Nash equilibrium.*

We next extend Theorem 3.6.2 to atomic splittable instances: every Nash flow has cost at most that of an optimal flow in which all players must route twice as much traffic.

Theorem 4.4.3 *Let (G, r, c) be an atomic splittable instance with semiconvex cost functions. If f is at Nash equilibrium for (G, r, c) and f^* is feasible for the atomic splittable instance $(G, 2r, c)$, then*

$$C(f) \leq C(f^*).$$

Proof: Let f and f^* satisfy the hypotheses of the theorem, and define the cost functions $\bar{c}$ as in the proof of Theorem 3.6.2. As in the proof of Theorem 3.6.2, evaluating f^* with cost functions $\bar{c}$, instead of c, increases its cost by at most an additive $C(f)$ factor.

Now view f and $(G, r, \bar{c})$ as standard nonatomic objects. The key claim is that f is an optimal (nonatomic) flow for the instance $(G, r, \bar{c})$. Suppose for contradiction that f is not optimal for $(G, r, \bar{c})$. We will show that the (atomic) flow f fails to be at Nash equilibrium for the atomic splittable instance (G, r, c).

The cost functions c are assumed to be semiconvex, and a simple calculation then shows that the modified cost functions $\bar{c}$ are also semiconvex. If the modified cost functions are also continuously differentiable, then the equivalence of statements (a) and (b) in Proposition 2.4.4 implies that, since f is not optimal for $(G, r, \bar{c})$,

(*) there is a user i, paths $P_1, P_2 \in \mathcal{P}_i$ with $f_{P_1}^{(i)} > 0$, and a sufficiently small $\delta \in (0, f_{P_1}^{(i)}]$ such that moving δ units of flow from P_1 to P_2 yields a flow feasible for $(G, r, \bar{c})$ with strictly smaller cost than f.

Unfortunately, the modified cost functions $\bar{c}$ are generally not everywhere differentiable. Nevertheless, semiconvexity is enough to ensure that (*) holds. The verification of this is left to the reader. Alternatively, the definition of the modified cost function $\bar{c}$ can be altered so that the functions are continuously differentiable. Again, details are left to the reader.

We now show that the local move suggested by (*) is beneficial for agent i in the atomic splittable instance (G, r, c). In the nonatomic instance $(G, r, \bar{c})$, the net global benefit of modifying the flow f by moving δ units of flow from the path P_1 to the path P_2 is the benefit

$$\left[\sum_{e \in P_1 \setminus P_2} [\bar{c}_e(f_e) f_e - \bar{c}_e(f_e - \delta)(f_e - \delta)] \right] \tag{4.5}$$

minus the cost

$$\left[\sum_{e \in P_2 \setminus P_1} [\bar{c}_e(f_e + \delta)(f_e + \delta) - \bar{c}_e(f_e) f_e] \right]. \tag{4.6}$$

Similarly, the net benefit to agent i of making the same local move in the instance

(G, r, c) is the benefit

$$\left[\sum_{e \in P_1 \setminus P_2} \left[c_e(f_e) f_e^{(i)} - c_e(f_e - \delta)(f_e^{(i)} - \delta) \right] \right] \tag{4.7}$$

minus the cost

$$\left[\sum_{e \in P_2 \setminus P_1} \left[c_e(f_e + \delta)(f_e^{(i)} + \delta) - c_e(f_e) f_e^{(i)} \right] \right]. \tag{4.8}$$

Since $c_e(f_e - \delta) \leq \bar{c}_e(f_e - \delta) = \bar{c}_e(f_e) = c_e(f_e)$ for all edges e, the global benefit (4.5) in $(G, r, \bar{c})$ cannot exceed the benefit (4.7) to agent i in (G, r, c). Similarly, since $\bar{c}_e(f_e) = c_e(f_e) \leq c_e(f_e + \delta) = \bar{c}_e(f_e + \delta)$ and $f_e^{(i)} \leq f_e$ for all edges e, the cost (4.8) of the local move to agent i in (G, r, c) cannot be more than the global cost (4.6) of the same local move in the instance $(G, r, \bar{c})$. Since the benefit (4.5) exceeds the cost (4.6) in $(G, r, \bar{c})$, this must be equally true for agent i in (G, r, c). The flow f is thus not a flow at Nash equilibrium, which provides the desired contradiction.

We have established that the flow f must be optimal for $(G, r, \bar{c})$. The flow f has the same cost $C(f)$ in both instances, (G, r, c) and $(G, r, \bar{c})$. Since every (nonatomic or atomic) flow feasible for $(G, r, \bar{c})$ has cost at least $C(f)$ and cost functions are nondecreasing, every flow f^* feasible for the atomic splittable instance $(G, 2r, \bar{c})$ must have cost at least $2C(f)$. Since the cost of f^* with respect to $\bar{c}$ exceeds its cost with respect to c by at most an additive $C(f)$ factor, the theorem follows. ∎

Theorem 3.6.2 can be regarded as the limiting case of Theorem 4.4.3, as the number of users tends to infinity and the amount of flow controlled by each user tends to 0.

In addition to the bicriteria bound above, the upper bound on the price of anarchy given in Theorem 3.3.7 carries over to atomic splittable instances with semiconvex cost functions.

Theorem 4.4.4 *Let $\mathcal{C}$ be a set of semiconvex cost functions with anarchy value $\alpha(\mathcal{C})$, and (G, r, c) an atomic splittable instance with cost functions in $\mathcal{C}$. If f and f^* are Nash and feasible flows for (G, r, c), respectively, then*

$$C(f) \leq \alpha(\mathcal{C}) \cdot C(f^*).$$

See Section 4.8 for further details.

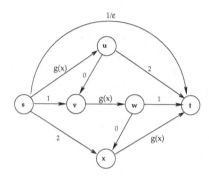

Figure 4.4
In atomic unsplittable instances, Nash flows can cost arbitrarily more than flows that send twice
as much traffic (Example 4.4.5). Edges are labeled with their cost functions.

4.4.2   Unsplittable Flow

We now briefly study *atomic unsplittable* instances, with a finite number of agents,
each of which has to route a nonnegligible portion of the traffic on a single path.
The definitions are the same as in Section 4.4.1, except that the vectors $f^{(i)}$ are
now required to take on a nonzero value for only one s_i-t_i path. Next is a negative
result, showing that there can be no extension of Theorems 3.6.2 and 4.4.3 to atomic
unsplittable instances.

Example 4.4.5   Consider the network shown in Figure 4.4, which is the same graph
as in Example 4.3.7 and Figure 4.3. The edges of the network are labeled with their
cost functions, where $g(x) = 1/(3 - x + \epsilon)$ and $\epsilon > 0$ is arbitrarily small. Three
users that each route two units of flow unsplittably from s to t using the paths
$s \to u \to t$, $s \to v \to w \to t$, and $s \to x \to t$ incur cost less than 18. On the other
hand, two agents routing one unit of flow on the path $s \to u \to v \to w \to x \to t$
and one user routing one unit of flow on the direct s-t link is a Nash flow with cost
at least $1/\epsilon$. Since $\epsilon > 0$ can be arbitrarily small, we conclude that the cost of a
Nash flow in an atomic unsplittable instance can be arbitrarily larger than that of
flow routing twice as much traffic.

A natural generalization of Example 4.4.5, similar to a construction described in
Section 5.2.2, shows that in atomic unsplittable instances, there can be Nash flows
that have cost arbitrarily larger than that of flows routing arbitrarily more traffic.

The upper bounds on the price of anarchy given in Chapter 3 also fail to carry over to atomic unsplittable instances. On the other hand, as for capacitated instances in Section 4.3, Nash flows are not unique in atomic unsplittable instances. Analogous to Section 4.3, the *best* Nash flow of such an instance obeys both the bicriteria bound (Theorem 3.6.2) and the upper bound on the price of anarchy stated in Theorem 3.3.7, at least if all cost functions are semiconvex and all commodities share the same source vertex. See Section 4.8 for more details on all of these results.

Finally, while the upper bound of Theorem 3.3.7 is false for the worst Nash flow of an atomic unsplittable instance, weaker bounds continue to hold. For example, in atomic unsplittable instances with cost functions that are polynomials with degree at most d and nonnegative coefficients, the price of anarchy is bounded above by a constant that is exponential in d but independent of the network size and the number of commodities. Again, see Section 4.8 for further details.

4.5   A Quick-and-Dirty Bound on the Price of Anarchy

The motivation for the definition of the anarchy value of a set of cost functions (Section 3.3.1) is now clear: for almost all sets C of cost functions, the anarchy value of C is precisely the price of anarchy of selfish routing in networks with cost functions in C. The complexity of the definition of the anarchy value, even in its simplified form in Proposition 3.3.2, reflects its far-reaching power. While the anarchy value can often be computed exactly, as in the applications in Section 3.5, easily computable estimates of the anarchy value are also useful. Such estimates are required when computing the anarchy value of a set is intractable, and they also can provide nontrivial information with shorter derivations than those demanded by the anarchy value. This section defines such an estimate. For example, this estimate implies that the price of anarchy in networks with cost functions that are polynomials with degree at most p and nonnegative coefficients is at most $p + 1$. While Proposition 3.5.1 shows that this upper bound is not the best possible, it can be derived with much less work than the proof of Proposition 3.5.1 required.

The development in this section mirrors that of the anarchy value in Section 3.3. We call the relaxation of the anarchy value the *incline*. The definition of incline is motivated by the nonlinear programming arguments in Sections 2.4 and 2.6. In particular, recall from Section 2.4 and Proposition 2.6.1 that the optimal flows of an instance (G, r, c) are the optimal solutions to the nonlinear program

$$\text{Min} \quad \sum_{e \in E} c_e(f_e) f_e$$

subject to:

(NLP)
$$\sum_{P \in \mathcal{P}_i} f_P = r_i \qquad \forall i \in \{1, \ldots, k\}$$

$$f_e = \sum_{P \in \mathcal{P}: e \in P} f_P \qquad \forall e \in E$$

$$f_P \geq 0 \qquad \forall P \in \mathcal{P},$$

while the Nash flows of (G, r, c) are the optimal solutions to a similar nonlinear program (CP), with the objective function $\sum_{e \in E} c_e(f_e) f_e$ replaced by

$$\sum_{e \in E} \int_0^{f_e} c(x)\, dx.$$

Thus, optimal and Nash flows differ only in the objective function that they minimize. The incline of a cost function measures the distortion it creates between these two objective functions.

Definition 4.5.1 The *incline* $\Gamma(c)$ of a cost function c is

$$\Gamma(c) = \sup_{x > 0} \frac{x \cdot c(x)}{\int_0^x c(t) dt},$$

with the understanding that $0/0 = 1$.

As in the definition of the anarchy value, the incline is a measure of the steepness of a cost function. The incline is simpler but coarser than the anarchy value. Since cost functions are nondecreasing, every cost function has incline at least 1.

Definition 4.5.2 If $\mathcal{C}$ is a set of cost functions, then the *incline* $\Gamma(\mathcal{C})$ of $\mathcal{C}$ is

$$\Gamma(\mathcal{C}) = \sup_{c \in \mathcal{C}} \Gamma(c).$$

We can now show that the incline $\Gamma(\mathcal{C})$ upper bounds the price of anarchy in every instance with cost functions in $\mathcal{C}$. This intuitively follows from the definition of incline, as Nash flows minimize an objective function that differs from the cost by at a most a multiplicative factor of $\Gamma(\mathcal{C})$.

Theorem 4.5.3 *Let $\mathcal{C}$ be a set of cost functions with incline $\Gamma(\mathcal{C})$, and (G, r, c) an* *instance with cost functions in* C. *Then*

$$\rho(G, r, c) \leq \Gamma(\mathcal{C}).$$

Proof: Let f and f^* denote Nash and optimal flows for (G, r, c), respectively. We then derive

$$
\begin{aligned}
C(f) &= \sum_{e \in E} c_e(f_e) f_e \\
&\leq \Gamma(\mathcal{C}) \cdot \sum_{e \in E} \int_0^{f_e} c_e(x) dx \\
&\leq \Gamma(\mathcal{C}) \cdot \sum_{e \in E} \int_0^{f_e^*} c_e(x) dx \\
&\leq \Gamma(\mathcal{C}) \cdot \sum_{e \in E} c_e(f_e^*) f_e^* \\
&= \Gamma(\mathcal{C}) \cdot C(f^*),
\end{aligned}
$$

where the first inequality follows from Definitions 4.5.1 and 4.5.2, the second inequality from the fact that the Nash flow f is an optimal solution for (CP), and the third inequality from the assumption that every cost function c_e is nondecreasing. ∎

Theorem 4.5.3 easily implies a nontrivial, if suboptimal, upper bound on the price of anarchy in networks with cost functions that are degree-bounded polynomials with nonnegative coefficients.

Corollary 4.5.4 *If every cost function of the instance* (G, r, c) *is a polynomial with nonnegative coefficients and degree at most* p, *then*

$$\rho(G, r, c) \leq p + 1.$$

Proof: By Theorem 4.5.3, it suffices to show that if $c(x) = \sum_{i=0}^{p} a_i x^i$ is a polynomial with degree at most p and nonnegative coefficients, then $\Gamma(c) \leq p + 1$. Establishing this inequality is a simple calculation: for every $x > 0$,

$$
\begin{aligned}
\frac{x \cdot c(x)}{\int_0^x c(t)dt} &= \frac{\sum_{i=0}^p a_i x^{i+1}}{\sum_{i=0}^p [a_i/(i+1)] x^{i+1}} \\
&\leq \frac{\sum_{i=0}^p a_i x^{i+1}}{\sum_{i=0}^p [a_i/(p+1)] x^{i+1}} \\
&= p + 1.
\end{aligned}
$$

■

4.6   Better Bounds for Many Traffic Rates

This section gives a non-trivial bound on the inefficiency of selfish routing in general networks by avoiding the usual worst-case comparison of Nash and optimal flows. Roughly, this section instead compares the cost of Nash and optimal flows in an instance with an arbitrary network and arbitrary cost functions, but in which *we are allowed to select the traffic rate*. The goal is to show that in every network, for "many" traffic rates the outcome of selfish routing is much better than in the worst case. This goal is similar in spirit to the bicriteria analysis of Section 3.6, since we are not restricting the edge cost functions but are nonetheless attempting to achieve a bound on the inefficiency of Nash flows via a novel type of comparison.

A strong guarantee for many traffic rates is of particular interest in networks where the traffic rate is changing over time. In such networks, inspiration can be taken from a popular saying about volatile weather:

if you don't like the performance of selfish routing, just wait a minute.

Example 4.6.1 We reap immediate benefits by considering the full range of traffic rates in the nonlinear variant of Pigou's example (Example 2.5.4). For traffic rates sufficiently close to 1, the cost of the Nash flow in that example continues to exceed that of the optimal flow by an exorbitant amount as the cost function degree bound p grows large. For traffic rates significantly below 1, the Nash and optimal flows in Example 2.5.4 are identical. As the traffic rate r goes to $+\infty$, the price of anarchy approaches 1. Moreover, the range of traffic rates for which a sufficiently large degree bound p induces an instance with price of anarchy at least ρ^* has length approaching zero as $\rho^* \to +\infty$. The price of anarchy in Example 2.5.4 is therefore upper bounded by a constant for almost all traffic rates.

Example 4.6.1 gives cause for hope. This section formalizes the intuition afforded by the example, that the worst-case inefficiency of selfish routing should be achieved by only a small portion of the possible traffic rates. For simplicity, this section considers only a particular finite range of traffic rates. For more general results, see Section 4.8.

First are a definition and two corollaries of the work described in Section 3.6.

Definition 4.6.2 Let (G, r, c) be a single-commodity instance. Let f and $f_{\frac{1}{2}}$ be Nash flows for (G, r, c) and $(G, r/2, c)$, respectively. Then, $\pi(G, r, c)$ is defined by

$$\pi(G, r, c) = \frac{C(f)}{C(f_{\frac{1}{2}})}.$$

Assuming for simplicity that $C(f_{\frac{1}{2}}) > 0$, Definition 4.6.2 makes sense because all Nash flows of an instance have equal cost (Proposition 2.2.6). The definition is interesting because the main bicriteria bound from the previous chapter (Theorem 3.6.2) can be rephrased in terms of the π-value of an instance.

Corollary 4.6.3 *In every instance* (G, r, c),

$$\rho(G, r, c) \leq \pi(G, r, c). \tag{4.9}$$

Proof: Expanding the definitions of ρ and π and rearranging terms shows that the corollary is equivalent to Theorem 3.6.2. ∎

As in Remark 3.6.4, Example 2.5.4 shows that Corollary 4.6.3 cannot be improved in the worst case. On the other hand, it gives us a yardstick by which to measure our progress: the right-hand side of (4.9) can be replaced with a sublinear function of $\pi(G, r, c)$ for many traffic rates r, then the goal is accomplished.

The next corollary is a consequence of Theorem 3.6.3. It states that an instance (G, r, c) has a large price of anarchy only if the cost of a Nash flow decreases rapidly with the traffic rate.

Corollary 4.6.4 *Let f and f_δ be Nash flows for the instances (G, r, c) and (G, r', c), respectively, where $r' \leq r/(1 + \delta)$ and $\delta > 0$. Then,*

$$C(f_\delta) \leq \frac{C(f)}{\delta \cdot \rho(G, r, c)}.$$

Proof: Let f^* be an optimal flow for (G, r, c). Theorem 3.6.3 then gives

$$
\begin{aligned}
C(f_\delta) &\leq \left(\frac{r}{r'} - 1\right)^{-1} \cdot C(f^*) \\
&\leq \frac{C(f^*)}{\delta} \\
&= \frac{C(f)}{\delta \cdot \rho(G, r, c)}.
\end{aligned}
$$

■

Corollary 4.6.4 allows us to control the range of traffic rates for which an instance has a large price of anarchy with its π-value. The statement of the next lemma and the rest of this section uses the asymptotic notation $O(\cdot)$ and $\Theta(\cdot)$ to suppress universal constants like $e \approx 2.718\ldots$. Terms that are instance- or parameter-dependent are not suppressed.

Lemma 4.6.5 *Suppose (G, r, c) is an instance and $\rho(G, \lambda r, c) \geq \rho^*$ for all λ in the interval $[1 - \ell, 1]$, where $\ell \leq 1/2$. Then*

$$
\ell \cdot \rho^* = O\left(\ln \pi(G, r, c)\right).
$$

Proof: Suppose $\rho(G, \lambda r, c) \geq \rho^*$ for all $\lambda \in [1 - \ell, 1]$, where $\ell \leq 1/2$. Set $\delta = 2/\rho^*$, which we can assume is less than 1. Corollary 4.6.4 then implies the following, by induction on $i \geq 1$: the cost of a Nash flow for (G, r, c) is at least 2^i times that of a Nash flow for $(G, \lambda r, c)$, provided $\lambda \leq (1 + \delta)^{-i}$ and $(1 + \delta)^{-(i-1)} \geq 1 - \ell$. Elementary calculations show that, since $\ell \leq 1/2$, $(1 + \delta)^{-(i-1)} \geq 1 - \ell$ whenever $i = O(\ell/\delta)$. Setting $i = \Theta(\ell/\delta) = \Theta(\ell \cdot \rho^*)$ and $\lambda = 1/2$ proves that $\pi(G, r, c) \geq 2^{\Theta(\ell \cdot \rho^*)}$. Taking logarithms then completes the proof. ■

Similar arguments, omitted here, extend Lemma 4.6.5 to the case where the set of λ for which $\rho(G, \lambda r, c) \geq \rho^*$ need not be an interval of the form $[1 - \ell, 1]$.

Theorem 4.6.6 *Suppose (G, r, c) is an instance and $\rho(G, \lambda r, c) \geq \rho^*$ for at least a 2ℓ fraction of the set $[\frac{1}{2}, 1]$ of possible values of λ. Then*

$$
\ell \cdot \rho^* = O\left(\ln \pi(G, r, c)\right).
$$

Theorem 4.6.6 provides a nice tradeoff between the severity of the inefficiency of selfish routing and the frequency of the traffic rates that achieve that degree of inefficiency: either one of the two quantities can be large, but they cannot both be large simultaneously. For example, a constant fraction of the traffic rates between $r/2$ and r yield an instance with ρ-value only $O(\ln \pi(G, r, c))$. This is an exponential improvement over the (best-possible) worst-case bound in Corollary 4.6.3.

Remark 4.6.7 Theorem 4.6.6 is tight in the following sense. There is an infinite family $\{(G_i, r_i, c_i)\}$ of single-commodity instances for which $\pi(G_i, r_i, c_i) \to \infty$ as $i \to \infty$ and, for each i, a constant fraction of the traffic rates r' in $[r_i/2, r_i]$ induce an instance with $\rho(G_i, r', c_i) = \Omega(\ln \pi(G_i, r_i, c_i))$.

4.7   Maximum Cost

Example 2.5.5 shows that defining the social objective function by aggregating the cost of all traffic, as in (2.2) and (2.3), can force the optimal flow to be "unfair." This section studies an alternative objective function, the maximum cost. In addition to forcing the optimal flow to be intuitively more fair, this new objective function serves as a case study on how the bounds on the price of anarchy in Chapter 3 depend on the definition of the social cost. See Section 4.8 for references on other natural objective functions and on alternative methods for measuring the fairness of a solution.

For a flow f feasible for an instance (G, r, c), define the maximum cost $M(f)$ by

$$M(f) = \max_{P \in \mathcal{P} : f_P > 0} c_P(f).$$

Unlike the equivalent definitions (2.2) and (2.3) of the cost, the maximum cost of a flow cannot be rewritten in terms of the induced flow on edges. In general, different path decompositions of a flow on edges can have different maximum costs. Example 2.5.3 provides one illustration of this subtlety.

Returning to Example 2.5.5, note that the Nash flow, which routes all traffic on the lower link, is the unique flow minimizing the maximum cost. The price of anarchy with respect to the maximum cost objective is therefore 1 in this example. This demonstrates how this objective refuses to reward flows that penalize some of the traffic in order to improve the rest.

Most basic properties of the cost are also satisfied by the maximum cost. For example, Proposition 2.2.2 and Corollary 2.6.2 imply that all Nash flows for an instance have equal maximum cost. Similarly, if there is a flow with maximum cost equal to 0, then every Nash flow also has maximum cost 0. Finally, since M is a continuous function, every instance admits a *max-optimal* flow, a flow that minimizes M over all feasible flows. The price of anarchy $\rho_M(G, r, c)$ of (G, r, c) with respect to the maximum cost is then defined by the ratio

$$\rho_M(G, r, c) = \frac{M(f)}{M(f^*)},$$

where f and f^* are Nash and max-optimal flows for (G, r, c), or by 1 if (G, r, c) admits a flow with zero maximum cost. Call ρ_M the *maximum price of anarchy*. As usual, the maximum price of anarchy $\rho_M(\mathcal{I})$ of a set $\mathcal{I}$ of instances is $\sup_{(G,r,c) \in \mathcal{I}} \rho_M(G, r, c)$.

The rest of this section discusses upper and lower bounds on the maximum price of anarchy. Two connections exist between this price of anarchy and previous results in the book. The first is lower bounds that arise from Braess's Paradox. To state these, let $d(G, r, c)$ denote the common cost of all flow paths in a Nash flow for a single-commodity instance (G, r, c). This definition makes sense by Proposition 2.2.2 and Corollary 2.6.2, and it is the same as the value $d(t)$ in the statement of Definition 2.7.5.

Proposition 4.7.1 *Suppose (G, r, c) is a single-commodity instance and H is a subgraph of G that contains an s-t path. Then,*

$$\rho_M(G, r, c) \geq \frac{d(G, r, c)}{d(H, r, c)},$$

with the understanding that $0/0 = 1$.

Proof: If f and f^* are Nash flows for (G, r, c) and (H, r, c), respectively, then f^* is also feasible for (G, r, c) and hence $\rho_M(G, r, c) \geq M(f)/M(f^*) = d(G, r, c)/d(H, r, c)$. ∎

For example, the following corollary is an immediate consequence of Example 2.5.2.

Corollary 4.7.2 *The maximum price of anarchy of single-commodity instances with linear cost functions is at least 4/3.*

In single-commodity instances, the price of anarchy for the cost upper bounds the price of anarchy for the maximum cost.

Proposition 4.7.3 *Let (G, r, c) be a single-commodity instance. Then,*

$$\rho_M(G, r, c) \leq \rho(G, r, c).$$

Proof: Let f, f^*, and f^M be Nash, optimal, and max-optimal flows for (G, r, c), respectively. Informally, the proposition follows from the facts that the maximum cost of a flow must be at least its average cost, and that the maximum and average costs of a Nash flow are equal in single-commodity instances. More precisely, by Proposition 2.2.4, $C(f) = r \cdot M(f)$. By the definition of f^*,

$$C(f^*) \leq C(f^M) = \sum_{P \in \mathcal{P}} c_P(f^M) f_P^M \leq \sum_{P \in \mathcal{P}} M(f^M) f_P^M = r \cdot M(f^M).$$

Hence,

$$\rho_M(G, r, c) = \frac{M(f)}{M(f^M)} \leq \frac{C(f)}{C(f^*)} = \rho(G, r, c).$$

∎

For example, Theorem 3.2.6 implies that the lower bound in Corollary 4.7.2 cannot be strengthened.

Corollary 4.7.4 *The maximum price of anarchy of single-commodity instances with linear cost functions is at most $4/3$.*

The maximum price of anarchy in single-commodity instances with other sets of restricted cost functions can be treated in a similar way. For example, Proposition 3.5.1 and examples given in Section 5.2.2 show that the maximum price of anarchy of single-commodity instances with cost functions that are polynomials with degree at most p and nonnegative coefficients is asymptotically $\Theta(p/\ln p)$ as $p \to \infty$.

Next, consider single-commodity instances in which the cost functions can be arbitrary. In this case, Proposition 4.7.3 offers no upper bound whatsoever on the maximum price of anarchy. Proposition 4.7.1 and a generalization of Example 2.5.2 given in Section 5.2.2 imply that the maximum price of anarchy in single-commodity instances with at most n vertices and arbitrary cost functions is at least $\lfloor n/2 \rfloor$, where $\lfloor x \rfloor$ denotes the largest integer equal to or less than x. Next is a stronger lower bound that is based on Example 2.5.3, rather than on Braess's Paradox.

Example 4.7.5 Let n be an integer greater than one. Let G be the network with

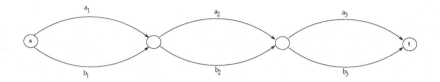

Figure 4.5
Lower bound on the maximum price of anarchy (Example 4.7.5 when $n = 4$). The maximum price of anarchy in single-commodity networks with n vertices and arbitrary cost functions is at least $n - 1$.

vertices $v_1, \ldots, v_n$, with $s = v_1$ and $t = v_n$, and with two edges, a_i and b_i, directed from v_i to v_{i+1} for each $i = 1, \ldots, n - 1$. See Figure 4.5. For each such i, edge a_i is given the constant cost function $c_{a_i}(x) = 1$ and edge b_i a cost function that satisfies $c_{b_i}((n-2)/(n-1)) = 0$ and $c_{b_i}(1) = 1$. The flow f that routes one unit of flow on edge b_i for all i is at Nash equilibrium for $(G, 1, c)$ with $M(f) = n - 1$. On the other hand, the flow f^* that routes $1/(n-1)$ units of flow on each of the $n - 1$ s-t paths of G that eschew exactly one edge of the form b_i is feasible for $(G, 1, c)$, and has maximum cost $M(f^*) = 1$.

Example 4.7.5 shows that the maximum price of anarchy in single-commodity instances with at most n vertices is at least $n - 1$. The next theorem is a matching upper bound.

Theorem 4.7.6 *If (G, r, c) is a single-commodity instance with $n \geq 2$ vertices, then*

$$\rho_M(G, r, c) \leq n - 1.$$

Proof: Let f be a Nash flow for (G, r, c), f^* a feasible flow for (G, r, c), and $d(v)$ the shortest-path distance from s to v with respect to edge lengths $c_e(f_e)$, as in Definition 2.7.5. By Proposition 2.2.2, $M(f) = d(t)$.

Let G have n vertices. Since all Nash flows have equal maximum cost, Proposition 2.7.4 implies that we can assume that f is a directed acyclic flow. By Proposition 2.7.8, we can therefore place an ordering $v_1, v_2, \ldots, v_n$ on the vertices of G that is f-monotone in the sense of Definition 2.7.5.

Let t appear as v_j in the f-monotone ordering. Let v_i, v_{i+1} be a pair of consecutive vertices with $i < j$ that maximizes the difference $d(v_{i+1}) - d(v_i)$. Since $d(t) = \sum_{i=1}^{j-1}[d(v_{i+1}) - d(v_i)]$ is the sum of $j - 1 \leq n - 1$ such differences, $d(v_{i+1}) - d(v_i) \geq d(t)/(n-1)$.

Let $S = \{v_1, \ldots, v_i\}$. By property (P1) of Definition 2.7.5, the set S is an s-t cut. By Proposition 2.7.2(a), $\sum_{e \in \delta^+(S)} f_e - \sum_{e \in \delta^-(S)} f_e = r$, where $\delta^+(S)$ is the set of edges with tail in S and head outside S and $\delta^-(S)$ is the set of edges with head inside S and tail outside S. Since vertices are sorted topologically with respect to f—property (P2) of Definition 2.7.5—no f-flow enters S and $\sum_{e \in \delta^-(S)} f_e = 0$. Hence, the amount of f-flow exiting S is precisely r: $\sum_{e \in \delta^+(S)} f_e = r$. By Proposition 2.7.2(a), the flow f^* must send at least r units of flow out of the cut S, so there must be an edge $e = (u, w)$ in $\delta^+(S)$ on which $f_e^* \geq f_e$ and $f_e^* > 0$, and hence $M(f^*) \geq c_e(f_e^*) \geq c_e(f_e)$. Moreover, by Proposition 2.7.7, $c_e(f_e) \geq d(w) - d(u)$. Since u is or precedes v_i in the f-monotone ordering, w is or succeeds v_{i+1} in the ordering, and property (P3) of Definition 2.7.5 ensures that d-values can only increase with the ordering, $d(w) - d(u) \geq d(v_{i+1}) - d(v_i)$. Thus,

$$M(f^*) \geq c_e(f_e) \geq d(v_{i+1}) - d(v_i) \geq d(t)/(n-1),$$

and the proof is complete. ∎

Corollary 4.7.4 and Theorem 4.7.6 do not carry over to multicommodity networks. In fact, even in two-commodity networks, the maximum price of anarchy can be linear in the size of a network with linear cost functions, and exponential in the size of a network with arbitrary cost functions. This provides a contrast to the work in Chapter 3, where single-commodity networks always determined the (original) price of anarchy. On the other hand, the maximum price of anarchy cannot be larger than exponential. See Section 4.8 for more details.

4.8   Notes

Section 4.1

While both nonatomic games and congestion games have long been studied in the game theory literature, as described below, Roughgarden and Tardos [349] were the first to consider the price of anarchy in such games. The extensions of Theorems 3.4.2, 3.4.9, and 3.6.2 described in Section 4.1 were first noted in [349], as was a slightly weaker version of the extension of Theorem 3.3.7. The stronger version of this last extension follows from work of Correa, Schulz, and Stier Moses [93]. Further extensions of these results to more general games—specifically, to nonatomic congestion games where the cost of an element can depend on the entire action distribution—have recently been given by Chau and Sim [75] and by Perakis [315].

The idealized assumption of a large population has figured prominently in economics since the birth of the field. Relatively recently, Schmeidler [353] initiated the study of general nonatomic noncooperative games. In [353], and in many subsequent research papers, nonatomic games are defined more generally than in Section 4.1. These papers model an outcome of a game by a *strategy profile*, defined as a Lebesgue-measurable function σ from a closed interval I to a finite-dimensional simplex of mixed strategies, rather than by an action distribution. For an introduction to Lebesgue measure and integration, see Aliprantis and Burkinshaw [6] or Bartle [33]. Multiple player types can be accommodated in this framework by replacing I with the product of several intervals. A strategy profile then naturally induces an action distribution x, with x_S obtained by integrating, with respect to Lebesgue measure, the coordinate of σ corresponding to strategy S over the interval I. Conversely, every action distribution is induced by some strategy profile. When all players select pure strategies, passing from strategy profiles to action distributions can be viewed as aggregating players according to their chosen strategies and ignoring their identities. Schmeidler [353] proved several existence results for equilibria in nonatomic games, which greatly generalize Proposition 2.2.5. These have subsequently been reformulated and refined by Mas-Colell [269] and Rath [327]. Section 4.1 does not explicitly consider strategy profiles, as it concerns only the cost of an equilibrium, a quantity that by definition depends only on the action distribution induced by a strategy profile.

Many types of games have been studied under the moniker of congestion games in the game theory literature. The salient feature of all such games is that the payoff to a player depends only on the player's strategy and on the number of other players choosing the same or some interfering strategy. Rosenthal [336] was the first to describe how the traffic model discussed in Chapter 2 naturally generalizes to a more abstract setting, and dubbed such games "congestion games." Additional applications of congestion games include firms competing for production processes [336], the migration of animals between different habitats [277, 323], and the evolution of attitudes toward risk [331].

Rosenthal [336] studied atomic games, where there are finitely many players of non-negligible size. Rosenthal [336] used a discretized version of the proof of Proposition 2.6.1 to show that when all players are the same size, there exists a Nash equilibrium in pure strategies, with each player deterministically picking a path for all of its traffic. This result also applies to networks with nonmonotone cost functions. Rosenthal [337] also showed that there need not exist a pure-strategy Nash equilibrium when players have different sizes. Libman and Orda [255] extended this counterexample to a single-commodity network. Section 4.4 of this book studies atomic games in some depth.

Rosenthal's work has been extended in several different directions. Perhaps the most influential of these generalizations is that of *potential games*, defined by Monderer and Shapley [283] as, essentially, the games for which a discretized version of the proof of Proposition 2.6.1 can be used to show the existence of a Nash equilibrium in pure strategies. The term *potential function* then refers to the analogue of the objective function of the convex program (CP) in Proposition 2.6.1. Subsequent work on potential games includes [139, 241, 242, 312, 386, 391, 392]. For other generalizations, refinements, and applications of congestion games, see [13, 198, 231, 232, 276, 322, 323, 362, 364, 391].

Most recently, congestion games have been studied in the theoretical computer science community from an algorithmic perspective. The focus of this work has been on the efficient computation of equilibria; see Fabrikant, Papadimitriou, and Talwar [138],

Papadimitriou and Roughgarden [305], and Papadimitriou [304] for more details.

Finally, many researchers explicitly considered nonatomic congestion games, or closely related concepts, prior to the aforementioned work on the price of anarchy in such games. See [53, 163, 184, 220, 265, 277, 278, 280, 290], for example, for a sampling of this research.

Section 4.2

Approximate Nash equilibria have been studied from many different perspectives by the game theory, transportation science, and computer science communities; a survey of this work is outside the scope of this book.

Section 4.2 is based on Roughgarden and Tardos [348]; in particular, Definition 4.2.1 and Theorem 4.2.3 are from [348]. A stronger version of Theorem 4.2.3 was incorrectly claimed in the preliminary version [347]. Example 4.2.4 is from Roughgarden [342], and Theorem 4.2.5 was first proved by Weitz [396].

Section 4.3

Section 4.3 is based on Schulz and Stier Moses [356] and its full version, Correa, Schulz, and Stier Moses [93]. In particular, all of the theorems in Section 4.3 were first proved in [356] or [93]. In [356], Theorem 4.3.4 was established only for semiconvex cost functions, because its proof was based on one of Roughgarden [343], which required semiconvexity. In [93], Theorems 4.3.4 and 4.3.9 were proved in their full generality.

Definition 4.3.1 and Proposition 4.3.2 are based on both [93] and on Marcotte, Nguyen, and Schoeb [266]. The discussion in Remark 4.3.5 is inspired by the paper of Anshelevich et al. [15]. Examples 4.3.3 and 4.3.7 are new.

For a sampling of earlier research in the transportation science literature that studied selfish routing in capacitated networks, see Daganzo [110, 111], Larsson and Patriksson [246, 248], and the references therein. In these earlier works, flows at Nash equilibrium were defined as the minimizers of the convex program (CAP) in the proof of Lemma 4.3.6, rather than game-theoretically and more generally via Definition 4.3.1.

Section 4.4

The atomic splittable model of Section 4.4.1 was first considered in the transportation science literature, long after the nonatomic model was proposed; see Harker [185], Catoni and Pallottino [74], and Bennett [41]. Subsequently but independently, Orda, Rom, and Shimkin [299] introduced the model to the networking literature. Fact 4.4.2 was proved in [185] using the theory of variational inequalities, and in [299] via a classical existence theorem of Rosen [335]. Since the publication of [299], research on the atomic splittable model has continued apace in the networking community. Several papers [11, 133, 234, 235, 254, 299] have studied Braess's Paradox in this model; these are discussed further in Section 5.4. Many researchers have pursued existence and uniqueness results for the atomic splittable model and several extensions [9, 8, 12, 58, 59, 132, 244, 299]. Korilis, Lazar, and Orda [233] also introduced the idea of Stackelberg routing strategies, the subject of Chapter 6, in the context of this model. Recently, La and Anantharam [244] considered a generalization of the atomic splittable model that includes an explicit temporal dimension, and Banner and Orda [31] studied the price of anarchy in atomic splittable instances with respect to a variation on the maximum cost objective of Section 4.7.

The inefficiency of selfish routing in the atomic splittable model was first studied by Roughgarden and Tardos [348]. In particular, Theorem 4.4.3 is from [348]. Theorem 4.4.4 is from Roughgarden [346]. Lastly, note that on a naive level these two theorems are highly intuitive: moving from a nonatomic instance to an atomic splittable one can be viewed as identifying groups of previously independent and noncooperative traffic into single users. Shouldn't the inefficiency of a Nash flow only decrease with the degree of cooperation? Unfortunately, Catoni and Pallottino [74] gave an example demonstrating that this intuition is erroneous. Theorems 4.4.3 and 4.4.4 can be interpreted as showing that the *worst-case* inefficiency of selfish routing is nonincreasing in the degree of cooperation, even though such monotonicity need not hold on an instance-by-instance basis.

The atomic unsplittable model of Section 4.4.2 was first studied by Rosenthal [336, 337], who showed that a Nash equilibrium in pure strategies exists when all players control the same amount of flow and need not exist when players control different amounts of flow. See also the notes on Section 4.1, above. Devarajan [117], Haurie and Marcotte [187, 188], and Milchtaich [278] showed formally how the nonatomic selfish routing model arises as the limit, as the number of players goes to infinity, of a sequence of atomic unsplittable instances. Libman and Orda [254, 255] studied several issues in the atomic unsplittable model, including the existence and uniqueness of Nash equilibria, conditions under which network users can quickly settle into a Nash equilibrium, and how a Nash equilibrium changes when edge cost functions are modified.

Example 4.4.5 is from Roughgarden and Tardos [348]. As mentioned after this example, researchers have very recently obtained bounds on the inefficiency of both the best and worst Nash flows of an atomic unsplittable instance. First, Anshelevich et al. [14] proved somewhat weaker analogues of the central upper bounds of Chapter 3 (Theorems 3.3.7 and 3.6.2) for the best flow at Nash equilibrium of an atomic unsplittable instance. Specifically, Anshelevich et al. [14] proved that in an atomic unsplittable instance with semiconvex cost functions in the set $\mathcal{C}$ and in which all commodities have a common source, there is some flow at Nash equilibrium with cost at most $\alpha(\mathcal{C})$ times the optimal cost, where $\alpha(\mathcal{C})$ is the anarchy value of $\mathcal{C}$ (Definition 3.3.3). For every atomic unsplittable instance with semiconvex cost functions in which all commodities have a common source, Anshelevich et al. [14] showed that there is a flow at Nash equilibrium with cost at most that of an optimal flow with twice as many players. The question of whether or not these bounds continue to hold in general atomic unsplittable instances is currently open.

Bounds on the price of anarchy of selfish routing in atomic unsplittable instances were obtained independently by Awerbuch, Azar, and Epstein [27] and by Christodoulou and Koutsoupias [78]. In particular, both groups of researchers proved that while the price of anarchy in such instances can be larger than in nonatomic or atomic splittable instances, qualitatively similar bounds hold. For example, the price of anarchy in atomic unsplittable instances with linear cost functions is precisely 5/2. With cost functions that are polynomials with nonnegative coefficients and degree at most p, the price of anarchy is $p^{\Theta(p)}$ as $p \to \infty$. Thus while the price of anarchy in such atomic unsplittable instances grows exponentially with the allowable degree, rather than polynomially as in the nonatomic and atomic splittable cases, it remains finite for each fixed p and is also independent of the network size and the number of commodities.

Section 4.5

The definitions and results in Section 4.5 are from Roughgarden and Tardos [348]. Analogues for nonatomic congestion games were given in [349].

Section 4.6

All of the definitions, examples, and results of Section 4.6 are from Friedman [164]. Details on the proof of Theorem 4.6.6, the family of examples mentioned in Remark 4.6.7, and an extension of Theorem 4.6.6 to more general ranges of traffic rates can also be found in [164].

Section 4.7

The maximum price of anarchy was first considered by Weitz [396]. Weitz [396] observed Propositions 4.7.1 and 4.7.3 and Corollaries 4.7.2 and 4.7.4, which were also noted independently by Roughgarden [338] in the context of Braess's Paradox (see also Sections 5.2 and 5.4). Weitz [396] also gave an example showing that the maximum price of anarchy can be $\Omega(n)$ in two-commodity, n-vertex networks with linear cost functions. Correa, Schulz, and Stier Moses [92] later gave a variation on this example.

Example 4.7.5 and Theorem 4.7.6, which resolve the maximum price of anarchy of single-commodity networks with arbitrary cost functions, are from Roughgarden [344]. Very recently. the maximum price of anarchy in multicommodity networks with arbitrary cost functions was analyzed by Lin et al. [257]. First, Lin et al. [257] showed that Braess's Paradox can be extremely severe in such networks: removing an edge from a two-commodity, n-vertex network with arbitrary cost functions can decrease the maximum price of anarchy by a $2^{\Omega(n)}$ multiplicative factor as $n \to \infty$. The family of networks that demonstrates this fact is an intricate generalization of Example 2.5.6. In contrast to the upper bound of Theorem 4.7.6 for single-commodity networks, Proposition 4.7.1 then implies that the maximum price of anarchy can be exponential in the number of vertices of a two-commodity network with arbitrary cost functions. On the other hand, Lin et al. [257] proved a nearly matching upper bound of $2^{O(kn)}$ on the maximum price of anarchy of k-commodity, n-vertex networks with arbitrary cost functions.

For still further aspects of selfish routing with respect to the maximum cost objective, see Correa, Schulz, and Stier Moses [92].

Finally, many recent papers address the unfairness of optimal flows using alternatives to the maximum cost objective. See Jahn et al. [203], Correa, Schulz, and Stier Moses [92], and Roughgarden [340] for several examples.

III COPING WITH SELFISHNESS

5 Bounding and Detecting Braess's Paradox

Part II developed techniques for bounding the worst-possible inefficiency of selfish routing. Part III attempts to address this inefficiency. Specifically, it considers two algorithmic approaches for *coping with selfishness*—using a modest degree of centralized control to ensure that selfish routing results in a socially desirable outcome. This chapter attempts to design networks that do not suffer from Braess's Paradox (Example 2.5.2), while Chapter 6 explores the power of routing a small portion of the network traffic centrally.

5.1 Overview

Braess's Paradox motivates a fundamental algorithmic question: how can we design networks that avoid the paradox? This chapter focuses on the following simple version of this problem: given a single-commodity instance (G, r, c), efficiently find a subgraph H of G that minimizes the common cost of all traffic in a Nash flow for (H, r, c). Letting $d(H, r, c)$ denote this common cost—as in Section 4.7, this is well defined by Propositions 2.2.2 and 2.6.1—we want a polynomial-time algorithm to solve the following problem in single-commodity instances:

$$\text{Given } (G, r, c), \text{ find a subgraph } H \text{ of } G \text{ that minimizes } d(H, r, c). \qquad (5.1)$$

Or course, Braess's Paradox (Example 2.5.2) shows that this problem is nontrivial, in the sense that the entire graph G need not be an optimal solution to the problem. Since the number of subgraphs H of G is in general exponential in the size of the instance (G, r, c), this problem cannot be solved in polynomial time by brute-force enumeration.

We will see that this network design problem is very difficult, and will therefore consider approximation algorithms.

Definition 5.1.1 A *c-approximation algorithm* for a minimization problem runs in polynomial time and returns a solution no more than c times as costly as an optimal solution. The value c is the *approximation ratio* or *performance guarantee* of the algorithm.

NP-hard optimization problems are widely believed to admit no exact polynomial-time algorithm, but many such problems do admit c-approximation algorithms for small values of c. On the other hand, there are also many *inapproximability* or *hardness results* for NP-hard optimization problems, which rule out c-approximation algorithms for reasonable values of c, assuming $P \neq NP$. This book equates a strong inapproximability result with a proof that a problem is "highly intractable," with the usual caveat that it does not rule out the existence of an algorithm that "usually" is fast and accurate but performs poorly in the worst case.

This chapter describes optimal inapproximability results and approximation algorithms for the network design problem (5.1). For example, Sections 5.2 and 5.3 prove the following, where $\lfloor x \rfloor$ is the largest integer equal to or less than x.

- There is a $\lfloor n/2 \rfloor$-approximation algorithm for the problem (5.1) for networks with at most n vertices, and no approximation algorithm with smaller performance guarantee exists, assuming that $P \neq NP$.
- There is a $\frac{4}{3}$-approximation algorithm for the problem (5.1) for instances with linear cost functions, and no approximation algorithm with smaller performance guarantee exists, assuming that $P \neq NP$.

Also in this chapter are analogous results for other sets of cost functions and for a more general network design problem.

This work also shows that an optimal approximation algorithm for these problems is the *trivial algorithm*: given a network of candidate edges, build the entire network. As a consequence, Braess's Paradox is impossible to detect efficiently, even in its worst-possible manifestations.

Proving upper and lower bounds on the approximation ratio of the trivial algorithm is tantamount to proving upper and lower bounds on the worst-possible severity of Braess's Paradox. Proofs of several such bounds are in Section 5.2. In particular, Section 5.2 shows that Braess's Paradox extends far beyond the simple network described in Example 2.5.2. Section 5.4 discusses Braess's Paradox in multicommodity networks and a multicommodity analogue of the network design problem (5.1).

5.2 Bounding Braess's Paradox

This section proves upper and lower bounds on the worst-possible severity of Braess's Paradox—on the largest factor by which removing edges from a network can decrease the cost incurred by traffic in a Nash flow. As in Chapter 3, these bounds depend on the set of allowable edge cost functions.

5.2.1   Upper Bounds on the Severity of Braess's Paradox

Since we are currently restricting our attention to single-commodity networks, upper bounds on the worst-possible severity of Braess's Paradox for restricted sets of allowable cost functions follow easily from the corresponding upper bounds on the price of anarchy described in Chapter 3. For example, by an argument similar to the proof of Proposition 4.7.3, the following upper bound for single-commodity instances with linear cost functions follows from Theorem 3.2.6.

Corollary 5.2.1 *If (G, r, c) is a single-commodity instance with linear cost functions and H is a subgraph of G, then*

$$d(G, r, c) \leq \frac{4}{3} \cdot d(H, r, c).$$

Proof: Let (G, r, c) be a single-commodity instance with linear cost functions and H a subgraph of G. Let f and f^* denote flows at Nash equilibrium for (G, r, c) and (H, r, c), respectively. By Proposition 2.2.4, we can write $C(f) = r \cdot d(G, r, c)$ and $C(f^*) = r \cdot d(H, r, c)$. Since f^* can be viewed as a feasible flow for (G, r, c), Theorem 3.2.6 implies that $C(f) \leq 4C(f^*)/3$ and hence $d(G, r, c) \leq 4d(H, r, c)/3$. ∎

The same proof, together with Proposition 3.5.1 and Theorem 4.5.3, gives analogous corollaries for networks with cost functions that are degree-bounded polynomials with nonnegative coefficients or that have bounded incline in the sense of Definition 4.5.1.

Corollary 5.2.2 *If (G, r, c) is a single-commodity instance with cost functions that are polynomials with degree at most p and nonnegative coefficients, and H is a subgraph of G, then*

$$d(G, r, c) \leq (1 - p \cdot (p+1)^{-(p+1)/p})^{-1} \cdot d(H, r, c).$$

Corollary 5.2.3 *If (G, r, c) is a single-commodity instance with $\Gamma(c_e) \leq \gamma$ for all edges e, and H is a subgraph of G, then*

$$d(G, r, c) \leq \gamma \cdot d(H, r, c).$$

For clarity, the rest of this chapter uses the following asymptotic version of Corollary 5.2.2.

Corollary 5.2.4 *There is a constant $c_1 > 0$ such that if (G,r,c) is a single-commodity instance with cost functions that are polynomials with degree at most p and nonnegative coefficients, and H is a subgraph of G, then*

$$d(G,r,c) \leq c_1 \frac{p}{\ln p} \cdot d(H,r,c).$$

The fourth and final set of allowable edge cost functions considered in this chapter is the set of all continuous, nondecreasing functions. Example 2.5.4 demonstrates that the proof approach in the preceding corollaries gives no finite upper bound on the severity of Braess's Paradox in this case, even in two-node, two-link networks. On the other hand, the network in Example 2.5.4 obviously does not suffer from Braess's Paradox at all. We therefore have set the bar unduly high by comparing the cost of a Nash flow to the cost of an optimal flow, as opposed to what we really care about, *the cheapest flow that arises as a Nash flow in a subgraph*. With this refined comparison, we can achieve the following upper bound on Braess's Paradox.

Theorem 5.2.5 *If (G,r,c) is a single-commodity instance with n vertices and H is a subgraph of G, then*

$$d(G,r,c) \leq \left\lfloor \frac{n}{2} \right\rfloor \cdot d(H,r,c).$$

We obtain Theorem 5.2.5 as a consequence of a more general theorem. The statement of this more general result uses the following definition.

Definition 5.2.6 Let (G,r,c) be a single-commodity instance and S a subset of the edges of G. The set S is *sparse* if:

(1) no two edges of S share an endpoint; and
(2) no edge of S is incident to s or t.

Our general bound on Braess's Paradox states that the size of the largest sparse set removed controls how much the cost of a Nash flow can decrease.

Theorem 5.2.7 *Let (G,r,c) be a single-commodity instance. Let H be a subgraph of G, and S the set of edges that are in G but not H. If every sparse subset of S contains at most k edges, then*

$$d(G,r,c) \leq (k+1) \cdot d(H,r,c).$$

Before proving Theorem 5.2.7, we show that it easily implies Theorem 5.2.5, as well as an upper bound on Braess's Paradox that is parameterized by the number of edges removed.

Proof of Theorem 5.2.5: Since there are only $n - 2$ nodes in G that are not s or t, every sparse set of edges has at most $\lfloor (n - 2)/2 \rfloor = \lfloor n/2 \rfloor - 1$ edges. Theorem 5.2.7 now implies the theorem. ∎

Corollary 5.2.8 *If (G, r, c) is a single-commodity instance and H is obtained from G by removing at most k edges, then*

$$d(G, r, c) \leq (k + 1) \cdot d(H, r, c).$$

Proof: Obvious from Definition 5.2.6 and Theorem 5.2.7. ∎

We now turn toward proving Theorem 5.2.7. We begin with a definition and a lemma.

Definition 5.2.9 Let f and $\tilde{f}$ be flows feasible for the instances (G, r, c) and $(G, \tilde{r}, c)$, respectively.

(a) An edge e of G is $(f, \tilde{f})$-*light* if $f_e \leq \tilde{f}_e$ and $\tilde{f}_e > 0$, $(f, \tilde{f})$-*heavy* if $f_e > \tilde{f}_e$, and $(f, \tilde{f})$-*useless* if $f_e = \tilde{f}_e = 0$.
(b) An undirected path is $(f, \tilde{f})$-*alternating* if it comprises only forward light edges and backward heavy edges.

When the context is clear, we drop the dependence on f and $\tilde{f}$ for the terms in Definition 5.2.9.

Example 5.2.10 Consider the Braess's Paradox network (Example 2.5.2). Let f be the Nash flow and $\tilde{f}$ the optimal flow. Then, edges (s, v), (v, w), and (w, t) are $(f, \tilde{f})$-heavy while edges (s, w) and (v, t) are $(f, \tilde{f})$-light. The unique $(f, \tilde{f})$-alternating s-t path is $s \to w \to v \to t$.

We now prove that an s-t alternating path exists, when comparing one flow to another at the same or an increased traffic rate.

Lemma 5.2.11 *Let f and $\tilde{f}$ be flows feasible for the single-commodity instances (G, r, c) and $(G, \tilde{r}, c)$, respectively, with $r \leq \tilde{r}$. Then, there is an $(f, \tilde{f})$-alternating* *s-t path. Moreover, if f is directed acyclic, then every such path begins and ends with a $(f, \tilde{f})$-light edge.*

Proof: Suppose for contradiction that there is no $(f, \tilde{f})$-alternating s-t path and let S denote the set of nodes reachable from s via such paths. The set S contains s and, by assumption, does not contain t; it is therefore an s-t cut. By Proposition 2.7.2(a),

$$\sum_{e \in \delta^+(S)} f_e - \sum_{e \in \delta^-(S)} f_e = r \tag{5.2}$$

and

$$\sum_{e \in \delta^+(S)} \tilde{f}_e - \sum_{e \in \delta^-(S)} \tilde{f}_e = \tilde{r}, \tag{5.3}$$

where $\delta^+(S)$ is the set of edges exiting S and $\delta^-(S)$ is the set of edges entering S.

Since vertices in S can be reached from s via $(f, \tilde{f})$-alternating paths and vertices outside S cannot, edges that exit S must be heavy or useless. In addition, one such edge must be heavy, since otherwise the left-hand side of (5.2) would be nonpositive. Similarly, edges that enter S are light or useless. These observations imply that the left-hand side of (5.2) is strictly greater than that of (5.3), contradicting the fact that $r \leq \tilde{r}$.

Moreover, if f is directed acyclic, then it sends no flow into s or out of t. Thus, the first and last edges of every $(f, \tilde{f})$-alternating s-t path must be light. ∎

To prepare for the proof of Theorem 5.2.7, we first prove an orthogonal monotonicity result, that $d(G, r, c)$ is nondecreasing in r.

Proposition 5.2.12 *For every network G with one source-destination pair and cost functions c, the value $d(G, r, c)$ is nondecreasing in r.*

While Proposition 5.2.12 is not directly used in this book, it nevertheless is a fundamental result (see Section 5.4).

Proof of Proposition 5.2.12: Let f and $\tilde{f}$ be Nash flows for (G, r, c) and $(G, \tilde{r}, c)$, respectively. For a vertex v, let $d(v)$ and $\tilde{d}(v)$ denote the shortest-path distance from s to v with respect to edge lengths $c_e(f_e)$ and $c_e(\tilde{f}_e)$, respectively. These are the same shortest-path distance labels as in Definition 2.7.5 and Proposition 2.7.7. By definition, $d(G, r, c) = d(t)$ and $d(G, \tilde{r}, c) = \tilde{d}(t)$. The proposition asserts that $d(t) \leq \tilde{d}(t)$.

We prove the stronger result that $d(v) \leq \tilde{d}(v)$ for all vertices v of an arbitrary $(f, \tilde{f})$-alternating s-t path P. At least one such path exists by Lemma 5.2.11. We proceed by induction. For the base case, $d(s) = \tilde{d}(s) = 0$. Now suppose that $d(v) \leq \tilde{d}(v)$ holds for some vertex v on P, and let w be the subsequent vertex on P. There are now two cases.

First, suppose that edge $e = (v, w)$ is $(f, \tilde{f})$-light. Then, $c_e(f_e) \leq c_e(\tilde{f}_e)$ and $\tilde{f}_e > 0$. Since f and $\tilde{f}$ are Nash flows, Proposition 2.7.7 and the inductive hypothesis imply that

$$d(w) \leq d(v) + c_e(f_e) \leq \tilde{d}(v) + c_e(\tilde{f}_e) = \tilde{d}(w).$$

Now suppose that edge $e = (w, v)$ is $(f, \tilde{f})$-heavy. Since $f_e > 0$ and f is a Nash flow, Proposition 2.7.7 implies that

$$d(v) = d(w) + c_e(f_e). \tag{5.4}$$

Similarly, for $\tilde{f}$ we have

$$\tilde{d}(v) \leq \tilde{d}(w) + c_e(\tilde{f}_e). \tag{5.5}$$

Since $d(v) \leq \tilde{d}(v)$ by the inductive hypothesis, and $c_e(\tilde{f}_e) \leq c_e(f_e)$ since e is $(f, \tilde{f})$-heavy, equation (5.4) and inequality (5.5) are only compatible if $d(w) \leq \tilde{d}(w)$. This completes the inductive step and therefore proves the proposition. ∎

Finally, we show how a refinement of the proof of Proposition 5.2.12 proves Theorem 5.2.7.

Proof of Theorem 5.2.7: Let f and $\tilde{f}$ be Nash flows for (G, r, c) and (H, r, c), respectively. We view $\tilde{f}$ as a flow, perhaps not at Nash equilibrium, in the larger network G in the obvious way. As in the proof of Proposition 5.2.12, let d and $\tilde{d}$ denote shortest-path distances with respect to the edge costs induced by f and $\tilde{f}$ in G and H, respectively. This proof must differ from that of Proposition 5.2.12, as $\tilde{f}$ is a Nash flow in H but not in G.

Let P be an $(f, \tilde{f})$-alternating s-t path, which exists by Lemma 5.2.11. A *segment* of P is a maximal subpath of P that contains only $(f, \tilde{f})$-light or only $(f, \tilde{f})$-heavy edges. Edges that are in G but not H are called *absent*. Since $\tilde{f}_e > 0$ on $(f, \tilde{f})$-light edges, absent edges can only reside in $(f, \tilde{f})$-heavy segments. The key claim is that if v is a vertex at the end of a segment of P, and k (heavy) segments of P between s and v contain an absent edge, then

$$d(v) \leq \tilde{d}(v) + k \cdot \tilde{d}(t). \tag{5.6}$$

This claim implies the theorem. To see why, first apply (5.6) to t to obtain

$$d(t) \leq \tilde{d}(t) + k \cdot \tilde{d}(t) = (k+1) \cdot \tilde{d}(t), \qquad (5.7)$$

where k is the number of segments of P that include an absent edge. Inequality (5.7) reduces the proof of the theorem to exhibiting a sparse set of k absent edges. By Definition 5.2.9 and Lemma 5.2.11, $(f, \tilde{f})$-heavy segments of P are disjoint from each other and from s and t. Picking one absent edge from each $(f, \tilde{f})$-heavy segment that contains one thus provides the desired sparse set.

We now prove (5.6) by induction on the segments of P. The inequality trivially holds when $v = s$, so suppose it holds for a vertex v that is last on a segment of P, or is equal to s. We wish to prove (5.6) for w, defined as the last vertex on the next segment. If no edges in the segment between v and w are absent, then (5.6) holds by the arguments in the penultimate or the final paragraph of the proof of Proposition 5.2.12, depending on whether the segment contains light or heavy edges, respectively.

Since absent edges can only be heavy, we can finish the proof by establishing the inductive hypothesis when the segment between v and w comprises heavy backward edges, at least one of which is absent. The inequality $\tilde{d}(w) \leq \tilde{d}(v) + c_e(\tilde{f}_e)$, crucial to the proof of Proposition 5.2.12, cannot be used here. It no longer applies because $\tilde{d}$ denotes shortest-path distance with respect to the edge costs induced by $\tilde{f}$ in H, but not in G. In exchange, the inductive hypothesis (5.6) bestows an extra additive factor of $\tilde{d}(t)$ on its right-hand side.

To finish the proof, first note that since there is a path of (heavy) edges from w to v, all with $f_e > 0$, Proposition 2.7.7 implies that $d(w) \leq d(v)$. Since the path P begins with a light edge (Lemma 5.2.11), $v \neq s$ and there is a light edge entering v. Since $\tilde{f}$ routes flow into v, it must route flow from v to t. By Proposition 2.7.7, $\tilde{d}(v) \leq \tilde{d}(t)$. Combining what we know with the inductive hypothesis, the proof of the inductive step is complete:

$$d(w) \leq d(v) \leq \tilde{d}(v) + k \cdot \tilde{d}(t) \leq (k+1) \cdot \tilde{d}(t) \leq \tilde{d}(w) + (k+1) \cdot \tilde{d}(t).$$

∎

5.2.2   Lower Bounds on the Severity of Braess's Paradox

This section shows that the upper bounds on the severity of Braess's Paradox in Section 5.2.1 are the best possible. For networks with linear cost functions, Example 2.5.2 already shows that the bound in Corollary 5.2.1 is tight.

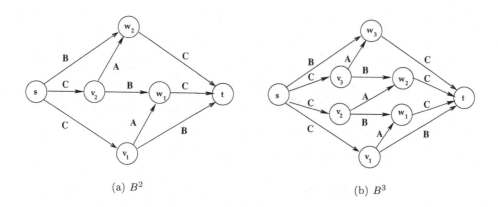

(a) B^2 (b) B^3

Figure 5.1
The second and third Braess graphs. Edges are labeled with their types.

Corollary 5.2.13 *There is a single-commodity instance (G, r, c) with linear cost functions and a subgraph H of G such that*

$$d(G, r, c) = \frac{4}{3} \cdot d(H, r, c).$$

To prove that the other three upper bounds in Section 5.2.1 are also optimal, this section introduces an infinite family of networks that generalizes Example 2.5.2. The following construction has been partially anticipated in Examples 4.3.7 and 4.4.5.

For a positive integer k, we define the *kth Braess graph*. Start with a set of $2k + 2$ vertices $V^k = \{s, v_1, \ldots, v_k, w_1, \ldots, w_k, t\}$. The edge set E^k is the union of three sets, $\{(s, v_i), (v_i, w_i), (w_i, t) : 1 \leq i \leq k\}$, $\{(v_i, w_{i-1}) : 2 \leq i \leq k\}$, and $\{(v_1, t)\} \cup \{(s, w_k)\}$ (see Figure 5.1). Call edges of the form (v_i, w_i) the *type A edges*, edges of the form (v_i, w_{i-1}), (s, w_k), and (v_1, t) the *type B edges*, and edges of the form (s, v_i) and (w_i, t) the *type C edges* (see Figure 5.1). Note that B^1 is the graph in which Braess's Paradox was first discovered (Figure 2.3).

The Braess graphs show that the upper bound of $\lfloor n/2 \rfloor$ for networks with arbitrary cost functions (Theorem 5.2.5) cannot be improved.

Theorem 5.2.14 *For every $n \geq 2$, there is an instance (G, r, c) in which G has n vertices and admits a subgraph H with*

$$d(G, r, c) = \lfloor n/2 \rfloor \cdot d(H, r, c).$$

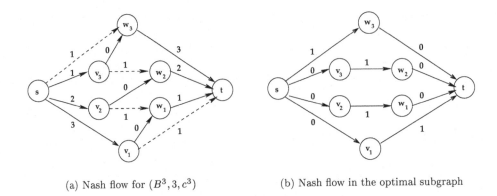

(a) Nash flow for $(B^3, 3, c^3)$ (b) Nash flow in the optimal subgraph

Figure 5.2
Proof of Theorem 5.2.14, when $k = 3$. Solid edges carry flow in the flow at Nash equilibrium, dashed edges do not. Edge costs are with respect to flows at Nash equilibrium.

Proof: We can assume that n is even, since the odd case reduces to the even case by adding an isolated vertex. We can also assume that n is at least 4. Write $n = 2k + 2$ for a positive integer k and define cost functions on the edges of the kth Braess graph B^k as follows.

(A) Type A edges are given the cost function $c_e^k(x) = 0$.

(B) Type B edges are given the cost function $c_e^k(x) = 1$.

(C) For each $i \in \{1, 2, \ldots, k\}$, the type C edges (w_i, t) and (s, v_{k-i+1}) are given a continuous, nondecreasing cost function $c_e^k(x)$ with $c_e^k(k/(k+1)) = 0$ and $c_e^k(1) = i$.

For $i = 1, \ldots, k$, let P_i denote the path $s \to v_i \to w_i \to t$. For $i = 2, \ldots, k$, let Q_i denote the path $s \to v_i \to w_{i-1} \to t$. Define Q_1 to be the path $s \to v_1 \to t$ and Q_{k+1} the path $s \to w_k \to t$. On one hand, routing one unit of flow on each of $P_1, \ldots, P_k$ yields a flow at Nash equilibrium for (B^k, k, c^k) demonstrating that $d(B^k, k, c^k) = k + 1$ (Figure 5.2(a)). On the other hand, if H is the subgraph obtained from B^k by deleting the k type A edges, then routing $k/(k+1)$ units of flow on each of $Q_1, \ldots, Q_{k+1}$ yields a flow at Nash equilibrium for (H, k, c^k) showing that $d(H, k, c^k) = 1$ (Figure 5.2(b)). Thus, $d(G)/d(H) = k + 1 = n/2$, completing the proof. ∎

In particular, Theorem 5.2.14 demonstrates the following fact when cost functions are unrestricted:

in large networks, Braess's Paradox can be arbitrarily severe.

The proof of Theorem 5.2.14 also shows that Theorem 5.2.7 and Corollary 5.2.8 are the best-possible parameterized bounds on Braess's Paradox.

Corollary 5.2.15 *For every $k \geq 1$, there is an instance (G, r, c) and a subgraph H obtainable from G by removing a sparse set of k edges that satisfy*

$$d(G, r, c) = (k + 1) \cdot d(H, r, c).$$

The Braess graphs also allow us to prove that Corollaries 5.2.2 and 5.2.3 are tight up to constant factors.

Theorem 5.2.16 *There is a constant $c_2 > 0$ such that for all $p \geq 1$, there is an instance (G, r, c) with cost functions that are polynomials with degree at most p and nonnegative coefficients and a subgraph H of G with*

$$d(G, r, c) \geq c_2 \frac{p}{\ln p} \cdot d(H, r, c).$$

Proof: The proof of Theorem 5.2.14 exploited the fact that general cost functions can be arbitrarily steep. Here, we simply adapt the argument in that proof as best we can, given that only low-degree polynomials are available.

For each sufficiently large integer p, we will define a parameter k and a set of cost functions c^k for the edges of the Braess graph B^k. We will choose the parameter k at the end of the proof. The functions c^k are identical to those in the proof of Theorem 5.2.14, except that for every $i \in \{1, 2, \ldots, k\}$, the type C edges (s, v_{k-i+1}) and (w_i, t) are given the cost function $c^k(x) = ix^p$. Now, consider the instance (B^k, k, c^k) and define paths $P_1, \ldots, P_k$ and $Q_1, \ldots, Q_{k+1}$ as in the proof of Theorem 5.2.14. On one hand, routing one unit of flow on each of $P_1, \ldots, P_k$ yields a flow at Nash equilibrium for (B^k, k, c^k) showing that $d(B^k, k, c^k) = k + 1$, as in Figure 5.2(a). On the other hand, if H is the subgraph obtained from B^k by deleting all of the type A edges, then routing $k/(k+1)$ units of flow on each of $Q_1, \ldots, Q_{k+1}$ yields a flow at Nash equilibrium for (H, k, c^k), showing that

$$d(H, k, c^k) = 1 + k \left(\frac{k}{k+1} \right)^p \leq 1 + k e^{-p/(k+1)},$$

as in Figure 5.2(b). For p sufficiently large, putting $k = \lfloor p/2 \ln p \rfloor - 1$ we obtain $d(H, k, c^k) \leq 2$ and $d(B^k, k, c^k) = \lfloor p/2 \ln p \rfloor$, and the proof is complete. ∎

Remark 5.2.17 The proof of Theorem 5.2.16 does not optimize constants in the interest of readability, and the rest of the chapter continues to make this tradeoff.

Similarly, the following theorem holds for instances with bounded incline.

Theorem 5.2.18 *For all $\gamma \geq 1$, there is an instance (G, r, c) with cost functions with incline at most γ and a subgraph H of G with*

$$d(G, r, c) \geq \frac{\gamma}{2} \cdot d(H, r, c).$$

The proof of Theorem 5.2.18 is the same as that for Theorem 5.2.16, except for two modifications. First, the parameter k, which controls the size of the underlying Braess graph, is set to $\lfloor \gamma \rfloor$. Second, the cost functions of the type C edges of the form (s, v_{k-i+1}) and (w_i, t) are changed from $c_e^k(x) = ix^p$ to the function g that is equal to $1/\gamma$ on $[0, \gamma/(\gamma+1)]$, and is linear on $[\gamma/(\gamma+1), 1]$, subject to $g(\gamma/(\gamma+1)) = 1/\gamma$ and $g(1) = 1$.

5.3   Detecting Braess's Paradox

This section shifts the focus from analyzing Braess's Paradox to designing algorithms for detecting it and for solving the network design problem (5.1) described at the beginning of this chapter. It studies four versions of (5.1): GENERAL NETWORK DESIGN, where networks can have arbitrary cost functions, LINEAR NETWORK DESIGN, where networks are permitted only linear cost functions, and the obvious analogues POLYNOMIAL(p) NETWORK DESIGN and INCLINE(γ) NETWORK DESIGN.

Proving bounds on the worst-possible severity of Braess's Paradox is tantamount to proving bounds on the approximation ratio of the trivial algorithm—the algorithm that, given an instance (G, r, c), returns the entire network G as a solution. Specifically, the work in Section 5.2 has the following corollaries.

Corollary 5.3.1 *The approximation ratio of the trivial algorithm for* LINEAR NETWORK DESIGN *is precisely 4/3.*

Corollary 5.3.2 *The approximation ratio of the trivial algorithm for* GENERAL NETWORK DESIGN *with networks with a most n vertices is precisely $\lfloor n/2 \rfloor$.*

Corollary 5.3.3 *The approximation ratio of the trivial algorithm for* POLYNOMIAL(p) NETWORK DESIGN *is asymptotically $\Theta(p/\ln p)$ as $p \to \infty$.*

Corollary 5.3.4 *The approximation ratio of the trivial algorithm for* INCLINE(γ) NETWORK DESIGN *is asymptotically $\Theta(\gamma)$ as $\gamma \to \infty$.*

While obviously uninteresting from an algorithmic perspective, the trivial algorithm does provide the weakest imaginable litmus test for approximation algorithms for the network design problem (5.1). For an approximation algorithm to have any merit whatsoever, it should improve upon the performance guarantees of the trivial algorithm listed in Corollaries 5.3.1–5.3.4.

Assuming $P \neq NP$, this section reports some bad news:

> *no polynomial-time algorithm outperforms the trivial algorithm.*

Of course, this statement is in the worst-case sense of approximation algorithms (Definition 5.1.1). While a polynomial-time algorithm may do much better than the trivial algorithm on many instances, there will also be instances on which it is just as clueless as the trivial algorithm.

The rest of this section is devoted to proving these negative results, and to extending them to a more general network design problem. Sections 5.3.1 and 5.3.2 contain complete proofs of the inapproximability results for LINEAR NETWORK DESIGN and GENERAL NETWORK DESIGN, respectively, which were claimed in Section 5.1. Section 5.3.3 states and briefly discusses the proofs of two more hardness of approximation results. Section 5.3.4 concludes with the aforementioned generalizations. The rest of this section assumes that the reader is at least somewhat familiar with polynomial-time reductions and the theory of NP-completeness; see Sections 1.5 for references on these topics.

5.3.1 Linear Cost Functions

The proof of inapproximability is particularly simple in the case of networks with linear cost functions.

Theorem 5.3.5 *Assuming $P \neq NP$, for every $\epsilon > 0$ there is no $(\frac{4}{3} - \epsilon)$-approximation algorithm for* LINEAR NETWORK DESIGN.

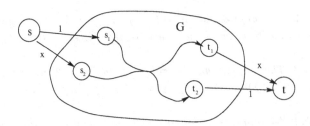

Figure 5.3
Proof of Theorem 5.3.5. In a "no" instance of 2DDP, the existence of s_1-t_1 and s_2-t_2 paths
implies the existence of an s_2-t_1 path.

Proof: The reduction will be from the NP-complete problem 2 DIRECTED DIS-
JOINT PATHS (2DDP): given a directed graph $G = (V, E)$ and distinct vertices
$s_1, s_2, t_1, t_2 \in V$, are there s_i-t_i paths P_i for $i = 1, 2$, such that P_1 and P_2 are
vertex-disjoint? We will show that a $(\frac{4}{3} - \epsilon)$-approximation algorithm for LINEAR
NETWORK DESIGN can be used to differentiate between "yes" and "no" instances
of 2DDP in polynomial time.

Consider an instance $\mathcal{I}$ of 2DDP, as above. Augment the vertex set V by an
additional source s and sink t, and include the directed edges (s, s_1), (s, s_2), (t_1, t),
and (t_2, t) (see Figure 5.3). Denote the new network by $G' = (V', E')$ and endow the
edges of E' with the following linear cost functions c: edges of E are given the cost
function $c(x) = 0$, edges (s, s_2) and (t_1, t) are given the cost function $c(x) = x$, and
edges (s, s_1) and (t_2, t) are given the cost function $c(x) = 1$. The instance $(G', 1, c)$
can be constructed from $\mathcal{I}$ in polynomial time.

To complete the proof, it suffices to show the following two statements.

(i) If $\mathcal{I}$ is a "yes" instance of 2DDP, then G' admits a subgraph H of G' with
$d(H, 1, c) = 3/2$.

(ii) If $\mathcal{I}$ is a "no" instance, then $d(H, 1, c) \geq 2$ for all subgraphs H of G'.

To prove (i), let P_1 and P_2 be vertex-disjoint s_1-t_1 and s_2-t_2 paths in G,
respectively, and obtain H by deleting all edges of G not contained in some P_i.
Then, H is a subgraph of G' with exactly two s-t paths, and routing half a unit of
flow along each yields a flow at Nash equilibrium in which each path has cost $3/2$
(cf., Figure 1.2(a)).

For (ii), we can assume that H contains an s-t path. If H has an s-t path P
containing an s_2-t_1 path, then routing all of the flow on P yields a Nash flow in
which every s-t path has cost 2 (cf., Figure 1.2(b)). Hence, $d(H) = 2$ for all such

subgraphs H. Otherwise, since $\mathcal{I}$ is a "no" instance of 2DDP, two sole possibilities remain (see Figure 5.3): either for precisely one $i \in \{1, 2\}$, H has an s-t path P containing an s_i-t_i path, or all s-t paths P in H contain an s_1-t_2 path of G. In either case, routing one unit of flow along such a path P provides a flow at Nash equilibrium showing that $d(H) = 2$. ∎

Corollary 5.2.1 and Theorem 5.3.5 imply that efficiently detecting Braess's Paradox in networks with linear cost functions is impossible, even in instances suffering from the most severe manifestations of the paradox. To make this statement precise, call an instance (G, r, c) with linear cost functions *paradox-free* if $d(G, r, c) \leq d(H, r, c)$ for all subgraphs H of G and *paradox-ridden* if for some subgraph H of G, $d(G, r, c) = 4d(H, r, c)/3$. Paradox-free instances do not suffer from Braess's Paradox and, by Corollary 5.2.1, paradox-ridden instances are precisely those incurring a worst-possible loss in network performance due to Braess's Paradox. The reduction in the proof of Theorem 5.3.5 then gives the following corollary.

Corollary 5.3.6 *Given an instance (G, r, c) that has linear cost functions and is either paradox-free or paradox-ridden, it is NP-hard to decide whether or not (G, r, c) is paradox-ridden.*

5.3.2   Arbitrary Cost Functions

The next proof shows that the trivial algorithm is the best approximation algorithm possible for GENERAL NETWORK DESIGN, in the sense that no $(\lfloor n/2 \rfloor - \epsilon)$-approximation algorithm exists, assuming $P \neq NP$. Of all the proofs included in this book, the one in this section is the most difficult.

An informal description of the reduction follows. In an instance of the NP-complete problem PARTITION, we are given q positive integers $\{a_1, a_2, \ldots, a_q\}$ and seek a subset $S \subseteq \{1, 2, \ldots, q\}$ such that $\sum_{j \in S} a_j = \frac{1}{2} \sum_{j=1}^{q} a_j$. The idea of the reduction is to start with a Braess graph (Section 5.2.2), and to replace the type A edges—edges of the form (v_i, w_i)—with a collection of parallel edges that represent an instance $\mathcal{I} = \{a_1, \ldots, a_q\}$ of PARTITION. We endow these edges with cost functions that simulate capacities, with an edge representing an integer a_j of $\mathcal{I}$ receiving capacity a_j. We then formalize the following three ideas. First, if too many edges are removed from the network, there will be insufficient remaining capacity to send flow cheaply. On the other hand, if too few edges are removed, the excess of capacity results in a Nash flow similar to that of Figure 5.2(a). Finally, these two cases can be avoided if and only if $\mathcal{I}$ is a "yes" instance of PARTITION, in which

case removing the appropriate collection of edges results in a network that admits
a Nash equilibrium similar to that of Figure 5.2(b).

Theorem 5.3.7 *Assuming $P \neq NP$, for every $\epsilon > 0$ there is no $(\lfloor n/2 \rfloor - \epsilon)$-
approximation algorithm for* GENERAL NETWORK DESIGN.

Proof: We prove, by a reduction from the NP-complete problem PARTITION, that
for every fixed $n \geq 2$, there is no $(\lfloor n/2 \rfloor - \epsilon)$-approximation algorithm for GENERAL
NETWORK DESIGN restricted to (multi)graphs with n vertices.

Fix $n \geq 2$. As in the proof of Theorem 5.2.14, we can assume that n is even
and at least four. Write $n = 2k + 2$ for a positive integer k. Consider an instance
$\mathcal{I} = \{a_j\}_{j=1}^q$ of PARTITION, with each a_j a positive integer. By scaling, there is no
loss of generality in assuming that each a_j is a multiple of 3. Put $A = \sum_{j=1}^q a_j$. We
are interested in the traffic rate

$$r = k\frac{A}{2} + k + 1. \tag{5.8}$$

Construct a graph G from the kth Braess graph B^k by replacing each edge of the
form (v_i, w_i) by q parallel edges, and denote these by $e_i^1, e_i^2, \ldots, e_i^q$.

The edge cost functions c are more complicated than in the proof of Theorem 5.2.14. We require a sufficiently small constant δ and a sufficiently large constant M. The following proof will be valid if we take $\delta = 1/A(q+k)$ and $M = n/2$.
The constant M should be interpreted as a substitute for $+\infty$, and is used to penalize a flow for violating an edge capacity constraint. We require the constant δ
to transform step functions—the type of function that would be most convenient
for our argument—into continuous functions. The parameter δ provides a small
window in which to smooth out the discontinuities of a step function. The cost
functions are defined next.

(A) An edge of the form e_i^j is given a cost function c with $c(x) = 0$ for $x \leq a_j - \delta$,
$c(a_j) = 1$, and $c(x) = M$ for $x \geq a_j + \delta$.
(B) Edges of the form (v_i, w_{i-1}), (s, w_k), and (v_1, t) receive a cost function c
satisfying $c(x) = 1$ for $x \leq 1$ and $c(x) = M$ for $x \geq 1 + \delta$.
(C) For each $i \in \{1, 2, \ldots, k\}$, the two edges (w_i, t) and (s, v_{k-i+1}) are given a cost
function c satisfying $c(x) = 0$ for $x \leq A/2 + 1$, $c(x) = i$ when $x = A/2 + (k+1)/k$,
and $c(x) = M$ for $x \geq A/2 + (k+1)/k + \delta$.

As usual, these cost functions can be defined arbitrarily outside of the regions
that we have prescribed, subject to the standard continuity and monotonicity

constraints. The instance (G, r, c) can be constructed in time polynomial in the size of the PARTITION instance $\mathcal{I}$. An edge of the form e_i^j is said to have *capacity* a_j, while edges of type B and C have capacity 1 and $A/2 + (k+1)/k$, respectively. Call an edge *oversaturated* by a flow if the amount of flow on it exceeds its capacity be at least an additive factor of δ. An oversaturated edge therefore has cost M.

Analogous to the proof of Theorem 5.3.5, it suffices to prove the following two statements.

(i) If $\mathcal{I}$ is a "yes" instance of PARTITION, then G admits a subgraph H with $d(H, r, c) = 1$.

(ii) If $\mathcal{I}$ is a "no" instance, then $d(H, r, c) \geq n/2$ for every subgraph H of G.

To prove (i), suppose that $\mathcal{I}$ admits a partition, and reindex the a_j's so that $\sum_{j=1}^{m} a_j = A/2$ for some $m \in \{1, 2, \ldots, q-1\}$. Obtain H from G by deleting all edges of the form e_i^j for $j > m$. For each $i = 1, \ldots, k$, the remaining edges of the form e_i^j have total capacity $A/2$. Define the paths $Q_1, \ldots, Q_{k+1}$ as in the proof of Theorem 5.2.14: for $i = 2, \ldots, k$, Q_i denotes the path $s \to v_i \to w_{i-1} \to t$, Q_1 is the path $s \to v_1 \to t$, and Q_{k+1} is the path $s \to w_k \to t$. Define a flow f feasible for (G, r, c) as follows: for each $i = 1, \ldots, k$ and $j = 1, \ldots, m$, route a_j units of flow on the unique path containing edge e_i^j, and route 1 unit of flow on the path Q_i for $i = 1, 2, \ldots, k+1$. The flow f is at Nash equilibrium for (H, r, c) and proves that $d(H, r, c) = 1$ (see Figure 5.4(a)).

Statement (ii) is more difficult. Recall that if a flow oversaturates an edge, then the edge has cost M. A simple but crucial observation is that if a Nash flow in the instance (H, r, c) oversaturates an edge, then $d(H, r, c) \geq M \geq n/2$. We next prove (ii) in two steps. First, we identify two sufficient conditions on the subgraph H that ensure that a Nash flow in (H, r, c) must oversaturate some edge and hence $d(H, r, c) \geq n/2$. Then, we give a separate argument that $d(H, r, c) \geq n/2$ for subgraphs H that do not meet these sufficient conditions.

The first claim is that if a subgraph H omits some type C edge, then a Nash flow in (H, r, c) must oversaturate an edge. To see why, observe that if H omits a type C edge incident to s, then the remaining capacity on edges incident to s is at most that of one type B edge and $k-1$ type C edges, which is

$$1 + (k-1)\left(\frac{1}{2}A + \frac{k+1}{k}\right) < (k-1)\frac{A}{2} + k + 1. \tag{5.9}$$

Since the right-hand side of (5.9) is less than the traffic rate (5.8), every feasible flow in (H, r, c) must oversaturate some edge incident to s, provided δ is sufficiently

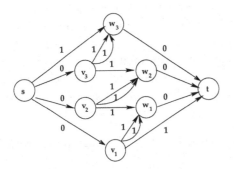

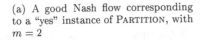

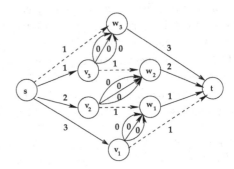

(a) A good Nash flow corresponding to a "yes" instance of PARTITION, with $m = 2$

(b) A bad Nash flow in a network with excess capacity

Figure 5.4
Proof of Theorem 5.3.7. Solid edges carry flow in the flow at Nash equilibrium, dashed edges do not. Edge costs are with respect to flows at Nash equilibrium.

small. The same argument shows that if H omits a type C edge incident to t, then every feasible flow for (H, r, c) oversaturates some edge.

The next claim is that if for some $i \in \{1, \ldots, k\}$, the total capacity A_i of edges of the form e_i^j in H is less than $A/2$, then every feasible flow in (H, r, c) oversaturates an edge. To see this, suppose $A_i < A/2$. Since every a_j is a multiple of 3, we must then have $A_i \leq A/2 - 3$. Besides edges of the form e_i^j, the only edge leaving the vertex v_i is the unit-capacity type B edge (v_i, w_{i-1}) (or (v_1, t), if $i = 1$). The total capacity out of the vertex v_i is therefore at most $A/2 - 2$. This in turn gives the edge (s, v_i) an effective capacity of $A/2 - 2$, in the sense that routing at least $A/2 - 2 + q\delta$ units of flow on (s, v_i) must oversaturate some edge out of v_i. The effective capacity of edges incident to s is thus only $A/2 - 2$ more than in the calculation in (5.9), which is at most

$$k\frac{A}{2} + k - 1 = r - 2.$$

As in the previous paragraph, for δ sufficiently small, every feasible flow in (H, r, c) must oversaturate some edge.

Finally, suppose that the subgraph H contains all type C edges and that the total capacity A_i of edges of the form e_i^j in H is at least $A/2$ for every i, Since $\mathcal{I}$ is a "no" instance of PARTITION and each a_j is a multiple of 3, $A_i \geq A/2 + 3$ for every i. Then, define a flow f in H as follows: for each $i = 1, \ldots, k$ and $j = 1, \ldots, q$

such that e_i^j is present in H, route

$$\frac{a_j}{A_i}\left(\frac{A}{2}+\frac{k+1}{k}\right)$$

units of flow along the unique s-t path containing e_i^j. Since $A_i \geq A/2 + 3$ for every i and $k \geq 1$, for δ sufficiently small, the cost of every edge of the form e_i^j in H is zero with respect to f. As shown in Figure 5.4(b), the flow f is at Nash equilibrium and proves that $d(H) = n/2$. ∎

As in Corollary 5.3.6, the matching upper and lower bounds of Theorems 5.2.5 and 5.3.7 have strong negative consequences for the problem of detecting Braess's Paradox. Defining an instance (G, r, c) with general cost functions and n vertices to be *paradox-free* if $d(G, r, c) \leq d(H, r, c)$ for all subgraphs H of G and *paradox-ridden* if for some subgraph H of G, $d(G, r, c) = \lfloor n/2 \rfloor \cdot d(H, r, c)$, we obtain the following corollary.

Corollary 5.3.8 *Given an instance (G, r, c) with general cost functions that is paradox-free or paradox-ridden, it is NP-hard to decide whether or not (G, r, c) is paradox-ridden.*

Remark 5.3.9 One of the constructions in Section 5.3.3 below yields a hardness result that is similar but incomparable to Theorem 5.3.7. Remark 5.3.12 for details.

5.3.3 Other Sets of Cost Functions

The strong hardness results of Sections 5.3.1 and 5.3.2 are not an aberration and extend beyond the particular sets of linear and general cost functions. The difficulty of designing a nontrivial algorithm for the network design problem (5.1) therefore seems to be intrinsic, rather than particular to certain sets of allowable cost functions.

The first result of this section states that the trivial algorithm is an optimal approximation algorithm for POLYNOMIAL(p) NETWORK DESIGN, up to a constant factor, assuming $P \neq NP$. Recall from Corollary 5.3.3 that the trivial algorithm has approximation ratio $\Theta(p/\ln p)$ for the problem, as $p \to \infty$.

Theorem 5.3.10 *Assuming $P \neq NP$, there is no $o(p/\ln p)$-approximation algorithm for POLYNOMIAL(p) NETWORK DESIGN.*

The proof of Theorem 5.3.10 is somewhat more difficult than that of Theorem 5.3.7. This added difficulty stems from the importance of implicit edge capacities in the proof of Theorem 5.3.7; these capacities are not entirely implementable with cost functions that are low-degree polynomials. Because of this, the proof of Theorem 5.3.10 adapts the arguments of Theorem 5.3.5 to larger Braess graphs. In particular, the reduction is from the 2 DIRECTED DISJOINT PATHS problem rather than from PARTITION. In essence, restricting the allowable cost functions forces a reduction to encode the intractability of an NP-hard problem into the network, rather than into the edge cost functions, of a network design instance. The basic idea of the reduction is to embed many copies of a 2DDP instance into a large Braess graph, in order to amplify the arguments used to prove Theorem 5.3.5. See Figure 5.5 for an illustration.

More specifically, Theorem 5.3.10 is proved by a construction, based on the network shown in Figure 5.5 with $\Theta(p/\ln p)$ copies of a 2DDP instance, with three properties analogous to those discussed before Theorem 5.3.7. If the construction begins with a "yes" instance of 2DDP, then deleting edges from the constructed instance (G, r, c) as in the proof of Theorem 5.3.5 yields a subgraph H with $d(H, r, c)$ equal to a small constant. If the construction begins with a "no" instance, then it produces an instance (G, r, c) for which all subgraphs H of G satisfy one of two conditions. Either enough edges are missing from H so that capacity considerations, analogous to those in the proof of Theorem 5.3.7, imply that $d(H, r, c) = \Omega(p/\ln p)$, or else there are enough edges present that a bad Nash flow in the spirit of Figure 5.2(b) can be defined, which again shows that $d(H, r, c) = \Omega(p/\ln p)$. The details of this argument are technical, and the proof of Theorem 5.3.10 is not discussed further here.

As mentioned in Remark 5.3.9, Theorem 5.3.10 has consequences for the GENERAL NETWORK DESIGN problem.

Corollary 5.3.11 *Assuming $P \neq NP$, for every $\epsilon > 0$ there is no $O(n^{1-\epsilon})$-approximation algorithm for* GENERAL NETWORK DESIGN.

Remark 5.3.12 discusses why Corollary 5.3.11 is not completely subsumed by Theorem 5.3.7. Next is a sketch of how Theorem 5.3.10 implies Corollary 5.3.11; the following argument can be made rigorous with little difficulty. Consider a 2DDP instance $\mathcal{I}$ with q vertices. Assume for simplicity that $\mathcal{I}$ is defined on a simple graph, with no parallel edges, and therefore has size polynomial in q. Let $\epsilon > 0$ be fixed but arbitrarily small. Invoking the construction in the proof of Theorem 5.3.10 using roughly $k = q^{1/\epsilon}$ copies of $\mathcal{I}$ produces an instance (G, r, c) with about

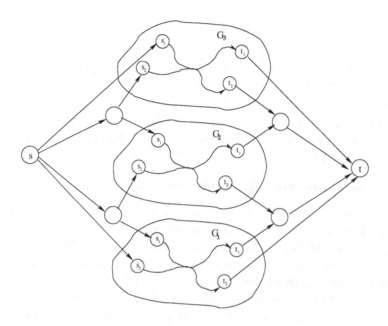

Figure 5.5
How to embed multiple copies of a 2DDP instance into a Braess graph.

$n = q^{(1+\epsilon)/\epsilon}$ vertices. Since $\epsilon > 0$ is fixed, this instance can be constructed from $\mathcal{I}$ in polynomial time. Moreover, the optimal subgraph H of G has value $d(H, r, c)$ a small constant if $\mathcal{I}$ is a "yes" instance of 2DDP, and has value $\Omega(q^{1/\epsilon})$ otherwise. Since $n^{1-\epsilon} = o(q^{1/\epsilon})$ for $\epsilon > 0$ fixed, an $O(n^{1-\epsilon})$-approximation algorithm for GENERAL NETWORK DESIGN can be used to differentiate between "yes" and "no" instances of 2DDP in polynomial time.

Remark 5.3.12 Corollary 5.3.11 is inferior to Theorem 5.3.7 in the obvious sense that it gives a weaker lower bound. On the other hand, Corollary 5.3.11 is superior to Theorem 5.3.7 in two respects. First, it applies to an easier problem, in which networks cannot have parallel edges, and cost functions must be polynomials with nonnegative coefficients. Second, the reduction in the proof of Corollary 5.3.11 shows that the problem GENERAL NETWORK DESIGN is a strongly NP-hard problem to approximate, while the reduction in the proof of Theorem 5.3.7 does not. See Section 5.4 for details on this distinction.

The final hardness result of this section is as follows.

Theorem 5.3.13 *Assuming $P \neq NP$, there is no $o(\gamma)$-approximation algorithm for* INCLINE(γ) NETWORK DESIGN.

The proof of Theorem 5.3.13 is similar to that of Theorem 5.3.10—in fact, a bit easier, due to the greater flexibility available for defining cost functions. Further details are omitted here.

5.3.4 Generalizing Edge Removals with Taxes

Most of the results in Section 5.3 carry over to a more general optimization problem, as follows. For a cost function c_e and a nonnegative real number τ_e, write $c_e + \tau_e$ to denote the shifted cost function $(c_e + \tau_e)(x) = c_e(x) + \tau_e$. Call the number τ_e a *tax*, though of course it need not represent any kind of money. Such taxes should be thought of as a tempered version of edge removals, as they give an algorithm the opportunity to make edges worse by whatever factors it sees fit.

We then have the natural generalization of the network design problem (5.1):

$$\text{Given } (G, r, c), \text{ find taxes } \tau \text{ that minimize } d(G, r, c + \tau). \qquad (5.10)$$

Here $d(G, r, c + \tau)$ denotes the common cost incurred by traffic in a Nash flow for $(G, r, c + \tau)$, where the cost is defined using the shifted cost functions $c + \tau$. An edge removal can always be simulated with a sufficiently large tax. Thus, the original network design problem (5.1) is the special case of (5.10) in which taxes are restricted to be either 0 or $+\infty$.

While taxes can only have more potential than edge removals for improving the cost of a Nash flow, the relationship between the problems (5.1) and (5.10) is less clear from a complexity-theoretic standpoint. Adding new feasible solutions to a problem can make it harder, because there are more options to take into account, or easier, because the new set of feasible solutions can have structure superior to the original one. A good example of the latter effect is provided by integer programs, which are typically intractable, and their linear relaxations, which have many more feasible solutions but are computationally solvable.

We therefore must reexamine both the upper and lower bounds on the approximability of the problem (5.1) in order to see what extends to the more general problem with taxes (5.10). We begin with the upper bounds, which present no surprises. There is clearly still a trivial algorithm for the new network design problem: set $\tau_e = 0$ for all edges e. The following are analogues of Corollaries 5.3.1–5.3.4.

Corollary 5.3.14 *The trivial algorithm is a $\frac{4}{3}$-approximation algorithm for the network design problem (5.10) in instances with linear cost functions.*

Corollary 5.3.15 *The trivial algorithm is an $\lfloor n/2 \rfloor$-approximation algorithm for the network design problem (5.10) in instances with a network with n vertices.*

Corollary 5.3.16 *The trivial algorithm is a $\Theta(p/\ln p)$-approximation algorithm for the network design problem (5.10) in instances with cost functions that are polynomials with degree at most p and nonnegative coefficients.*

Corollary 5.3.17 *The trivial algorithm is a $\Theta(\gamma)$-approximation algorithm for the network design problem (5.10) in instances with cost functions that have incline at most γ.*

All four corollaries are easy to prove, given what we already know. The lower bounds in all four corollaries follow immediately from the lower bounds on the severity of Braess's Paradox in Section 5.2.2. The upper bounds in Corollaries 5.3.14, 5.3.16, and 5.3.17 follow from the corresponding results in Chapter 3 that bound the price of anarchy, by the same reasoning as in the proofs of Corollaries 5.2.1–5.2.3. The upper bound in Corollary 5.3.15 can be proved by making minor modifications to the proof of Theorem 5.2.5; these are left to the reader.

Extending the hardness of approximation results described earlier in this section is not quite as trivial, though Theorem 5.3.5, Theorem 5.3.10 and its consequence, Corollary 5.3.11, and Theorem 5.3.13 extend to the more general network design problem (5.10).

Theorem 5.3.18 *Assuming $P \neq NP$, for every $\epsilon > 0$ there is no $(\frac{4}{3} - \epsilon)$-approximation algorithm for the network design problem (5.10) in instances with linear cost functions.*

Theorem 5.3.19 *Assuming $P \neq NP$, there is no $o(p/\ln p)$-approximation algorithm for the network design problem (5.10) in instances with cost functions that are polynomials with degree at most p and nonnegative coefficients.*

Corollary 5.3.20 *Assuming $P \neq NP$, for every $\epsilon > 0$ there is no $O(n^{1-\epsilon})$-approximation algorithm for the network design problem (5.10) in instances with a network with n vertices.*

Theorem 5.3.21 *Assuming $P \neq NP$, there is no $o(\gamma)$-approximation algorithm for the network design problem (5.10) in instances with cost functions with incline at most γ.*

The reductions used to prove these four hardness results are identical to those earlier in this section, as are the arguments that "yes" instances of 2DDP or PARTITION lead to network design instances that admit a solution with small cost. The added power of taxes, however, slightly increases the difficulty of arguing that "no" instances result in network design instances in which all possible solutions have large cost. To illustrate this point, the following is a sketch of the proof of Theorem 5.3.18, which the reader should compare to the proof of Theorem 5.3.5.

Proof of Theorem 5.3.18: The reduction is from 2DDP and is identical to the one in the proof of Theorem 5.3.5, shown in Figure 5.3. Suppose the reduction creates the instance (G', r, c) with linear cost functions from the 2DDP instance $\mathcal{I} = \{G, s_1, s_2, t_1, t_2\}$. Following the proof of Theorem 5.3.5, if $\mathcal{I}$ is a "yes" instance with vertex-disjoint s_1-t_1 and s_2-t_2 paths P_1 and P_2, respectively, then setting $\tau_e = 1$ for edges in G that are not in P_1 or P_2, and $\tau_e = 0$ for other edges, we obtain a tax τ with $d(G, r, c + \tau) = 3/2$.

Now suppose that $\mathcal{I}$ is a "no" instance of 2DDP, and consider an arbitrary tax τ on the edges of G'. In the proof of Theorem 5.3.5, there was a dichotomy between subgraphs H of G' with too many edges and those with too few edges. With taxes, we do not have this dichotomy at our disposal. We instead make use of the distance labels first introduced in Definition 2.7.5 and Proposition 2.7.7.

Let f be a Nash flow for $(G', r, c + \tau)$ and let $d(v)$ denote the length, with respect to edge lengths $c_e(f_e) + \tau_e$, of a shortest path from s to v. We must show that the common cost $d(t)$ incurred by all traffic in f is at least 2. Assume for simplicity that f has a flow path P_1 that includes s_1 and t_1 and a flow path P_2 that includes s_2 and t_2; the other cases can be treated by similar analyses.

Since $\mathcal{I}$ is a "no" instance of 2DDP, paths P_1 and P_2 intersect at a vertex v. Since path P_1 uses the edge (s, s_1) and subsequently arrives at the vertex v, Proposition 2.7.7 implies that, irrespective of τ, $d(v) \geq 1$. Since path P_2 uses the edge (t_2, t) after departing the vertex v, Proposition 2.7.7 implies that $d(t) \geq d(v) + 1 \geq 2$. ∎

The added power of taxes has a more dramatic effect for instances with arbitrary cost functions. A notable omission from the list of four hardness results is an analogue of Theorem 5.3.7, which rules out the existence of an $(\lfloor n/2 \rfloor - \epsilon)$-

approximation algorithm for GENERAL NETWORK DESIGN in networks with n vertices. In fact, the reduction in the proof of Theorem 5.3.7 does not prove *any* lower bound on the approximability of problem (5.10) in instances with arbitrary cost functions. To see why, recall that one component of the proof of Theorem 5.3.7 is that the reduction in the proof transforms a "no" instance of PARTITION into an instance (G, r, c) of GENERAL NETWORK DESIGN for which $d(H, r, c) \geq n/2$ for all subgraphs H of G. For this instance, there *is* a set of taxes τ for which $d(G, r, c + \tau) = 1$. Adopting the notation in the proof of Theorem 5.3.7, these taxes τ are easy to describe: add 1 to the cost functions of all of the parallel edges of the form e_i^j. These taxes compensate for the excess capacity in the network, and thereby allow the flow pictured in Figure 5.4(a) to arise as a Nash flow for $(G, r, c + \tau)$.

While the problems (5.1) and (5.10) have comparable computational complexity, the discussion in the previous paragraph demonstrates how the potential benefit of taxes can far outpace that of merely removing edges.

Theorem 5.3.22 *For all $n \geq 2$, there is an instance (G, r, c) for which $d(H, r, c) \geq \lfloor n/2 \rfloor$ for all subgraphs H of G, and yet there is a tax τ for which $d(G, r, c + \tau) = 1$.*

The upper bound on the approximation ratio of the trivial algorithm given in Corollary 5.3.15 implies that no larger gap between the benefits of taxes and of edge removals is possible.

On the other hand, no analogue of Theorem 5.3.22 holds in networks with linear cost functions: taxes offer no benefit beyond that of removing edges from the network.

Theorem 5.3.23 *If (G, r, c) is an instance with linear cost functions, then for every tax τ there is a subgraph H with*

$$d(H, r, c) \leq d(G, r, c + \tau).$$

The proof of Theorem 5.3.23 is technical and not discussed here. The theorem is mentioned only because the contrast between it and Theorem 5.3.22 is somewhat surprising. In all other analyses in this book, the difference between linear and nonlinear cost functions has been a quantitative one, as in the different bounds on the price of anarchy (Table 3.1), rather than a qualitative one. For example, the phenomena illustrated in Section 2.5—the inefficiency of Nash flows, the possibility of Braess's Paradox, the unfairness of optimal flows, and so on—occur with both linear and with nonlinear cost functions. By contrast, Theorems 5.3.22 and 5.3.23

show that the linearity or nonlinearity of the allowable cost functions fundamentally affects the relative power of taxes and of edge removals.

Remark 5.3.24 While taxes have long been used to improve the performance of a flow at Nash equilibrium, their use in this section is unconventional. Traditionally, taxes are assumed to influence selfish behavior as above without contributing to the cost of a flow. See Section 6.7 for further details.

5.4   Notes

Following the comments on each of the sections in this chapter is a discussion of Braess's Paradox in multicommodity networks, as well as additional background on the network design problem (5.1), on approximation algorithms for network design problems, and on paradoxes in networks.

Section 5.1

Definition 5.1.1 is standard. See [25, 172, 195, 361, 387] for more on approximation algorithms and [19, 20, 25, 29, 200, 210] for further details on inapproximability results.

Section 5.2

Corollaries 5.2.1–5.2.4 are explicit in Roughgarden [338], but many researchers noted that the price of anarchy translates to a bound on Braess's Paradox. In particular, this proof approach was noted independently by Weitz [396]. Theorem 5.2.5 was first proved by Roughgarden [338], but the proof in this section is from Lin, Roughgarden, and Tardos [256]. Theorem 5.2.7, Corollary 5.2.8, Lemma 5.2.11, and the proof of Proposition 5.2.12 are also from [256]. Theorem 5.2.7 was first conjectured by H. Kameda (personal communication, June 2002). Corollary 5.2.13 is due to L. Schulman (personal communication, October 1999). The Braess graphs, Theorems 5.2.14, 5.2.16, and 5.2.18, and Corollary 5.2.15 are from Roughgarden [338]. Kameda [212] independently proved Theorems 5.2.5 and 5.2.14 in the special case of four-node networks.

Proposition 5.2.12 was first proved by Hall [182]. In fact, Hall [182] proved the following more general statement for multicommodity networks: in every instance (G, r, c), the common cost incurred by commodity i's traffic is nondecreasing in r_i. Other papers that perform similar sensitivity analyses of Nash flows include [100, 107, 182, 401]. One application of Proposition 5.2.12 occurs in the proof of Theorem 5.3.10, which appears in [338].

Section 5.3

All of the results from Sections 5.3.1–5.3.3 first appeared in Roughgarden [338]. In particular, full proofs of Theorem 5.3.10 and Corollary 5.3.11 can be found in [338].

The 2DDP problem was proved NP-complete by Fortune, Hopcroft, and Wyllie [158]. The PARTITION problem was one of the first problems to be proved NP-complete, see Karp [218]. The proofs of Theorems 5.3.5, 5.3.7, 5.3.10, and 5.3.13, which use a reduction from an NP-complete problem to prove an inapproximability result, are typically called *gap reductions*. Gap reductions are related to but slightly different from *approximation preserving reductions* [19] and the *L-reductions* of Papadimitriou and Yannakakis [307]. While the reductions in Section 5.3 are relatively direct, many of the hardness results discovered in the last ten to fifteen years are based on long chains of gap and approximation preserving reductions, some of which can be very sophisticated. Reductions based on so-called *probabilistically checkable proofs* [21, 22, 140] are prime examples.

Remark 5.3.12 alludes to a distinction between "strongly NP-hard" and "weakly NP-hard" problems. Informally, a problem is strongly NP-hard if it remains NP-hard even when all of the numerical parameters in the problem instance are restricted to be small. Here, "small" means that the magnitude of each number should be polynomial in the size of the rest of the problem instance. For example, the 2DDP problem must be strongly NP-hard since it has no numerical parameters whatsoever. On the other hand, the magnitudes of the n numbers in an instance of PARTITION can be superpolynomial in n. In fact, PARTITION instances with numbers that are small in the above sense are solvable in polynomial time, by a technique called dynamic programming (see e.g. Cormen et al. [91]). For this reason, the PARTITION problem is only weakly NP-hard. Since the reduction in the proof of Theorem 5.3.10 produces an instance in which the numerical values—the degrees and coefficients of the cost functions—are comparable to the size of the network, it proves that approximating the GENERAL NETWORK DESIGN problem to within an $O(n^{1-\epsilon})$ factor is strongly NP-hard for all $\epsilon > 0$. Since the proof of Theorem 5.3.7 is a reduction from PARTITION, it does not imply that approximating the GENERAL NETWORK DESIGN problem to within an $\lfloor n/2 \rfloor - \epsilon$ factor, or any smaller factor, is strongly NP-hard. For rigorous definitions of strongly and weakly NP-hard, see the book by Garey and Johnson [172], or the original research paper, also by Garey and Johnson [171].

All of the results in Section 5.3.4 are due to Cole, Dodis, and Roughgarden [86, 88]. For more traditional applications of taxes to selfish routing networks, see Section 6.7.

Braess's Paradox in Multicommodity Networks

Example 2.5.6 touched on Braess's Paradox in multicommodity networks, and demonstrated that removing an edge from a two-commodity network can increase the cost of some of the traffic by an unbounded amount. As mentioned at the end of Section 4.8, Lin et al. [257] recently studied Braess's Paradox in multicommodity networks in depth. First, Lin et al. [257] greatly generalized Example 2.5.6 to show another sense in which Braess's Paradox can be much more severe in multicommodity networks than in single-commodity ones: in two-commodity, n-vertex networks, removing a single edge can decrease the cost incurred by *all* of the traffic by a $2^{\Omega(n)}$ multiplicative factor as $n \to \infty$. On the other hand, removing any number of edges can only decrease the cost of all of the traffic of a k-commodity, n-vertex network by a factor of $2^{O(kn)}$ [257]. Finally, Lin et al. [257] showed that the trivial algorithm continues to be (nearly) optimal for the following analogue of the network design problem (5.1): given a multicommodity instance, find a subgraph that minimizes the maximum cost incurred by traffic in a Nash flow. The aforementioned upper bound on the worst-case severity of Braess's Paradox implies that the trivial algorithm is a $2^{O(kn)}$-approximation algorithm for this network design problem, and Lin et al. [257] showed that there is no $2^{o(n)}$-approximation algorithm for the problem (assuming $P \neq NP$). The proof of this hardness result is similar to that of Theorem 5.3.7.

Network Design

Motivated by the discovery of Braess's Paradox [64, 285] and evidence of similarly counterintuitive and counterproductive traffic behavior following the construction of new roads in congested cities [148, 228, 229, 285], researchers have long developed network design strategies to avoid Braess's Paradox and have in particular tried to solve variants of the problem (5.1). Because of the problem's difficulty, early computational work on the problem either focused on very small networks [250, 311], assumed that cost functions were constant [62, 124, 194, 330, 357, 399], or made other simplifying assumptions [2, 109, 115, 263, 321, 372, 378]. The survey of Magnanti and Wong [261] gives more details on computational approaches to the problem.

On the theoretical side, many papers studied restricted versions of problem (5.1). For example, several [161, 212, 310, 313] considered only the four-node network of Figure 1.2(a), while Frank [162] considered a limited generalization. Dafermos and Nagurney [106], Steinberg and Zangwill [374], and Taguchi [379] studied Braess's Paradox in general networks. However, all of these papers allowed only restricted classes of edge removals that rendered (5.1) algorithmically trivial—solvable in polynomial-time by enumerating the allowable subgraphs, using Fact 2.4.9 to compute the Nash flow in each, and picking the best solution. On the other hand, all of these papers had ambitions beyond a polynomial-time algorithm—each sought closed-form analytical conditions that would detect whether removing an edge would improve the Nash flow. Roughgarden [338] was the first to theoretically study the general network design problem (5.1) with arbitrary edge removals allowed, and to study the problem solely from the perspective of computational complexity. Of course, the negative results described in Section 5.3 for the general problem provide one way to validate previous efforts that focused only on restricted, and hopefully more tractable, versions of the problem.

One variant of the network design problem (5.1) is described by Milchtaich [279], who investigated which undirected graphs, unadorned with cost functions, are vulnerable to Braess's Paradox in the sense that *some* assignment of cost functions to edges causes Braess's Paradox to arise. Milchtaich [279] characterized the graphs with this property, which confirmed an unproven assertion by Murchland [285]. The analogue of this problem for directed graphs, however, is not yet well understood.

A second variant of (5.1) considers the atomic splittable model described in Section 4.4.1 and the M/M/1 delay functions discussed in Section 3.5. Recall that an M/M/1 delay function has the form $c(x) = 1/(u - x)$, where u is the edge capacity. Several researchers [11, 133, 234, 235, 254] have studied how to allocate a fixed amount of capacity to the network edges to minimize the cost of the resulting Nash flow. Again, this problem appears to be difficult because of Braess's Paradox. Papers in this area have therefore focused on efficiently solvable special cases of the problem. See also Marcotte [264] for approximation algorithms for a related variant of (5.1).

Finally, approximation algorithms for network design problems have long been a popular topic in theoretical computer science. However, most of the previous work in this area, some of which is surveyed in [177, 222, 324, 387], designs and analyzes algorithms for finding the smallest or cheapest network satisfying desiderata such as high connectivity or small diameter. Problems of this sort are only nontrivial in the presence of nonzero costs on the network vertices or edges—otherwise, the best solution is simply to build the largest possible network. Braess's Paradox shows that the network design problem (5.1) has a rather different flavor: there are no costs in the problem, and yet it is not at all clear which subgraph is the optimal one.

Paradoxes

This section concludes with a few of the many reverberations of Braess's Paradox. Braess's Paradox has intrigued researchers ever since its discovery in 1968 [64], and has appeared frequently in textbooks [94, 404, 236, 288, 296, 359] and in the popular science literature [18, 36, 37, 80, 229, 317]. In addition, Braess's Paradox has spawned many further research developments. For example, it has catalyzed the search for other "paradoxes" in traffic networks [17, 74, 112, 147, 181, 213, 214, 221, 365, 373, 402], and for analogues of Braess's Paradox in queueing networks [71, 83, 84, 398] as well as in seemingly unrelated contexts [38, 70, 82, 219], such as the networks of strings and springs described in Section 1.3.3. It has helped increase interest in the Downs-Thomson paradox [69, 127, 383] and the Vickrey paradox [389]. It has even stirred debate over its implications for classical philosophical problems [201, 267]. For a current catalogue of papers on Braess's Paradox, see D. Braess's Web page [65].

6 Stackelberg Routing

This final chapter considers a second technique for coping with selfishness, one which applies to networks used by both selfish individuals and by some central authority. The focus will be on the following question: in such a network, how should the centrally controlled traffic be routed to induce good, albeit selfish, behavior from the noncooperative users?

6.1   Overview

To model networks with both centrally and selfishly controlled traffic, this chapter borrows a concept from game theory, *Stackelberg games*. In general, Stackelberg games model multistage games in which some players must choose their strategy before others. Of interest here is a Stackelberg game in which one player, responsible for routing the centrally controlled traffic and interested in minimizing the cost of all of the traffic, acts as a *leader*. We assume that the leader is the owner or manager of the network and is capable of controlling some of the network's traffic. This assumption is motivated by applications in computer networking; see Section 6.7 for details. The leader holds its routing of the centrally controlled traffic—its *Stackelberg strategy*—fixed while all other players—the *followers*—react independently and selfishly to the Stackelberg strategy, reaching a flow at Nash equilibrium relative to it. To clarify, the network manager's routing strategy is not fixed once and for all; instead, this Stackelberg game takes place each time the manager updates its strategy.

This chapter studies Stackelberg strategies through the following two questions.

(1) How much can Stackelberg strategies reduce the price of anarchy?

(2) Can a Stackelberg strategy that minimizes the price of anarchy be computed efficiently?

In these two questions and the rest of this chapter, the *price of anarchy* of a given strategy in a given instance is the ratio between the cost of an induced flow at Nash equilibrium and that of an optimal flow.

After a formal treatment of these notions in Section 6.2 and several examples in Section 6.3, Section 6.4 describes the main positive result of this chapter. Namely, it answers question (1) and shows that in a network of parallel links and arbitrary cost functions, carefully routing a β fraction of the traffic centrally ensures that the cost of all of the traffic is no more than $1/\beta$ times that of an optimal flow.

Thus, in such networks, controlling a constant fraction of the traffic is sufficiently powerful to approximate the cost to within a constant factor. This guarantee stands in sharp contrast to the nonlinear version of Pigou's example (Example 2.5.4), which shows that in the absence of centrally routed traffic, the cost of a Nash flow can be arbitrarily larger than that of an optimal flow, even in networks of parallel links.

Of course, networks of parallel links are significantly less general than the networks considered in all previous chapters. Sections 6.5 and 6.6 host negative results that partially justify this strong restriction on the network topology. Section 6.5 gives an example that shows that the $1/\beta$ guarantee for networks of parallel links does not carry over to more general networks and notes that no guarantee is possible for one formulation of multicommodity Stackelberg strategies. Section 6.6 answers question (2) in the negative by proving that finding an optimal Stackelberg strategy is an NP-hard problem, even in networks of parallel links with linear cost functions.

6.2 Stackelberg Strategies and Induced Equilibria

This section defines Stackelberg routing games and considers two examples. It focuses on single-commodity networks, although a brief discussion of multicommodity networks is given in Section 6.5.

The next two definitions formalize the idea of a hierarchical game, where a leader routes centrally controlled traffic and, holding this strategy fixed, the network users react in a selfish manner. A *Stackelberg instance* (G, r, c, β) is a single-commodity instance (G, r, c) in the sense of Section 2.1, together with a parameter $\beta \in (0, 1)$ specifying the fraction of the network traffic that is centrally controlled.

Definition 6.2.1 A *Stackelberg strategy*, or simply a *strategy*, for the Stackelberg instance (G, r, c, β) is a flow feasible for $(G, \beta r, c)$.

Definition 6.2.2 Let f be a strategy for the Stackelberg instance (G, r, c, β), and define $\tilde{c}_e$ by

$$\tilde{c}_e(x) = c_e(f_e + x)$$

for each edge $e \in E$. An *equilibrium induced by strategy* f is a flow g at Nash equilibrium for the instance $(G, (1 - \beta)r, \tilde{c})$. We then say that $f + g$ is a *flow induced by f* for (G, r, c, β).

Existence and essential uniqueness of induced equilibria follow easily from Propositions 2.2.4 and 2.2.5 and Corollary 2.6.2.

Proposition 6.2.3 *Let f be a strategy for a Stackelberg instance. Then there exists a flow induced by f, and every two flows induced by f have equal cost.*

The following simple observation about induced equilibria in networks of parallel links will be useful in Section 6.4.

Proposition 6.2.4 *Let f be a strategy for the Stackelberg instance (G, r, c, β) inducing equilibrium g, where G is a network of parallel links. If i and j are two edges and $g_i > 0$, then $c_i(f_i + g_i) \leq c_j(f_j + g_j)$.*

Next consider two examples that demonstrate both the usefulness and the limitations of Stackelberg strategies.

Example 6.2.5 Recall that in Pigou's example (Example 2.5.1 and Figure 2.2), the price of anarchy is 4/3. Suppose that half of the traffic is controlled by the network manager, so $\beta = 1/2$, and consider the strategy of routing all centrally controlled traffic on the link with cost function $c(x) = 1$. Then, the selfishly controlled traffic will travel on the link with cost function $c(x) = x$ in the induced equilibrium, resulting in the optimal flow. Thus, in Pigou's example, Stackelberg strategies suffice to recover the optimal flow.

Example 6.2.6 Now consider modifying Example 6.2.5 by replacing the cost function $c(x) = x$ of the lower edge in Figure 2.2 by the cost function $c(x) = 2x$. The flow at Nash equilibrium puts half of the traffic on each edge and has cost 1, while the optimal flow routes only 1/4 units of traffic on the lower edge, for a cost of 7/8. If the network manager again is allowed to route half of the traffic, then for *every* strategy f, the flow induced by f is the flow at Nash equilibrium and hence is not optimal. In this example, there is no available strategy by which the network manager can improve the price of anarchy.

6.3   Three Stackelberg Strategies

6.3.1   Two Natural Strategies

Our investigation of Stackelberg strategies begins with a consideration of two natural but suboptimal strategies. To keep things simple, this section considers networks of parallel links with linear cost functions, in which half of the traffic is centrally controlled ($\beta = 1/2$).

First consider the following strategy for an instance $(G, r, c, 1/2)$: if f^* is the optimal flow for instance $(G, r/2, c)$, put $f = f^*$. That is, we choose the strategy of minimum cost, ignoring the existence of traffic that is not centrally controlled. Accordingly, we call this the *Aloof* strategy. Pigou's example (Example 2.5.1) shows that this strategy performs poorly: in that network, the Aloof strategy routes all flow on the edge with cost function $c(x) = x$, and so the induced flow is the same as the inefficient Nash flow. As shown in Example 6.2.5, routing all flow on the edge with cost function $c(x) = 1$ induces the optimal flow. Applying this type of argument to the nonlinear variant of Pigou's example (Example 2.5.4) also shows that the Aloof strategy can perform arbitrarily badly in networks with arbitrary cost functions.

Here is a second attempt at a good strategy: if f^* is the optimal flow for (G, r, c), put $f = f^*/2$. We call this the *Scale* strategy, since it is simply the optimal flow, suitably scaled. To understand why the Scale strategy is not satisfactory, modify Pigou's example (Example 2.5.1) by replacing the cost function $c_2(x) = x$ by the cost function $c_2(x) = 3x/2$. The optimal flow routes $2/3$ units of flow on the first link and the rest on the second link, for a cost of $5/6$, so the Scale strategy will route $1/3$ units of flow on the first link and $1/6$ units on the second link. All selfish traffic flocks to the second link, which induces a flow with cost 1. Given the enduring appeal of the second link to selfish users, we can conclude that the Scale strategy routed too much flow on it. Indeed, the strategy that instead routes all centrally controlled traffic on the first link induces a flow with the superior cost of $7/8$. In addition, a slightly more complicated example shows that the Scale strategy can perform arbitrarily badly in networks with arbitrary cost functions.

6.3.2   The Largest Cost First (LCF) Strategy

Intuitively, both the Aloof and Scale strategies suffer from a common flaw: both route traffic on edges that will subsequently be inundated in any induced equilibrium, while routing too little traffic on edges that selfish users are prone to ignore. This observation suggests that a good strategy should give priority to the edges that are least appealing to selfish users—edges with relatively high cost. In networks of parallel links, such a strategy is easy to define. We call the following strategy for a Stackelberg instance (G, r, c, β) with a network of parallel links G the *Largest Cost First* or *LCF* strategy.

(1) Compute an optimal flow f^* for (G, r, c).

(2) Label the edges of G from 1 to m so that

$$c_1(f_1^*) \leq \cdots \leq c_m(f_m^*).$$

(3) Let $j \leq m$ be minimal with $\sum_{i=j+1}^{m} f_i^* \leq \beta r$.

(4) Put $f_i = f_i^*$ for $i > j$, $f_j = \beta r - \sum_{i=j+1}^{m} f_i^*$, and $f_i = 0$ for $i < j$.

Call an edge i *saturated* by a strategy f if $f_i = f_i^*$. The LCF strategy thus saturates edges one-by-one, in order from the largest cost with respect to f^* to the smallest, until there is no centrally controlled traffic remaining. Steps (2)–(4) are trivial to implement. If the link cost functions are semiconvex in the sense of Definition 2.4.2(d), then Fact 2.4.9 implies that step (1), and hence the LCF strategy, can be computed to arbitrary precision in polynomial time. Fact 2.4.12 implies that some kind of restriction must be placed on the cost functions for the LCF strategy to be efficiently implementable.

The next section proves that the LCF strategy always induces a flow with near-optimal cost in networks of parallel links.

6.4   Upper Bounds for Networks of Parallel Links

This section uses the LCF strategy to prove the following moral for Stackelberg instances with a network of parallel links and a constant fraction of centrally controlled traffic:

Stackelberg routing reduces the price of anarchy to a constant.

Again, Example 2.5.4 shows that no bound on the price of anarchy is possible in such networks when no traffic is centrally controlled.

A simple variation on Example 6.2.6 demonstrates the limitations of Stackelberg strategies in networks of parallel links with arbitrary cost functions.

Example 6.4.1 In a two-node, two-link instance with $\beta = 1/2$ and cost functions $c_1(x) = 1$ and $c_2(x) = 2^p x^p$ for a positive integer p, every Stackelberg strategy induces the Nash flow, with half of the flow routed on each link for a cost of 1. On the other hand, the optimal flow routes $\frac{1}{2} + \delta_p$ units of flow on the first link and the rest on the second link, for a cost of $\frac{1}{2} + \epsilon_p$, where $\delta_p, \epsilon_p \to 0$ as $p \to \infty$. The minimum cost of an induced flow can therefore be arbitrarily close to twice as costly as an optimal flow.

Minor modifications to Example 6.4.1 show that for every $\beta \in (0,1)$, there is an instance in which every induced flow is at least $1/\beta$ times as costly as an optimal flow.

The main result of this section is that the LCF strategy always induces a flow with cost no more than $1/\beta$ times that of an optimal flow. A rough outline of the proof is as follows. The goal is to exploit the iterative structure of the LCF strategy and proceed by induction on the number of edges. If the LCF strategy first saturates the mth edge, a natural idea is to apply the inductive hypothesis to the remainder of the LCF strategy on the first $m-1$ edges to derive a performance guarantee. This idea nearly succeeds, but there are two difficulties. First, the LCF strategy might not saturate any edges. This case turns out to be easy to analyze and will cause us no trouble. Second, obtaining a clean application of the inductive hypothesis to the first $m-1$ edges requires that the optimal and LCF-induced flows route the same amount of flow on these edges—that the LCF-induced equilibrium eschews the mth edge. This can fail in trivial cases, as in the next example.

Example 6.4.2 Consider a two-node, two-link network in which both edges have the cost function $c(x) = 1$ and put $r = 1$ and $\beta = 1/2$. One particular optimal assignment is $(2/3, 1/3)$, and a corresponding LCF strategy is $(1/6, 1/3)$. One particular induced flow is then $(1/3, 2/3)$. Even though the LCF strategy saturated the second machine, the induced equilibrium uses it.

The following lemma states that saturation by the LCF strategy drives away selfish traffic, except in similarly trivial examples.

Lemma 6.4.3 Let (G, r, c, β) denote a Stackelberg instance on a network of m parallel links. Let f^* be an optimal flow for (G, r, c). Label the edges of G from 1 to m so that $c_m(f_m^*) \geq c_i(f_i^*)$ for all $i \in \{1, 2, \ldots, m\}$. If f is a strategy with $f_m = f_m^*$, then there exists an induced equilibrium g with $g_m = 0$.

Proof: Consider an arbitrary induced equilibrium g and suppose that $g_m > 0$. The plan is to prove that this scenario only occurs when several cost functions—that of the mth edge, and others—are locally constant. In this case, traffic routed on edge m in the induced equilibrium can be evacuated to other edges with locally constant cost functions to provide a new induced equilibrium.

By Proposition 6.2.4, all edges i with $g_i > 0$ have a common cost L with respect to $f + g$, and all other edges have cost at least L with respect to $f + g$. Since $f + g$ and f^* route the same amount of traffic, there is some edge i for which $f_i^* \geq f_i + g_i$

and hence $c_i(f_i^*) \geq c_i(f_i + g_i)$. Since all edges have cost at least L with respect to $f + g$ and at most $c_m(f_m^*)$ with respect to f^*, $c_m(f_m^*) \geq L$. On the other hand, since $g_m > 0$ and f^* saturates edge m, $c_m(f_m^* + g_m) = c_m(f_m + g_m) = L$. Since c_m is nondecreasing, it must be locally constant, with c_m equal to L on $[f_m^*, f_m^* + g_m]$.

Next, let E' denote the subgraph of edges on which $f_i + g_i < f_i^*$. Since f^* and $f + g$ are flows at the same rate and $f_m + g_m$ exceeds f_m^* by g_m, E' is nonempty and

$$\sum_{i \in E'} [f_i^* - (f_i + g_i)] \geq g_m. \tag{6.1}$$

For each edge $i \in E'$, we have $c_i(f_i + g_i) \geq L$, $c_i(f_i^*) \leq c_m(f_m^*) = L$, and c_i nondecreasing. Hence, c_i is equal to L on $[f_i + g_i, f_i^*]$. Finally, consider modifying g as follows: move all traffic previously routed on edge m to edges in E', subject to the constraint $f_i + g_i \leq f_i^*$ for each $i \in E'$. Inequality (6.1) guarantees sufficient room on the edges in E' for this operation, and all cost functions are constant in the domain of the modifications. We have thus exhibited a new induced equilibrium with no traffic routed on edge m, completing the proof. ∎

We are now prepared to prove the main result of this section.

Theorem 6.4.4 *Let $\mathcal{I} = (G, r, c, \beta)$ denote a Stackelberg instance on a network of parallel links. If f is an LCF strategy for $\mathcal{I}$ inducing an equilibrium g, and f^* is an optimal flow for the instance (G, r, c), then*

$$C(f + g) \leq \frac{1}{\beta} \cdot C(f^*).$$

Proof: We proceed by induction on the number of edges m. For each fixed m, we prove the theorem for arbitrary c, r, and β. The case of a single edge is trivial.

Fix a Stackelberg instance $\mathcal{I} = (G, r, c, \beta)$ with at least two edges. Via the change of variable $\tilde{c}_i(x) = c_i(rx)$, we can assume that $r = 1$. Let f^* denote an optimal flow for the instance (G, r, c), f a corresponding LCF strategy, and g an equilibrium induced by f. Label the edges 1 to m so that

$$c_1(f_1^*) \leq c_2(f_2^*) \leq \cdots \leq c_m(f_m^*).$$

By Proposition 6.2.4, every edge i with $g_i > 0$ has a common cost L with respect to $f + g$, and all other edges have cost at least L with respect to $f + g$.

Case 1: Suppose $g_i = 0$ for some edge i. Let E_1 denote the edges i for which $g_i = 0$ and E_2 the edges for which $g_i > 0$. Both of these sets are nonempty. Let G_1 and G_2

denote the corresponding subgraphs of G. For $j = 1, 2$, let β_j denote the amount of centrally controlled traffic routed on edges in E_j and C_j the cost incurred by $f + g$ on edges in E_j. Restricting f^* to E_2 gives an optimal flow for $(G_2, 1 - \beta_1, c)$, where we are abusing notation and using c to denote the original cost functions restricted to G_2. Restricting the flow f to E_2 is therefore an LCF strategy for the instance $\mathcal{I}_2 = (G_2, 1 - \beta_1, c, \beta')$, where

$$\beta' = \frac{\beta_2}{1 - \beta_1}, \tag{6.2}$$

and $f + g$ restricted to E_2 is a corresponding induced equilibrium. Applying the inductive hypothesis to $\mathcal{I}_2$ and using the fact that $f_i^* \geq f_i = f_i + g_i$ for all $i \in E_1$, we obtain

$$C(f^*) \geq C_1 + \beta' C_2.$$

Proving that

$$C(f + g) \leq \frac{1}{\beta} \cdot C(f^*)$$

thus reduces to showing

$$\beta(C_1 + C_2) \leq C_1 + \beta' C_2.$$

By the definition of L, we have $C_2 = (1 - \beta_1)L$ and $C_1 \geq \beta_1 L$. Since $\beta \leq 1$, we can therefore complete the proof by verifying the inequality

$$\beta(\beta_1 L + (1 - \beta_1)L) \leq \beta_1 L + \beta'(1 - \beta_1)L. \tag{6.3}$$

Dividing through by L and using (6.2) reduces (6.3) to

$$\beta(\beta_1 + (1 - \beta_1)) \leq \beta_1 + \frac{\beta_2}{1 - \beta_1}(1 - \beta_1),$$

which is obviously true, since both sides equal β.

Case 2: Suppose $g_i > 0$ for every edge i; since $r = 1$, $C(f + g) = L$. We can assume that the LCF strategy failed to saturate edge m; otherwise, by the essential uniqueness of induced flows (Proposition 6.2.3), we can finish the proof by applying the previous case to the better-behaved induced equilibrium guaranteed by Lemma 6.4.3. Thus, $\beta < f_m^*$.

As in the proof of Lemma 6.4.3, we must have $c_m(f_m^*) \geq L$; otherwise, $c_i(f_i^*) < L$ for all edges i while $c_i(f_i + g_i) = L$ for all i, contradicting that f^* and $f + g$ route the same amount of traffic. Having established that edge m has large cost with respect to f^* and that f_m^* is fairly large, it is now a simple matter to lower bound $C(f^*)$:

$$C(f^*) \geq f_m^* c_m(f_m^*) \geq \beta L = \beta \cdot C(f + g).$$

∎

As noted above, the bound of $1/\beta$ in Theorem 6.4.4 is the best possible in networks of parallel links with arbitrary cost functions, for all values of β.

Improved versions of Theorem 6.4.4 can be established for networks of parallel links with restricted cost functions. For example, the following is true.

Theorem 6.4.5 *Let $\mathcal{I} = (G, r, c, \beta)$ denote a Stackelberg instance on a network of parallel links with linear cost functions. If f is an LCF strategy for $\mathcal{I}$ inducing an equilibrium g, and f^* is an optimal flow for (G, r, c), then*

$$C(f + g) \leq \frac{4}{3 + \beta} \cdot C(f^*).$$

Theorem 6.4.5 includes as special cases the bound of 4/3 that follows from Theorem 3.2.6 for the $\beta = 0$ case, and the trivial result that the price of anarchy is 1 when $\beta = 1$. Minor variations of Example 6.2.6 show that the guarantee in Theorem 6.4.5 is the best possible for all values of β.

Like the proof of Theorem 6.4.4, the proof of Theorem 6.4.5 proceeds by induction on the number of machines, with the inductive hypothesis breaking down into two cases. The case in which there is some edge on which the induced equilibrium routes no flow is nearly identical to the first case in the proof of Theorem 6.4.4: the desired performance guarantee can easily be extracted from the inductive guarantee for the smaller instance induced by the edges on which the induced equilibrium routes flow. The second case, in which the induced equilibrium routes traffic on all of the edges, is substantially more complicated. The simple approach in the proof of Theorem 6.4.4 does not use any inductive guarantee in this case and is not strong enough to prove a guarantee better than $1/\beta$. A key idea in the proof of Theorem 6.4.5 is a different way to apply the inductive hypothesis in this second case. The details of the proof are technical and are omitted here.

6.5   Lower Bounds in More General Networks

Theorem 6.4.4 unfortunately applies only to networks of parallel links. Even worse, it is not known whether the main moral of Section 6.4—that controlling a constant fraction of the traffic reduces the price of anarchy to a constant—holds in more

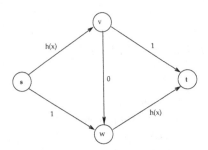

Figure 6.1
A network showing that the $1/\beta$ guarantee of Theorem 6.4.4 does not carry over to general networks (Example 6.5.1).

general networks. This section describes two examples that provide some evidence that Stackelberg strategies are less powerful in general networks than in networks of parallel links. The first example will show that the guarantee given in Theorem 6.4.4 cannot be extended to general network topologies.

Example 6.5.1 Consider the network of Braess's Paradox (Example 2.5.2), shown in Figure 6.1. As usual, edges (s, w) and (v, t) have the cost function $c(x) = 1$, and the edge (v, w) is given the cost function $c(x) = 0$. The remaining two edges (s, v) and (w, t) are both given some cost function h with $h(x) = 0$ for x in $[0, \frac{3}{4} - \epsilon]$ and $h(x) = 1 - \epsilon$ for $x \geq 3/4$, where $\epsilon > 0$ is small. Routing $\frac{1}{2} - 2\epsilon$ units of flow on the three-hop path and $\frac{1}{4} + \epsilon$ units of flow on each of the two-hop paths defines a flow feasible for $(G, 1, c)$ that has cost approaching $1/2$ as $\epsilon \to 0$. We complete the example by arguing that every flow induced by a Stackelberg strategy for $(G, 1, c, 1/2)$ has cost bounded away from 1 as $\epsilon \to 0$.

Let f be a Stackelberg strategy for $(G, 1, c, 1/2)$. First observe that all selfish traffic will be routed on the three-hop path $s \to v \to w \to t$, independent of f. Let g denote this induced equilibrium. Next, $f + g$ must route a total of one unit of flow on the two edges incident to the source s. The cost of $f + g$ on these two edges must be at least $1/4$, and is 1 unless at least $\frac{1}{4} + \epsilon$ units of (centrally controlled) traffic is routed on the edge (s, w). Similarly, the cost of $f + g$ on the two edges incident to t is at least $1/4$, and is 1 unless $\frac{1}{4} + \epsilon$ units of flow are routed on the edge (v, t). Since (s, w) and (v, t) do not lie in a common path and only centrally routed flow uses them, the half unit of centrally controlled flow is not sufficient to avoid an induced flow with cost at least $5/4$.

Of course, Example 6.5.1 does not rule out a version of Theorem 6.4.4 with the guarantee of $1/\beta$ replaced by a larger function of β, such as $2/\beta$. While it is tempting to believe that the Braess graphs of Section 5.2.2 could provide a family of instances that excludes such a positive result, no such generalization of Example 6.5.1 is currently known.

For multicommodity instances, there are two different natural extensions of the definition of a Stackelberg strategy.

Definition 6.5.2 A *weak Stackelberg strategy* for a multicommodity Stackelberg instance (G, r, c, β) is a flow feasible for $(G, \beta r, c)$.

In other words, a weak Stackelberg strategy routes at most a β fraction of the traffic of each commodity.

Definition 6.5.3 A *strong Stackelberg strategy* for a multicommodity Stackelberg instance (G, r, c, β) is a flow feasible for an instance $(G, \{\beta_i r_i\}_{i=1}^k, c)$, where $\beta_i \in [0, 1]$ for all commodities i and

$$\sum_{i=1}^k \beta_i r_i = \beta \sum_{i=1}^k r_i.$$

A strong Stackelberg strategy thus routes a β fraction of the overall traffic, and in addition is permitted to choose how much flow of each commodity is centrally controlled.

Definitions 6.5.2 and 6.5.3 coincide in single-commodity networks, but strong Stackelberg strategies are strictly more general than weak ones in multicommodity networks. The second example of this section, which is a simple modification of Example 6.2.6, shows that weak Stackelberg strategies can be utterly ineffective in arbitrary multicommodity instances.

Example 6.5.4 Consider the two-commodity network shown in Figure 6.2. The traffic rates are $r_1 = 1$ and $r_2 = M$ for M large. Edge (s_1, t_1) has the cost function $c(x) = 1$, edges (s_1, s_2) and (t_2, t_1) are given the cost function $c(x) = 0$, and the edge (s_2, t_2), which is the villain of this example, has the cost function $c(x) = h(x) = \max\{0, (x - M)/(1 - \beta)\}$, where $\beta \in (0, 1)$ is arbitrary. There is only one way for the second commodity's traffic to be routed. The optimal flow has a cost of 1, with all of the first commodity's traffic routed on edge (s_1, t_1). For every weak Stackelberg strategy, at least $1 - \beta$ units of the first commodity's flow will be routed

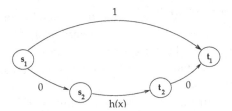

Figure 6.2
Weak Stackelberg strategies cannot guarantee a bounded price of anarchy (Example 6.5.4).

on the path $s_1 \to s_2 \to t_2 \to t_1$, resulting in a flow with a cost of at least M. Since M can be arbitrarily large and β arbitrarily close to 1, weak Stackelberg strategies cannot guarantee a bounded price of anarchy in multicommodity networks, even allowing arbitrarily large dependence on β and on the network size.

Example 6.5.4 does not give any lower bound on the power of strong Stackelberg strategies. In fact, determining the power of such strategies remains an interesting open question.

6.6   The Complexity of Computing Optimal Strategies

This section provides evidence that Stackelberg strategies seem intrinsically more difficult to analyze than flows at Nash equilibrium. Unlike the rest of this chapter, which measured the performance of a Stackelberg strategy by comparing the cost of the corresponding induced flow to the cost of the optimal flow, this section focuses on the induced flow with minimum cost. In other words, it considers the problem of computing the best Stackelberg strategy, with no regard as to what an optimal flow can achieve.

The LCF strategy, in spite of its commendable traits studied in Section 6.4, does not always compute an optimal Stackelberg strategy.

Example 6.6.1 Consider a network G of three parallel links, with the cost functions $c_1(x) = x$, $c_2(x) = 1 + x$, and $c_3(x) = 1 + x$. In the instance $(G, 1, c, 1/6)$, the optimal flow routes two thirds of the traffic on the first edge and splits the remaining traffic equally between the last two edges. The LCF strategy routes all of the centrally controlled traffic on one of the last two links. The rest of the traffic then gets routed on the first edge, and the induced flow has cost $8/9$. On the other hand, the Stackelberg strategy that splits the centrally controlled traffic evenly between the second and third links induces a flow with cost only 7/8.

Example 6.6.1 raises an obvious question: if the LCF strategy is not the optimal strategy, what is? The main result in this section is negative, stating that for networks of parallel links with linear cost functions, there is no polynomial-time algorithm that always computes an optimal Stackelberg strategy, assuming $P \neq NP$.

Theorem 6.6.2 *The problem of computing the optimal Stackelberg strategy is NP-hard, even for instances in networks of parallel links with linear cost functions.*

Proof: The reduction of the proof will be from the NP-complete problem $\frac{1}{3}$-$\frac{2}{3}$ PARTITION: given n positive integers $a_1, a_2, \ldots, a_n$, is there a subset $S \subseteq \{1, 2, \ldots, n\}$ satisfying

$$\sum_{i \in S} a_i = \frac{1}{3} \sum_{i=1}^{n} a_i?$$

We will show that deciding the problem $\frac{1}{3}$-$\frac{2}{3}$ PARTITION reduces to deciding whether or not a given Stackelberg instance on a network of parallel links with linear cost functions admits a Stackelberg strategy that induces a flow with a given cost.

Given an arbitrary instance $\mathcal{I}$ of $\frac{1}{3}$-$\frac{2}{3}$ PARTITION specified by positive integers $a_1, \ldots, a_n$, put $A = \sum_{i=1}^{n} a_i$. Define a Stackelberg instance $\mathcal{I}' = (G, 2A, c, 1/4)$ on a network G of $n + 1$ parallel links and with linear cost functions as follows. For an edge $i \in \{1, \ldots, n\}$, define its cost function by $c_i(x) = x/a_i + 4$, and give edge $n + 1$ the cost function $c_{n+1}(x) = 3x/A$. The instance $\mathcal{I}'$ can be constructed from $\mathcal{I}$ in polynomial time. The key claim is that $\mathcal{I}$ admits a $\frac{1}{3}$-$\frac{2}{3}$ partition if and only if there is a Stackelberg strategy for the instance $\mathcal{I}'$ that induces a flow with cost at most $35A/4$.

First suppose that $\mathcal{I}$ is a "yes" instance, with the subset $S \subseteq \{1, 2, \ldots, n\}$ satisfying $\sum_{i \in S} a_i = 2A/3$. Define the strategy f by $f_i = 3a_i/4$ for $i \in S$ and $f_i = 0$ otherwise. This routes $A/2$ units of flow. The induced equilibrium is then $g_i = 0$ for $i \in S$, $g_i = a_i/4$ for $i \in \{1, 2, \ldots, n\} \setminus S$, and $g_{n+1} = 17A/12$. The cost of $f + g$ is $35A/4$.

Now suppose that $\mathcal{I}$ is a "no" instance. Let f be a Stackelberg strategy for $\mathcal{I}'$ and g an induced equilibrium. We need to show that $C(f + g) > 35A/4$.

Recall the notion of a marginal cost function, which was introduced in Definition 2.4.5. For a linear cost function $c(x) = ax + b$, the corresponding marginal cost function is $c^*(x) = 2ax + b$. Call an edge $i \in \{1, 2, \ldots, n+1\}$ *heavy* if $g_i = 0$ and *light* otherwise. We claim that we can assume that all heavy edges have the same cost with respect to $f + g$ (or f). Since all light edges also have the same cost (Proposition 6.2.4), this claim will facilitate the calculation of the cost of $f + g$. The claim follows from three observations. First, edge $n + 1$ must be light. Second, two edges in $\{1, 2, \ldots, n\}$ have equal cost if and only if they have equal marginal cost. Third, we can assume that every two heavy edges have equal marginal cost, since rerouting some centrally controlled traffic from a heavy edge with large marginal cost to a heavy edge with small marginal cost does not affect the induced equilibrium and can only decrease the cost of the induced flow.

Let $S \subseteq \{1, 2, \ldots, n\}$ denote the set of heavy edges. If $S = \emptyset$ then $f + g$ is the Nash flow for $\mathcal{I}'$ with $f_i + g_i = a_i/2$ for $i \in \{1, 2, \ldots, n\}$ and $f_{n+1} + g_{n+1} = 3A/2$, in which case $C(f+g) = 9A > 35A/4$. So, suppose S is nonempty and define $\lambda \in (0, 1]$ by the equation $\sum_{i \in S} a_i = \lambda A$ and $\mu \in (0, \frac{1}{2}]$ by the equation $\sum_{i \in S} f_i = \mu A$. The aim is to lower bound the cost of $f + g$ as a function of the parameters λ and μ.

Since all heavy edges have equal cost, for i heavy we must have $f_i + g_i = f_i = \mu a_i/\lambda$ with $c_i(f_i + g_i) = 4 + \mu/\lambda$. Since all light edges have equal cost, we can solve for λ and μ and compute $C(f + g)$. The calculations are left the reader. The result is that the cost of $f + g$ is

$$C(f + g) = A \left(8 + \frac{(4 - 3\lambda)\mu^2 + \lambda(2 - \mu)(2 - 3\mu)}{\lambda(4 - 3\lambda)} \right). \tag{6.4}$$

Routine calculus shows that (6.4) is minimized only when $\mu = 1/2$ and $\lambda = 2/3$, in which case (6.4) equals $35A/4$. Since $\mathcal{I}$ admits no $\frac{1}{3}$-$\frac{2}{3}$ partition, $\lambda \neq 2/3$, and (6.4) is greater than $35A/4$. ∎

Recall from Fact 2.4.9 and Corollary 2.6.7 that Nash and optimal flows are computationally tractable, with the former always computable in polynomial time, and the latter efficiently computable under the weak assumption of semiconvex cost functions. By contrast, Theorem 6.6.2 rules out polynomial-time algorithms for computing an optimal Stackelberg strategy, even in networks with linear cost functions, assuming $P \neq NP$. This suggests that optimal Stackelberg strategies are harder to analyze than Nash and optimal flows, which in turn could be a partial explanation for the paucity of upper and lower bounds on the power of Stackelberg strategies outside of networks of parallel links. Of course, this reasoning is only heuristic. For example, the bounds on the price of anarchy of selfish routing described in Chapter 3 do not depend fundamentally on a semiconvexity assumption, even though the computational complexity of computing an optimal flow does.

This chapter concludes with an algorithmic result. Having established Theorem 6.6.2, we are justified in considering approximations algorithms, which were introduced in Definition 5.1.1. The next definition describes a certain type of approximation algorithm.

Definition 6.6.3 A *fully polynomial-time approximation scheme (FPTAS)* for a minimization problem is an algorithm $\mathcal{A}$ with the following property for some bivariate polynomial $p(\cdot, \cdot)$: given an error parameter $\epsilon > 0$ and a problem instance $\mathcal{I}$ with size $|\mathcal{I}|$, $\mathcal{A}$ returns a feasible solution to $\mathcal{I}$ with objective function value at most $1 + \epsilon$ times that of optimal in time at most $p(|\mathcal{I}|, \epsilon^{-1})$.

A fully polynomial-time approximation scheme is not a polynomial-time algorithm in the usual sense, because the natural encoding length of the error parameter ϵ is logarithmic in $1/\epsilon$, while the running time of the algorithm can be exponential in this quantity. On the other hand, existence of an FPTAS is typically as good as it gets for an NP-hard optimization problem. In particular, if a problem admits an FPTAS, then it admits a $(1 + \epsilon)$-approximation algorithm for all constant $\epsilon > 0$. The network design problems described in Chapter 5, for example, do not admit an FPTAS unless $P = NP$, due to the hardness results proved in Section 5.3. The following fact thus provides some consolation for Theorem 6.6.2.

Fact 6.6.4 *There is a fully polynomial-time approximation scheme for the problem of computing an optimal Stackelberg strategy for instances in networks of parallel links with cost functions that are polynomials with nonnegative coefficients.*

The proof of Fact 6.6.4 is technical and is omitted here.

6.7   Notes

Section 6.1

Stackelberg games are named after von Stackelberg [390], who was interested in a new formulation of the *duopoly game*, which models two competing firms. Von Stackelberg [390] introduced the idea of a two-stage game, with the leader choosing a strategy in the first stage, and the follower choosing a strategy in the second stage, with full knowledge of the leader's strategy. Stackelberg games continue to play an important role in game theory; see Başar and Olsder [34] or Fudenberg and Tirole [166] for further reading.

Stackelberg games and Stackelberg equilibria also have been extensively studied in engineering applications. Fields of application include control theory, as surveyed in [30, 95, 96, 308], competitive facility location [329, 358], and networking [35, 125, 126, 130, 233].

In most of these papers, and in contrast to the work described in this chapter, every agent is interested in optimizing its personal objective function, rather than the social objective function. This is also the more traditional use of Stackelberg games. Douligeris and Mazumdar [125] appear to be the first researchers to suggest Stackelberg games to model a system manager with partial control over the system, though similar ideas are implicit in Dafermos [102] and Bennett [41]. Douligeris and Mazumdar [125] were interested in applications to flow control. Korilis, Lazar, and Orda [233], on the other hand, studied the atomic splittable selfish routing model described in Section 4.4.1. That paper was the main motivation for the work described in this chapter. Korilis, Lazar, and Orda [233] were interested in characterizing the instances in which a Stackelberg strategy can recover the optimal flow, as in Example 6.2.5, rather than in proving worst-case approximation guarantees that apply to all instances. They studied Stackelberg routing because of its application to so-called *virtual private networks (VPNs)*. A VPN is a set of paths that are preassigned for the ongoing use of the traffic of a network user. Assuming that these paths are chosen by the network manager, the traffic of this user is centrally controlled. For more on virtual private networks and their applications, see, for example, Birman [52].

Sections 6.2–6.4

These three sections are all based on Roughgarden [345]. A full proof of Theorem 6.4.5 can also be found in [345].

Section 6.5

Example 6.5.1 is from Roughgarden [342], and the rest of this section is previously unpublished.

Section 6.6

Theorem 6.6.2 was proved by Roughgarden [345]. The proof in [345] is more detailed than that given here. The NP-hardness of the $\frac{1}{3}$-$\frac{2}{3}$ PARTITION problem follows from the same reduction used by Karp [218] to reduce the PARTITION problem to the NP-complete SUBSET SUM problem. See also Kozen [240, P.129] for this reduction.

Fact 6.6.4 was proved by Kumar and Marathe [243], who also extended Fact 6.6.4 to a somewhat more general class of graphs. For more on fully polynomial-time approximation schemes and their close relatives, see Garey and Johnson [172].

Coping with Selfishness via Economic Incentives

Part III of this book analyzes two ideas for "coping with selfishness"—removing edges to avoid Braess's Paradox and carefully routing a fraction of the traffic centrally. However, it completely ignores what is perhaps the most natural and well-studied approach to improving the performance of selfish routing: economic incentives.

Even a brief survey of the literature on economic incentives in selfish routing is beyond the scope of this book. Accordingly, this section will only mention a few references on two topics—edge taxes and mechanism design—that can serve as a starting point for further reading.

Edge taxes, as in Section 5.3.4, have been extensively studied in many different communities. The easiest way to include edge taxes into the basic selfish routing model is to allow a tax τ_e for each edge e and to then assume that network users choose paths to minimize the sum of the edge costs plus the sum of the taxes on a path. This idea was discussed in Pigou [320], if not earlier. Beckmann, McGuire, and Winsten [40], via Corollary 2.4.6, made the benefit of taxes precise: if (G, r, c) is an instance with continuously differentiable, semiconvex cost functions, f^* is optimal for (G, r, c), and $\tau_e = f_e^* \cdot c_e'(f_e^*)$ for each e, then f^* is a Nash flow for $(G, r, c + \tau)$. In other words, under the *marginal cost taxes* $\tau_e = f_e^* \cdot c_e'(f_e^*)$, the optimal flow f^* arises as a flow at Nash equilibrium. This statement continues to hold if cost functions are not semiconvex [40].

The preceding result assumes that taxes do not contribute to the objective function—the goal is to minimize the cost of a flow, and no attention is paid to the amount of taxes levied. This fact is typically justified by assuming that the collected taxes can be feasibly returned—possibly indirectly, for example via investment in the network infrastructure—to the network users. The model in Section 5.3.4 includes the taxes paid into the objective function, which is more appropriate when refunding the collected taxes to the network users is not possible, or if taxes represent quantities of a nonmonetary, nonrefundable good such as time delays.

A sampling of references that include further discussion, and variants on and generalizations of the above research on edge taxes follows. See [18, 43, 68, 104, 119, 120, 121, 122, 144, 192, 245, 247, 252, 367], for example, for papers in the transportation science literature; see [88, 87, 149, 150, 215] for recent work in theoretical computer science; and see [10, 79, 176, 223], for example, for work on edge taxes in networking applications. Much of this work also can be interpreted in the context of general microeconomic theory; see the survey by Mirrlees [281], for example, for discussion and references on this point.

Mechanism design, also known as *implementation theory,* is "inverse game theory" in the sense that the goal is to design a game in which noncooperative players will achieve a desirable outcome. As with edge taxes, achieving this goal typically requires taxes and subsidies to the players, and these are assumed to be independent of the social objective function. While edge pricing can be viewed as one example of the mechanism design paradigm, mechanism design is a broad field of economics with many other applications, including auctions. While selfish routing has not yet been explicitly studied from a mechanism design perspective, the classical techniques of mechanism design have been successfully adapted to several network models. Introductions to the field can be found in Mas-Colell, Whinston, and Green [270] and Osbourne and Rubinstein [300]. For surveys of recent mechanism design research in the theoretical computer science community, which places greater emphasis on network applications and on computational constraints, see [16, 141, 186, 298, 303, 309, 334, 351].

References

[1] H. Z. Aashtiani and T. L. Magnanti. Equilibria on a congested transportation network. *SIAM Journal on Algebraic and Discrete Methods*, 2(3):213–226, 1981.

[2] M. Abdulaal and L. J. LeBlanc. Continuous equilibrium network design models. *Transportation Research, Part B*, 13(1):19–32, 1979.

[3] M. Abdulaal and L. J. LeBlanc. Methods for combining modal split and equilibrium assignment models. *Transportation Science*, 13(4):292–314, 1979.

[4] A. V. Aho, J. E. Hopcroft, and J. D. Ullman. *The Design and Analysis of Computer Algorithms*. Addison-Wesley, 1974.

[5] R. K. Ahuja, T. L. Magnanti, and J. B. Orlin. *Network Flows: Theory, Algorithms, and Applications*. Prentice-Hall, 1993.

[6] C. D. Aliprantis and O. Burkinshaw. *Principles of Real Analysis*. Academic Press, 1981. Third Edition, 1998.

[7] N. Alon and J. H. Spencer. *The Probabilistic Method*. Wiley, 1991. Second Edition, 2000.

[8] E. Altman, T. Başar, T. Jiménez, and N. Shimkin. Routing into two parallel links: Game-theoretic distributed algorithms. *Journal of Parallel and Distributed Computing*, 61(9):1367–1381, 2001.

[9] E. Altman, T. Başar, T. Jiménez, and N. Shimkin. Competitive routing in networks with polynomial costs. *IEEE Transactions on Automatic Control*, 47(1):92–96, 2002.

[10] E. Altman, T. Boulogne, R. El Azouzi, T. Jiménez, and L. Wynter. A survey on networking games in telecommunications. *Computers & Operations Research*, 2005. To appear.

[11] E. Altman, R. El Azouzi, and O. Pourtallier. Avoiding paradoxes in multi-agent competitive routing. *Computer Networks*, 43(2):133–146, 2003.

[12] E. Altman and H. Kameda. Equilibria for multiclass routing in multi-agent networks. In *Proceedings of the 40th Annual IEEE Conference on Decision and Control (CDC)*, pages 604–609, 2001.

[13] S. P. Anderson, J. K. Goeree, and C. A. Holt. Minimum-effort coordination games: Stochastic potential and logit equilibrium. *Games and Economic Behavior*, 34(2):177–199, 2001.

[14] E. Anshelevich, A. Dasgupta, J. Kleinberg, É. Tardos, T. Wexler, and T. Roughgarden. The price of stability for network design with fair cost allocation. In *Proceedings of the 45th Annual Symposium on Foundations of Computer Science (FOCS)*, pages 295–304, 2004.

[15] E. Anshelevich, A. Dasgupta, É. Tardos, and T. Wexler. Near-optimal network design with selfish agents. In *Proceedings of the 35th Annual ACM Symposium on Theory of Computing (STOC)*, pages 511–520, 2003.

[16] A. F. Archer. *Mechanisms for Discrete Optimization with Rational Agents*. PhD thesis, Cornell University, 2004.

[17] R. Arnott, A. De Palma, and R. Lindsey. Properties of dynamic traffic equilibrium involving bottlenecks, including a paradox and metering. *Transportation Science*, 27(2):148–160, 1993.

[18] R. Arnott and K. Small. The economics of traffic congestion. *American Scientist*, 82(5):446–455, 1994.

[19] S. Arora. The approximability of NP-hard problems. In *Proceedings of the 30th Annual ACM Symposium on Theory of Computing (STOC)*, pages 337–348, 1998.

[20] S. Arora and C. Lund. Hardness of approximations. In D. S. Hochbaum, editor, *Approximation Algorithms for NP-Hard Problems*, chapter 10, pages 399–446. PWS Publishing Company, 1997.

[21] S. Arora, C. Lund, R. Motwani, M. Sudan, and M. Szegedy. Proof verification and the hardness of approximation problems. *Journal of the ACM*, 45(3):501–555, 1998.

[22] S. Arora and S. Safra. Probabilistic checking of proofs: A new characterization of NP. *Journal of the ACM*, 45(1):70–122, 1998.

[23] R. Asmuth, B. C. Eaves, and E. L. Peterson. Computing economic equilibria on affine networks with Lemke's algorithm. *Mathematics of Operations Research*, 4(3):209–214, 1979.

[24] J. Aspnes, K. Chang, and A. Yampolskiy. Inoculation strategies for victims of viruses and the sum-of-squares partition problem. In *Proceedings of the 16th Annual ACM-SIAM Symposium on Discrete Algorithms (SODA)*, 2005. To appear.

[25] G. Ausiello, P. Crescenzi, G. Gambosi, V. Kann, A. Marchetti-Spaccamela, and M. Protasi. *Complexity and Approximation*. Springer, 1999.

[26] I. Austen. Like a swerving commuter, a selfish router slows traffic. *New York Times*, page G7, April 24 2003.

[27] B. Awerbuch, Y. Azar, and L. Epstein. The price of routing unsplittable flow. In *Proceedings of the 37th Annual ACM Symposium on Theory of Computing (STOC)*, 2005. To appear.

[28] B. Awerbuch, Y. Azar, Y. Richter, and D. Tsur. Tradeoffs in worst-case equilibria. In *Proceedings of the First Workshop on Approximation and Online Algorithms (WAOA)*, pages 41–52, 2003.

[29] L. Babai. Transparent proofs and limits to approximations. In A. Joseph, F. Mignot, F. Murat, B. Prum, and R. Rentschler, editors, *Proceedings of the First European Congress of Mathematics*, volume I, pages 31–91. Birkhauser, 1994.

[30] A. Bagchi. *Stackelberg Differential Games in Economic Models*. Springer, 1984.

[31] R. Banner and A. Orda. Bottleneck games in noncooperative networks. Manuscript, 2004.

[32] R. J. Barro and P. M. Romer. Ski-lift pricing, with applications to labor and other markets. *American Economic Review*, 77(5):875–890, 1987.

[33] R. G. Bartle. *The Elements of Integration and Lebesgue Measure*. Wiley, 1995.

[34] T. Başar and G. J. Olsder. *Dynamic Noncooperative Game Theory*. Society for Industrial and Applied Mathematics, 1982. Second Edition, 1999.

[35] T. Başar and R. Srikant. A Stackelberg network game with a large number of followers. *Journal of Optimization Theory and Applications*, 115(3):479–490, 2002.

[36] T. Bass. Road to ruin. *Discover*, 13(5):56–61, 1992.

[37] N. G. Bean. Secrets of network success. *Physics World*, pages 30–33, February 1996.

[38] N. G. Bean, F. P. Kelly, and P. G. Taylor. Braess's paradox in a loss network. *Journal of Applied Probability*, 34(1):155–159, 1997.

[39] M. J. Beckmann. On the theory of traffic flow in networks. *Traffic Quarterly*, 21:109–117, 1967.

[40] M. J. Beckmann, C. B. McGuire, and C. B. Winsten. *Studies in the Economics of Transportation*. Yale University Press, 1956.

[41] L. D. Bennett. The existence of equivalent mathematical programs for certain mixed equilibrium traffic assignment problems. *European Journal of Operational Research*, 71(2):177–187, 1993.

[42] P. Berenbrink, L. A. Goldberg, P. Goldberg, and R. Martin. Utilitarian resource assignment. Manuscript, 2004.

[43] P. Bergendorff, D. W. Hearn, and M. V. Ramana. Congestion toll pricing of traffic networks. In P. M. Pardalos, D. W. Hearn, and W. W. Hager, editors, *Network Optimization*, pages 51–71. Springer, 1997.

[44] P. Berman and C. Coulstron. Speed is more powerful than clairvoyance. *Nordic Journal of Computing*, 6(2):181–193, 1999.

[45] D. P. Bertsekas. *Network Optimization: Continuous and Discrete Models*. Athena Scientific, 1998.

[46] D. P. Bertsekas and D. El Baz. Distributed asynchronous relaxation methods for convex network flow problems. *SIAM Journal on Control and Optimization*, 25(1):74–85, 1987.

[47] D. P. Bertsekas and E. M. Gafni. Projection methods for variational inequalities with application to the traffic assignment problem. *Mathematical Programming Study*, 17:139–159, 1982.

[48] D. P. Bertsekas and E. M. Gafni. Projected Newton methods and optimization of multicommodity flows. *IEEE Transactions on Automatic Control*, 28(12):1090–1096, 1983.

[49] D. P. Bertsekas, E. M. Gafni, and R. G. Gallager. Second derivative algorithms for minimum delay distributed routing in networks. *IEEE Transactions on Communications*, 32(8):911–919, 1984.

[50] D. P. Bertsekas and R. G. Gallager. *Data Networks*. Prentice-Hall, 1987. Second Edition, 1991.

[51] D. P. Bertsekas and J. N. Tsitsiklis. *Parallel and Distributed Computation: Numerical Methods*. Prentice-Hall, 1989. Second Edition, Athena Scientific, 1997.

[52] K. P. Birman. *Building Secure and Reliable Network Applications*. Manning, 1996.

[53] M. Blonski. Anonymous games with binary actions. *Games and Economic Behavior*, 28(2):171–180, 1999.

[54] B. Bollobás. *Modern Graph Theory*. Springer, 1998.

[55] K. C. Border. *Fixed Point Theorems with Applications to Economics and Game Theory*. Cambridge University Press, 1985.

[56] A. Borodin and R. El-Yaniv. *Online Computation and Competitive Analysis.* Cambridge University Press, 1998.

[57] R. Bott and R. J. Duffin. On the algebra of networks. *Transactions of the AMS,* 74(1):99–109, 1953.

[58] T. Boulogne and E. Altman. Competitive routing in multicast communications. Manuscript, 2001.

[59] T. Boulogne, E. Altman, H. Kameda, and O. Pourtallier. Mixed equilibrium for multiclass routing games. *IEEE Transactions on Automatic Control,* 47(6):903–916, 2002.

[60] D. E. Boyce, B. N. Janson, and R. W. Eash. The effect on equilibrium trip assignment of different link congestion functions. *Transportation Research, Part A,* 15(3):223–232, 1981.

[61] D. E. Boyce, H. S. Mahmassani, and A. Nagurney. A retrospective of Beckmann, McGuire, and Winsten's *Studies in the Economics of Transportation. Papers in Regional Science,* 2005. To appear.

[62] D. E. Boyce and J. L. Soberanes. Solutions to the optimal network design problem with shipments related to transportation cost. *Transportation Research, Part B,* 13(1):65–80, 1979.

[63] P. G. Bradford. On worst-case equilibria for the Internet. Manuscript, 2001. Cited in [99].

[64] D. Braess. Über ein Paradoxon aus der Verkehrsplanung. *Unternehmensforschung,* 12:258–268, 1968. Available from [65].

[65] D. Braess. http://homepage.ruhr-uni-bochum.de/ Dietrich.Braess/, Homepage, 2005.

[66] D. Braess and G. Koch. On the existence of equilibria in asymmetrical multiclass-user transportation networks. *Transportation Science,* 13(1):56–63, 1979.

[67] D. Branston. Link capacity functions: A review. *Transportation Research,* 10(4):223–236, 1976.

[68] L. Brotcorne, M. Labbé, P. Marcotte, and G. Savard. A bilevel model for toll optimization on a multicommodity transportation network. *Transportation Science,* 35(4):345–358, 2001.

[69] B. Calvert. The Downs-Thomson effect in a Markov process. *Probability in the Engineering and Informational Sciences,* 11:327–340, 1997.

[70] B. Calvert and G. Keady. Braess's paradox and power-law nonlinearities in networks. *Journal of the Australian Mathematical Society, Series B,* 35(1):1–22, 1993.

[71] B. Calvert, W. Solomon, and I. Ziedins. Braess's paradox in a queueing network with state-dependent routing. *Journal of Applied Probability,* 34(1):134–154, 1997.

[72] D. G. Cantor and M. Gerla. Optimal routing in a packet-switched computer network. *IEEE Transactions on Computers,* 23(10):1062–1069, 1974.

[73] M. Carey. Optimal time-varying flows on congested networks. *Operations Research,* 35(1):58–69, 1987.

[74] S. Catoni and S. Pallottino. Traffic equilibrium paradoxes. *Transportation Science,*

25(3):240–244, 1991.

[75] C. K. Chau and K. M. Sim. The price of anarchy for non-atomic congestion games with symmetric cost maps and elastic demands. *Operations Research Letters*, 31(5):327–334, 2003.

[76] J. Chen, P. Druschel, and D. Subramanian. A new approach to routing with dynamic metrics. In *Proceedings of the 18th INFOCOM Conference*, pages 661–670, 1999.

[77] H. Chernoff. A measure of asymptotic efficiency for tests of a hypothesis based on the sum of observations. *Annals of Mathematical Statistics*, 23(4):493–507, 1952.

[78] G. Christodoulou and E. Koutsoupias. The price of anarchy of finite congestion games. In *Proceedings of the 37th Annual ACM Symposium on Theory of Computing (STOC)*, 2005. To appear.

[79] R. Cocchi, S. J. Shenker, D. Estrin, and L. Zhang. Pricing in computer networks: Motivation, formulation, and example. *IEEE/ACM Transactions on Networking*, 1(6):614–627, 1993.

[80] J. E. Cohen. The counterintuitive in conflict and cooperation. *American Scientist*, 76(6):576–584, 1988.

[81] J. E. Cohen. Cooperation and self-interest: Pareto-inefficiency of Nash equilibria in finite random games. *Proceedings of the National Academy of Science*, 95(17):9724–9731, 1998.

[82] J. E. Cohen and P. Horowitz. Paradoxical behavior of mechanical and electrical networks. *Nature*, 352(8):699–701, 1991.

[83] J. E. Cohen and C. Jeffries. Congestion resulting from increased capacity in single-server queueing networks. *IEEE/ACM Transactions on Networking*, 5(2):305–310, 1997.

[84] J. E. Cohen and F. P. Kelly. A paradox of congestion in a queuing network. *Journal of Applied Probability*, 27:730–734, 1990.

[85] R. M. Cohn. The resistance of an electrical network. *Proceedings of the AMS*, 1(3):316–324, 1950.

[86] R. Cole, Y. Dodis, and T. Roughgarden. How much can taxes help selfish routing? In *Proceedings of the Fourth ACM Conference on Electronic Commerce (EC)*, pages 98–107, 2003. Preliminary version of [88].

[87] R. Cole, Y. Dodis, and T. Roughgarden. Pricing network edges for heterogeneous selfish users. In *Proceedings of the 35th Annual ACM Symposium on Theory of Computing (STOC)*, pages 521–530, 2003.

[88] R. Cole, Y. Dodis, and T. Roughgarden. How much can taxes help selfish routing? *Journal of Computer and Systems Sciences*, 2005. To appear.

[89] R. Cole, Y. Dodis, and T. Roughgarden. Throughput-competitive selfish routing. In preparation, 2005.

[90] W. J. Cook, W. H. Cunningham, W. R. Pulleyblank, and A. Schrijver. *Combinatorial Optimization*. Wiley, 1998.

[91] T. H. Cormen, C. E. Leiserson, R. L. Rivest, and C. Stein. *Introduction to*

Algorithms. MIT Press, 2001.

[92] J. R. Correa, A. S. Schulz, and N. E. Stier Moses. Computational complexity, fairness, and the price of anarchy of the maximum latency problem. In *Proceedings of the 10th Conference on Integer Programming and Combinatorial Optimization (IPCO),* volume 3064 of *Lecture Notes in Computer Science,* pages 59–73, 2004.

[93] J. R. Correa, A. S. Schulz, and N. E. Stier Moses. Selfish routing in capacitated networks. *Mathematics of Operations Research,* 29(4):961–976, 2004.

[94] R. W. Cottle, J. Pang, and R. E. Stone. *The Linear Complementarity Problem.* Academic Press, 1992.

[95] J. B. Cruz, Jr. Leader-follower strategies for multilevel systems. *IEEE Transactions on Automatic Control,* 23(2):244–255, 1978.

[96] J. B. Cruz, Jr. Survey of leader-follower concepts in hierarchical decision-making. In *Proceedings of the 4th International Conference on the Analysis and Optimization of Systems,* pages 384–396, 1980.

[97] A. Czumaj. Selfish routing on the Internet. In J. Leung, editor, *Handbook of Scheduling: Algorithms, Models, and Performance Analysis,* chapter 42. CRC Press, 2004.

[98] A. Czumaj, P. Krysta, and B. Vöcking. Selfish traffic allocation for server farms. In *Proceedings of the 34th Annual ACM Symposium on Theory of Computing (STOC),* pages 287–296, 2002.

[99] A. Czumaj and B. Vöcking. Tight bounds for worst-case equilibria. In *Proceedings of the 13th Annual ACM-SIAM Symposium on Discrete Algorithms (SODA),* pages 413–420, 2002.

[100] S. C. Dafermos. An extended traffic assignment model with applications to two-way traffic. *Transportation Science,* 5(4):366–389, 1971.

[101] S. C. Dafermos. The traffic assignment problem for multiclass-user transportation networks. *Transportation Science,* 6(1):73–87, 1972.

[102] S. C. Dafermos. Toll patterns for multiclass-user transportation networks. *Transportation Science,* 7(3):211–223, 1973.

[103] S. C. Dafermos. Traffic equilibrium and variational inequalities. *Transportation Science,* 14(1):42–54, 1980.

[104] S. C. Dafermos. A multicriteria route-mode choice traffic equilibrium model. In *Proceedings of the Frontiers in Transportation Equilibrium and Supply Models Symposium,* 1981.

[105] S. C. Dafermos. The general multimodal network equilibrium problem with elastic demand. *Networks,* 12(1):57–72, 1982.

[106] S. C. Dafermos and A. Nagurney. On some traffic equilibrium theory paradoxes. *Transportation Research, Part B,* 18(2):101–110, 1984.

[107] S. C. Dafermos and A. Nagurney. Sensitivity analysis for the asymmetric network equilibrium problem. *Mathematical Programming,* 28(2):174–184, 1984.

[108] S. C. Dafermos and F. T. Sparrow. The traffic assignment problem for a general network. *Journal of Research of the National Bureau of Standards, Series B,* 73(2):91–118, 1969.

[109] S. C. Dafermos and F. T. Sparrow. Optimal resource allocation and toll patterns in user-optimised transport networks. *Journal of Transport Economics and Policy*, 5(2):184–200, 1971.

[110] C. F. Daganzo. On the traffic assignment problem with flow dependent costs–I. *Transportation Research*, 11(6):433–437, 1977.

[111] C. F. Daganzo. On the traffic assignment problem with flow dependent costs–II. *Transportation Research*, 11(6):439–441, 1977.

[112] C. F. Daganzo. Queue spillovers in transportation networks with a route choice. *Transportation Science*, 32(1):3–11, 1998.

[113] C. F. Daganzo and Y. Sheffi. On stochastic models of traffic assignment. *Transportation Science*, 11(3):253–274, 1977.

[114] G. C. D'Ans and D. C. Gazis. Optimal control of oversaturated store-and-forward transportation networks. *Transportation Science*, 10(1):1–19, 1976.

[115] G. B. Dantzig, R. P. Harvey, Z. F. Lansdowne, D. W. Robinson, and S. F. Maier. Formulating and solving the network design problem by decomposition. *Transportation Research, Part B*, 13(1):5–17, 1979.

[116] N. R. Devanur, N. Garg, R. Khandekar, V. Pandit, A. Saberi, and V. V. Vazirani. Price of anarchy, locality gap, and a network service provider game. Manuscript, 2003.

[117] S. Devarajan. A note on network equilibrium and noncooperative games. *Transportation Research, Part B*, 15(6):421–426, 1981.

[118] R. B. Dial. A probabilistic multipath traffic assignment model which obviates path enumeration. *Transportation Research*, 5(2):83–111, 1971.

[119] R. B. Dial. Minimal-revenue congestion pricing: Part I: A fast algorithm for the single-origin case. *Transportation Research, Part B*, 33(3):189–202, 1999.

[120] R. B. Dial. Network-optimized road pricing: Part I: A parable and a model. *Operations Research*, 47(1):54–64, 1999.

[121] R. B. Dial. Network-optimized road pricing: Part II: Algorithms and examples. *Operations Research*, 47(2):327–336, 1999.

[122] R. B. Dial. Minimal-revenue congestion pricing: Part II: An efficient algorithm for the general case. *Transportation Research, Part B*, 34(8):645–665, 2000.

[123] R. Diestel. *Graph Theory*. Springer, 1997. Second Edition, 2000.

[124] R. Dionne and M. Florian. Exact and approximate algorithms for optimal network design. *Networks*, 9(1):37–59, 1979.

[125] C. Douligeris and R. Mazumdar. Multilevel flow control of queues. In *Proceedings of the Johns Hopkins Conference on Information Sciences and Systems*, page 21, 1989.

[126] C. Douligeris and R. Mazumdar. A game theoretic perspective to flow control in telecommunication networks. *Journal of the Franklin Institute*, 329(2):383–402, 1992.

[127] A. Downs. The law of peak-hour expressway congestion. *Traffic Quarterly*, 16:393–409, 1962.

[128] P. Dubey. Inefficiency of Nash equilibria. *Mathematics of Operations Research*, 11(1):1–8, 1986.

[129] R. J. Duffin. Nonlinear networks. *Bulletin of the AMS*, 53:963–971, 1947.

[130] A. A. Economides and J. A. Silvester. Priority load sharing: An approach using Stackelberg games. In *Proceedings of the 28th Annual Allerton Conference on Communications, Control, and Computing*, pages 674–683, 1990.

[131] J. Edmonds. Scheduling in the dark. *Theoretical Computer Science*, 235(1):109–141, 2000.

[132] R. El Azouzi and E. Altman. Constrained traffic equilibrium in routing. *IEEE Transactions on Automatic Control*, 48(9):1656–1660, 2003.

[133] R. El Azouzi, E. Altman, and O. Pourtallier. Properties of equilibria in competitive routing with several user types. In *Proceedings of the 41st Annual IEEE Conference on Decision and Control (CDC)*, volume 4, pages 3646–3651, 2002.

[134] S. Enke. Equilibrium among spatially separated markets: Solution by electric analogue. *Econometrica*, 19(1):40–47, 1951.

[135] S. P. Evans. Derivation and analysis of some models for combining trip distribution and assignment. *Transportation Research*, 10(1):37–57, 1976.

[136] E. Even-Dar, A. Kesselman, and Y. Mansour. Convergence time to Nash equilibria. In *Proceedings of the 30th Annual International Colloquium on Automata, Languages, and Programming (ICALP)*, volume 2719 of *Lecture Notes in Computer Science*, pages 502–513, 2003.

[137] A. Fabrikant, A. Luthra, E. Maneva, C. H. Papadimitriou, and S. J. Shenker. On a network creation game. In *Proceedings of the 22nd ACM Symposium on Principles of Distributed Computing (PODC)*, pages 347–351, 2003.

[138] A. Fabrikant, C. H. Papadimitriou, and K. Talwar. The complexity of pure Nash equilibria. In *Proceedings of the 36th Annual ACM Symposium on Theory of Computing (STOC)*, pages 604–612, 2004.

[139] G. Facchini, F. van Megan, P. Borm, and S. Tijs. Congestion models and weighted Bayesian potential games. *Theory and Decision*, 42(2):193–206, 1997.

[140] U. Feige, S. Goldwasser, L. Lovász, S. Safra, and M. Szegedy. Interactive proofs and the hardness of approximating cliques. *Journal of the ACM*, 43(2):268–292, 1996.

[141] J. Feigenbaum and S. J. Shenker. Distributed algorithmic mechanism design: Recent results and future directions. In *Proceedings of the 6th International Workshop on Discrete Algorithms and Methods for Mobile Computing and Communications*, pages 1–13, 2002.

[142] R. Feldmann, M. Gairing, T. Lücking, B. Monien, and M. Rode. Nashification and the coordination ratio for a selfish routing game. In *Proceedings of the 30th Annual International Colloquium on Automata, Languages, and Programming (ICALP)*, volume 2719 of *Lecture Notes in Computer Science*, pages 514–526, 2003.

[143] R. Feldmann, M. Gairing, T. Lücking, B. Monien, and M. Rode. Selfish routing in non-cooperative networks: A survey. In *Proceedings of the 28th International Symposium on Mathematical Foundations of Computer Science (MFCS)*, volume 2747 of *Lecture Notes in Computer Science*, pages 21–45, 2003.

[144] P. Ferrari. Road network toll pricing and social welfare. *Transportation Research, Part B*, 36(5):471–483, 2002.

[145] P. M. Ferreira. *Interconnected Communication Networks Provisioned Selfishly.* PhD thesis, Carnegie Mellon University, 2004.

[146] S. Fischer and B. Vöcking. On the evolution of selfish routing. In *Proceedings of the 12th Annual European Symposium on Algorithms (ESA)*, pages 323–334, 2004.

[147] C. Fisk. More paradoxes in the equilibrium assignment problem. *Transportation Research, Part B*, 13(4):305–309, 1979.

[148] C. Fisk and S. Pallottino. Empirical evidence for equilibrium paradoxes with implications for optimal planning strategies. *Transportation Research, Part A*, 15(3):245–248, 1981.

[149] L. K. Fleischer. Linear tolls suffice: New bounds and algorithms for tolls in single source networks. In *Proceedings of the 31st Annual International Colloquium on Automata, Languages, and Programming (ICALP)*, volume 3142 of *Lecture Notes in Computer Science*, pages 544–554, 2004.

[150] L. K. Fleischer, K. Jain, and M. Mahdian. Tolls for heterogeneous selfish users in multicommodity networks and generalized congestion games. In *Proceedings of the 45th Annual Symposium on Foundations of Computer Science (FOCS)*, pages 277–285, 2004.

[151] M. Florian. A traffic equilibrium model of travel by car and public transit modes. *Transportation Science*, 11(2):166–179, 1977.

[152] M. Florian. An introduction to network models used in transportation planning. In M. Florian, editor, *Transportation Planning Models*, pages 137–152. North-Holland, 1984.

[153] M. Florian. Nonlinear cost network models in transportation analysis. *Mathematical Programming Study*, 26:167–196, 1986.

[154] M. Florian and D. W. Hearn. Network equilibrium models and algorithms. In M. O. Ball, T. L. Magnanti, C. L. Monma, and G. L. Nemhauser, editors, *Network Routing*, chapter 6, pages 485–550. North-Holland, 1995.

[155] M. Florian and S. Nguyen. A method for computing network equilibrium with elastic demands. *Transportation Science*, 8(4):321–332, 1974.

[156] M. Florian and S. Nguyen. An application and validation of equilibrium trip assignment methods. *Transportation Science*, 10(4):374–390, 1976.

[157] L. R. Ford and D. R. Fulkerson. *Flows in Networks.* Princeton University Press, 1962.

[158] S. Fortune, J. E. Hopcroft, and J. Wyllie. The directed subgraph homeomorphism problem. *Theoretical Computer Science*, 10(2):111–121, 1980.

[159] D. Fotakis, S. C. Kontogiannis, E. Koutsoupias, M. Mavronicolas, and P. G. Spirakis. The structure and complexity of Nash equilibria for a selfish routing game. In *Proceedings of the 29th Annual International Colloquium on Automata, Languages, and Programming (ICALP)*, volume 2380 of *Lecture Notes in Computer Science*, pages 123–134, 2002.

[160] D. Fotakis, S. C. Kontogiannis, and P. G. Spirakis. Selfish unsplittable flows. In *Proceedings of the 31st Annual International Colloquium on Automata, Languages, and Programming (ICALP)*, volume 3142 of *Lecture Notes in Computer Science*, pages 593–605, 2004.

[161] M. Frank. The Braess paradox. *Mathematical Programming*, 20(3):283–302, 1981.

[162] M. Frank. Cost-deceptive links on ladder networks. *Methods of Operations Research*, 45:75–86, 1983.

[163] E. J. Friedman. Dynamics and rationality in ordered externality games. *Games and Economic Behavior*, 16(1):65–76, 1996.

[164] E. J. Friedman. Genericity and congestion control in selfish routing. In *Proceedings of the 43rd Annual IEEE Conference on Decision and Control (CDC)*, pages 4667–4672, 2004.

[165] T. L. Friesz, D. Bernstein, N. J. Mehta, R. L. Tobin, and S. Ganjalizadeh. Day-to-day dynamic network disequilibria and idealized traveler information systems. *Operations Research*, 42(6):1120–1136, 1994.

[166] D. Fudenberg and J. Tirole. *Game Theory*. MIT Press, 1991.

[167] M. Gairing, T. Lücking, M. Mavronicolas, and B. Monien. Computing Nash equilibria for scheduling on restricted parallel links. In *Proceedings of the 36th Annual ACM Symposium on Theory of Computing (STOC)*, pages 613–622, 2004.

[168] M. Gairing, T. Lücking, M. Mavronicolas, B. Monien, and M. Rode. Nash equilibria in discrete routing games with convex latency functions. In *Proceedings of the 31st Annual International Colloquium on Automata, Languages, and Programming (ICALP)*, volume 3142 of *Lecture Notes in Computer Science*, pages 645–657, 2004.

[169] M. Gairing, T. Lücking, M. Mavronicolas, B. Monien, and P. G. Spirakis. Extreme Nash equilibria. In *Proceedings of the 8th Italian Conference on Theoretical Computer Science (ICTCS)*, volume 2841 of *Lecture Notes in Computer Science*, pages 1–20, 2003.

[170] R. G. Gallager. A minimum delay routing algorithm using distributed computation. *IEEE Transactions on Communications*, 25(1):73–85, 1977.

[171] M. R. Garey and D. S. Johnson. "Strong" NP-completeness results: Motivation, examples, and implications. *Journal of the ACM*, 25(3):499–508, 1978.

[172] M. R. Garey and D. S. Johnson. *Computers and Intractability: A Guide to the Theory of NP-Completeness*. Freeman, 1979.

[173] N. H. Gartner. Optimal traffic assignment with elastic demands: A review; Part I. Analysis framework. *Transportation Science*, 14(2):174–191, 1980.

[174] N. H. Gartner. Optimal traffic assignment with elastic demands: A review; Part II. Algorithmic approaches. *Transportation Science*, 14(2):192–208, 1980.

[175] C. Gawron. An iterative algorithm to determine the dynamic user equilibrium in a traffic simulation model. *International Journal of Modern Physics C*, 9(3):393–407, 1998.

[176] R. J. Gibbens and F. P. Kelly. Resource pricing and the evolution of congestion control. *Automatica*, 35(12):1969–1985, 1999.

[177] M. X. Goemans and D. P. Williamson. The primal-dual method for approximation algorithms and its application to network design problems. In D. S. Hochbaum, editor, *Approximation Algorithms for NP-Hard Problems*, chapter 4, pages 144–191. PWS Publishing Company, 1997.

[178] G. R. Grimmett and D. R. Stirzaker. *Probability and Random Processes*. Oxford University Press, 1982. Third Edition, 2001.

[179] D. Gross and C. M. Harris. *Fundamentals of Queueing Theory*. Wiley, 1974. Third Edition, 1998.

[180] M. Grötschel, L. Lovász, and A. Schrijver. *Geometric Algorithms and Combinatorial Optimization*. Springer, 1988. Second Edition, 1993.

[181] J. N. Hagstrom and R. A. Abrams. Characterizing Braess's paradox for traffic networks. In *Proceedings of the 2001 IEEE Conference on Intelligent Transportation Systems*, pages 836–841, 2001.

[182] M. A. Hall. Properties of the equilibrium state in transportation networks. *Transportation Science*, 12(3):208–216, 1978.

[183] M. M. Halldórsson, J. Y. Halpern, E. L. Li, and V. S. Mirrokni. On spectrum sharing games. In *Proceedings of the 23rd Annual ACM Symposium on Principles of Distributed Computing (PODC)*, pages 107–114, 2004.

[184] P. T. Harker. A variational inequality approach for the determination of oligopolistic market equilibrium. *Mathematical Programming*, 30(1):105–111, 1984.

[185] P. T. Harker. Multiple equilibrium behaviors on networks. *Transportation Science*, 22(1):39–46, 1988.

[186] J. D. Hartline. *Optimization in the Private Value Model: Competitive Analysis Applied to Auction Design*. PhD thesis, University of Washington, 2003.

[187] A. Haurie and P. Marcotte. On the relationship between Nash-Cournot and Wardrop equilibria. *Networks*, 15(3):295–308, 1985.

[188] A. Haurie and P. Marcotte. A game-theoretic approach to network equilibrium. *Mathematical Programming Study*, 26:252–255, 1986.

[189] D. W. Hearn and S. Lawphongpanich. Convex programming formulations of the asymmetric traffic assignment problem. *Transportation Research, Part B*, 18(4/5):357–365, 1984.

[190] D. W. Hearn, S. Lawphongpanich, and J. A. Ventura. Restricted simplicial decomposition: Computation and extensions. *Mathematical Programming Study*, 31:99–118, 1987.

[191] D. W. Hearn and J. Ribera. Convergence of the Frank-Wolfe method for certain bounded variable traffic assignment problems. *Transportation Research, Part B*, 15(6):437–442, 1981.

[192] D. W. Hearn and M. B. Yildirim. A toll pricing framework for traffic assignment problems with elastic demand. In *Transportation and Network Analysis Current Trends: Miscellanea in Honor of Michael Florian*, chapter 9. Kluwer, 2002.

[193] F. S. Hillier and G. J. Lieberman. *Introduction to Operations Research*. McGraw-Hill, 1967. Seventh Edition, 2001.

[194] H. H. Hoc. A computational approach to the selection of an optimal network. *Management Science*, 19(5):488–498, 1973.

[195] D. S. Hochbaum, editor. *Approximation Algorithms for NP-Hard Problems*. PWS Publishing Company, 1997.

[196] D. S. Hochbaum and J. G. Shanthikumar. Convex separable optimization is not much harder than linear optimization. *Journal of the ACM*, 37(4):843–862, 1990.

[197] W. Hoeffding. Probability inequalities for sums of bounded random variables. *Journal of the American Statistical Association*, 58(1):13–30, 1963.

[198] R. Holzman and N. Law-Yone. Strong equilibrium in congestion games. *Games and Economic Behavior*, 21(1-2):85–101, 1997.

[199] J. L. Horowitz. The stability of stochastic equilibrium in a two-link transportation network. *Transportation Research, Part B*, 18(1):13–28, 1984.

[200] S. Hougardy, H. J. Prömel, and A. Steger. Probabilistically checkable proofs and their consequences for approximation algorithms. *Discrete Mathematics*, 136(1-3):175–223, 1994.

[201] A. D. Irvine. How Braess' paradox solves Newcomb's problem. *International Studies in the Philosophy of Science*, 7(2):141–160, 1993.

[202] M. O. Jackson. A survey of models of network formation: Stability and efficiency. In G. Demange and M. Wooders, editors, *Group Formation in Economics; Networks, Clubs, and Coalitions*, chapter 1. Cambridge University Press, 2005.

[203] O. Jahn, R. Möhring, A. S. Schulz, and N. E. Stier Moses. System-optimal routing of traffic flows with user constraints in networks with congestion. *Operations Research*, 2005. To appear.

[204] B. N. Janson. Dynamic traffic assignment for urban road networks. *Transportation Research, Part B*, 25(2/3):143–161, 1991.

[205] R. Johari, S. Mannor, and J. N. Tsitsiklis. Efficiency loss in a network resource allocation game: The case of elastic supply. Technical Report 2605, MIT LIDS, 2004.

[206] R. Johari and J. N. Tsitsiklis. Routing and peering in a competitive Internet. Technical Report 2570, MIT LIDS, 2003.

[207] R. Johari and J. N. Tsitsiklis. Efficiency loss in a Cournot mechanism for network resource allocation. Manuscript, 2004.

[208] R. Johari and J. N. Tsitsiklis. Efficiency loss in a network resource allocation game. *Mathematics of Operations Research*, 29(3):407–435, 2004.

[209] D. S. Johnson. Approximation algorithms for combinatorial problems. *Journal of Computer and System Sciences*, 9(3):256–278, 1974.

[210] D. S. Johnson. The NP-completeness column: An ongoing guide. *Journal of Algorithms*, 13(3):502–524, 1992.

[211] B. Kalyanasundaram and K. Pruhs. Speed is as powerful as clairvoyance. *Journal of the ACM*, 47(4):617–643, 2000.

[212] H. Kameda. How harmful the paradox can be in the Braess/Cohen-Kelly-Jeffries networks. In *Proceedings of the 21st INFOCOM Conference*, volume 1, pages 437–445, 2002.

[213] H. Kameda, E. Altman, T. Kozawa, and Y. Hosokawa. Braess-like paradoxes in distributed computer systems. *IEEE Transactions on Automatic Control*, 45(9):1687–1691, 2000.

[214] H. Kameda and O. Pourtallier. Paradoxes in distributed decisions on optimal load balancing for networks of homogeneous computers. *Journal of the ACM*, 49(3):407–433, 2002.

[215] G. Karakostas and S. G. Kolliopoulos. Edge pricing of multicommodity networks for heterogeneous selfish users. In *Proceedings of the 45th Annual Symposium on Foundations of Computer Science (FOCS)*, pages 268–276, 2004.

[216] S. Karlin and H. M. Taylor. *A Second Course in Stochastic Processes*. Academic Press, 1981.

[217] N. Karmarkar. A new polynomial-time algorithm for linear programming. *Combinatorica*, 4(4):373–395, 1984.

[218] R. M. Karp. Reducibility among combinatorial problems. In R. E. Miller and J. W. Thatcher, editors, *Complexity of Computer Computations*, pages 85–103. Plenum Press, 1972.

[219] G. Keady. The Colebrook-White formula for pipe networks. *Journal of Hydraulic Engineering*, 124(1):96–97, 1998.

[220] M. J. Kearns and Y. Mansour. Efficient Nash computation in large population games with bounded influence. In *Proceedings of the 18th Conference on Uncertainty in Artificial Intelligence*, pages 259–266, 2002.

[221] F. P. Kelly. Network routing. *Philosophical Transactions of the Royal Society of London, Series A*, 337(3):343–367, 1991.

[222] F. P. Kelly. Charging and rate control for elastic traffic. *European Transactions on Telecommunications*, 8(1):33–37, 1997.

[223] F. P. Kelly, A. K. Maulloo, and D. K. H. Tan. Rate control for communication networks: Shadow prices, proportional fairness and stability. *Journal of the Operational Research Society*, 49(3):237–252, 1998.

[224] S. Keshav. *An Engineering Approach to Computer Networking*. Addison-Wesley, 1997.

[225] L. G. Khachiyan. A polynomial algorithm in linear programming. *Soviet Mathematics Doklady*, 20(1):191–194, 1979.

[226] A. Khanna and J. A. Zinky. The revised ARPANET routing metric. In *Proceedings of the 1989 ACM SIGCOMM Symposium on Communications, Architecture, and Protocols (SIGCOMM)*, pages 45–56, 1989.

[227] F. H. Knight. Some fallacies in the interpretation of social cost. *Quarterly Journal of Economics*, 38(4):582–606, 1924.

[228] W. Knödel. *Graphentheoretische Methoden und ihre Anwendungen*. Springer, 1969.

[229] G. Kolata. What if they closed 42nd Street and nobody noticed? *New York Times*, page 38, December 25 1990.

[230] H. Konishi. Uniqueness of user equilibrium in transportation networks with heterogeneous commuters. *Transportation Science*, 2005. To appear.

[231] H. Konishi, M. Le Breton, and S. Weber. Equilibria in a model with partial rivalry. *Journal of Economic Theory*, 72(1):225–237, 1997.

[232] H. Konishi, M. Le Breton, and S. Weber. Pure strategy Nash equilibrium in a group formation game with positive externalities. *Games and Economic Behavior*, 21(1/2):161–182, 1997.

[233] Y. A. Korilis, A. A. Lazar, and A. Orda. Achieving network optima using Stackelberg routing strategies. *IEEE/ACM Transactions on Networking*, 5(1):161–173, 1997.

[234] Y. A. Korilis, A. A. Lazar, and A. Orda. Capacity allocation under noncooperative routing. *IEEE Transactions on Automatic Control*, 42(3):309–325, 1997.

[235] Y. A. Korilis, A. A. Lazar, and A. Orda. Avoiding the Braess paradox in non-cooperative networks. *Journal of Applied Probability*, 36(1):211–222, 1999.

[236] T. W. Körner. *The Pleasures of Counting*. Cambridge University Press, 1996.

[237] B. Korte and J. Vygen. *Combinatorial Optimization: Theory and Algorithms*. Springer, 2000. Second Edition, 2002.

[238] E. Koutsoupias, M. Mavronicolas, and P. G. Spirakis. Approximate equilibria and ball fusion. *Theory of Computing Systems*, 36(6):683–693, 2003. Preliminary version in *SIROCCO '02*.

[239] E. Koutsoupias and C. H. Papadimitriou. Worst-case equilibria. In *Proceedings of the 16th Annual Symposium on Theoretical Aspects of Computer Science (STACS)*, volume 1563 of *Lecture Notes in Computer Science*, pages 404–413, 1999.

[240] D. C. Kozen. *The Design and Analysis of Algorithms*. Springer, 1992.

[241] N. S. Kukushkin. Potential games: A purely ordinal approach. *Economics Letters*, 64(3):279–283, 1999.

[242] N. S. Kukushkin. Perfect information and potential games. *Games and Economic Behavior*, 38(2):306–317, 2002.

[243] V. S. Anil Kumar and M. V. Marathe. Improved results for Stackelberg scheduling strategies. In *Proceedings of the 29th Annual International Colloquium on Automata, Languages, and Programming (ICALP)*, volume 2380 of *Lecture Notes in Computer Science*, pages 776–787, 2002.

[244] R. J. La and V. Anantharam. Optimal routing control: Repeated game approach. *IEEE Transactions on Automatic Control*, 47(3):437–450, 2002.

[245] M. Labbé, P. Marcotte, and G. Savard. A bilevel model of taxation and its application to optimal highway pricing. *Management Science*, 44(12):1608–1622, 1998.

[246] T. Larsson and M. Patriksson. An augmented Lagrangean dual algorithm for link capacity side constrained traffic assignment problems. *Transportation Research, Part B*, 29(6):433–455, 1995.

[247] T. Larsson and M. Patriksson. Side constrained traffic equilibrium models—traffic management through link tolls. In P. Marcotte and S. Nguyen, editors, *Equilibrium and Advanced Transportation Modelling*, chapter 7, pages 125–151. Kluwer, 1998.

[248] T. Larsson and M. Patriksson. Side constrained traffic equilibrium models: Analysis, computation and applications. *Transportation Research, Part B*, 33(4):233–264, 1999.

[249] S. Lawphongpanich and D. W. Hearn. Simplicial decomposition of the asymmetric traffic assignment problem. *Transportation Research, Part B*, 18(2):123–133, 1984.

[250] L. J. LeBlanc. An algorithm for the discrete network design problem. *Transportation Science*, 9(3):183–199, 1975.

[251] L. J. LeBlanc and E. K. Morlok. An analysis and comparison of behavioral assumptions in traffic assignment. In *Proceedings of the 1974 International Symposium on Traffic Equilibrium Methods*, pages 413–425, 1976.

[252] F. Leurent. Cost versus time equilibrium over a network. *European Journal of Operational Research*, 71(2):205–221, 1993.

[253] T. Leventhal, G. Nemhauser, and L. Trotter, Jr. A column generation algorithm for optimal traffic assignment. *Transportation Science*, 7(2):168–176, 1973.

[254] L. Libman and A. Orda. The designer's perspective to atomic noncooperative networks. *IEEE/ACM Transactions on Networking*, 7(6):875–884, 1999.

[255] L. Libman and A. Orda. Atomic resource sharing in noncooperative networks. *Telecommunication Systems*, 17(4):385–409, 2001.

[256] H. Lin, T. Roughgarden, and É. Tardos. A stronger bound on Braess's Paradox. In *Proceedings of the 15th Annual ACM-SIAM Symposium on Discrete Algorithms (SODA)*, pages 333–334, 2004.

[257] H. Lin, T. Roughgarden, É. Tardos, and A. Walkover. Braess's Paradox, Fibonacci numbers, and exponential inapproximability. Manuscript, 2005.

[258] N. Linial. Game-theoretic aspects of computing. In R. J. Aumann and S. Hart, editors, *Handbook of Game Theory with Economic Applications*, volume 2, chapter 38, pages 1339–1395. North-Holland, 1994.

[259] T. Lücking, M. Mavronicolas, B. Monien, M. Rode, P. Spirakis, and I. Vrto. Which is the worst-case Nash equilibrium? In *Proceedings of the 28th International Symposium on Mathematical Foundations of Computer Science (MFCS)*, volume 2747 of *Lecture Notes in Computer Science*, pages 551–561, 2003.

[260] T. L. Magnanti. Models and algorithms for predicting urban traffic equilibria. In M. Florian, editor, *Transportation Planning Models*, pages 153–185. North-Holland, 1984.

[261] T. L. Magnanti and R. T. Wong. Network design and transportation planning: Models and algorithms. *Transportation Science*, 18(1):1–55, 1984.

[262] H. S. Mahmassani. Dynamic models of commuter behavior: Experimental investigation and application to the analysis of planned traffic disruptions. *Transportation Research, Part A*, 24(6):465–484, 1990.

[263] P. Marcotte. Network optimization with continuous control parameters. *Transportation Science*, 17(2):181–197, 1983.

[264] P. Marcotte. Network design problem with congestion effects: A case of bilevel programming. *Mathematical Programming*, 34(2):142–162, 1986.

[265] P. Marcotte. Algorithms for the network oligopoly problem. *Journal of the Operational Research Society*, 38(11):1051–1065, 1987.

[266] P. Marcotte, S. Nguyen, and A. Schoeb. A strategic flow model of traffic assignment in static capacitated networks. *Operations Research*, 52(2):191–212, 2004.

[267] L. Marinoff. How Braess' paradox solves Newcomb's problem: not! *International Studies in the Philosophy of Science*, 10(3):217–237, 1996.

[268] J. E. Marsden and M. J. Hoffman. *Elementary Classical Analysis*. Freeman, 1974. Second Edition, 1993.

[269] A. Mas-Colell. On a theorem of Schmeidler. *Journal of Mathematical Economics*, 13(3):201–206, 1984.

[270] A. Mas-Colell, M. D. Whinston, and J. R. Green. *Microeconomic Theory*. Oxford University Press, 1995.

[271] L. G. Mason. Equilibrium flows, routing patterns and algorithms for store-and-forward networks. *Large Scale Systems*, 8:187–209, 1985.

[272] M. Mavronicolas and P. Spirakis. The price of selfish routing. In *Proceedings of the 33rd Annual ACM Symposium on Theory of Computing (STOC)*, pages 510–519, 2001.

[273] J. McCullough and E. Torng. SRPT optimally utilizes faster machines to minimize flow time. In *Proceedings of the 15th Annual ACM-SIAM Symposium on Discrete Algorithms (SODA)*, pages 343–351, 2004.

[274] D. K. Merchant and G. L. Nemhauser. A model and an algorithm for the dynamic traffic assignment problems. *Transportation Science*, 12(3):183–199, 1978.

[275] D. K. Merchant and G. L. Nemhauser. Optimality conditions for a dynamic traffic assignment model. *Transportation Science*, 12(3):200–207, 1978.

[276] I. Milchtaich. Congestion games with player-specific payoff functions. *Games and Economic Behavior*, 13(1):111–124, 1996.

[277] I. Milchtaich. Congestion models of competition. *American Naturalist*, 147(5):760–783, 1996.

[278] I. Milchtaich. Generic uniqueness of equilibrium in large crowding games. *Mathematics of Operations Research*, 25(3):349–364, 2000.

[279] I. Milchtaich. Network topology and the efficiency of equilibrium. Working paper 12-01, Department of Economics, Bar-Ilan University, 2001.

[280] I. Milchtaich. Social optimality and cooperation in nonatomic congestion games. *Journal of Economic Theory*, 114:56–87, 2004.

[281] J. A. Mirrlees. The theory of optimal taxation. In K. J. Arrow and M. D. Intriligator, editors, *Handbook of Mathematical Economics*, volume 3, chapter 24, pages 1197–1249. North-Holland, 1986.

[282] V. S. Mirrokni and A. Vetta. Convergence issues in competitive games. In *Proceedings of the 7th International Workshop on Approximation Algorithms for Combinatorial Optimization Problems (APPROX)*, pages 183–194, 2004.

[283] D. Monderer and L. S. Shapley. Potential games. *Games and Economic Behavior*, 14(1):124–143, 1996.

[284] R. Motwani and P. Raghavan. *Randomized Algorithms*. Cambridge University Press, 1995.

[285] J. D. Murchland. Braess's paradox of traffic flow. *Transportation Research*, 4(4):391–394, 1970.

[286] A. Nagurney. Comparative tests of multimodal traffic equilibrium methods. *Transportation Research, Part B*, 18(6):469–485, 1984.

[287] A. Nagurney. *Network Economics: A Variational Inequality Approach*. Kluwer, 1993. Second Edition, 1999.

[288] A. Nagurney. *Sustainable Transportation Networks*. Edward Elgar, 2000.

[289] A. Nagurney and J. Dong. A multiclass, multicriteria traffic network equilibrium model with elastic demand. *Transportation Research, Part B*, 36(5):445–469, 2002.

[290] A. Nagurney, J. Dong, and D. Zhang. A supply chain network equilibrium model. *Transportation Research, Part E*, 38(5):281–303, 2002.

[291] A. Nagurney and D. Zhang. Projected dynamical systems in the formulation, stability analysis, and computation of fixed-demand traffic network equilibria. *Transportation Science*, 31(2):147–158, 1997.

[292] J. F. Nash. Equilibrium points in *N*-person games. *Proceedings of the National Academy of Science*, 36(1):48–49, 1950.

[293] J. F. Nash. Non-cooperative games. *Annals of Mathematics*, 54(2):286–295, 1951.

[294] Y. Nesterov. Stable traffic equilibria: Properties and applications. *Optimization and Engineering*, 1(1):29–50, 2000.

[295] Y. Nesterov and A. de Palma. Stable dynamics in transportation systems. CORE Discussion Paper 00/27, 2000.

[296] G. F. Newell. *Traffic Flow on Transportation Networks*. MIT Press, 1980.

[297] S. Nguyen and C. Dupuis. An efficient method for computing traffic equilibria in networks with asymmetric transportation costs. *Transportation Science*, 18(2):185–202, 1984.

[298] N. Nisan. Algorithms for selfish agents: Mechanism design for distributed computation. In *Proceedings of the 16th Annual Symposium on Theoretical Aspects of Computer Science (STACS)*, pages 1–15, 1999.

[299] A. Orda, R. Rom, and N. Shimkin. Competitive routing in multiuser communication networks. *IEEE/ACM Transactions on Networking*, 1(5):510–521, 1993.

[300] M. J. Osborne and A. Rubinstein. *A Course in Game Theory*. MIT Press, 1994.

[301] G. Owen. *Game Theory*. Academic Press, 1968. Third Edition, 1995.

[302] C. H. Papadimitriou. *Computational Complexity*. Addison-Wesley, 1994.

[303] C. H. Papadimitriou. Algorithms, games, and the Internet. In *Proceedings of the 33rd Annual ACM Symposium on Theory of Computing (STOC)*, pages 749–753, 2001.

[304] C. H. Papadimitriou. Computing correlated equilibria in multi-player games. To appear, 2005.

[305] C. H. Papadimitriou and T. Roughgarden. Computing equilibria in multi-player games. In *Proceedings of the 16th Annual ACM-SIAM Symposium on Discrete Algorithms (SODA)*, 2005. To appear.

[306] C. H. Papadimitriou and K. Steiglitz. *Combinatorial Optimization: Algorithms and Complexity*. Prentice-Hall, 1982. Dover Edition, 1998.

[307] C. H. Papadimitriou and M. Yannakakis. Optimization, approximation, and complexity classes. *Journal of Computer and System Sciences*, 43(3):425–440, 1991.

[308] G. P. Papavassilopoulos. Algorithms for static Stackelberg games with linear costs and polyhedra constraints. In *Proceedings of the 21st Annual IEEE Conference on Decision and Control (CDC)*, volume 2, pages 647–652, 1982.

[309] D. C. Parkes. *Iterative Combinatorial Auctions: Achieving Economic and Computational Efficiency.* PhD thesis, University of Pennsylvania, 2001.

[310] E. I. Pas and S. L. Principio. Braess' paradox: Some new insights. *Transportation Research, Part B*, 31(3):265–276, 1997.

[311] A. D. Pearman. The structure of the solution set to network optimisation problems. *Transportation Research, Part B*, 13(1):81–90, 1979.

[312] B. Peleg, J. Potters, and S. Tijs. Minimality of consistent solutions for strategic games, in particular for potential games. *Economic Theory*, 7(1):81–93, 1996.

[313] C. M. Penchina. Braess paradox: Maximum penalty in a minimal critical network. *Transportation Research, Part A*, 31(5):379–388, 1997.

[314] C. M. Penchina and L. J. Penchina. The Braess paradox in mechanical, traffic, and other networks. *American Journal of Physics*, 71(5):479–482, 2003.

[315] G. Perakis. The price of anarchy when costs are non-separable and asymmetric. In *Proceedings of the 10th Conference on Integer Programming and Combinatorial Optimization (IPCO)*, volume 3064 of *Lecture Notes in Computer Science*, pages 46–58, 2004.

[316] A. L. Peressini, F. E. Sullivan, and J. J. Uhl, Jr. *The Mathematics of Nonlinear Programming.* Springer, 1988.

[317] I. Peterson. Strings and springs net mechanical surprise. *Science News*, 140(8):118, 1991.

[318] L. L. Peterson and B. S. Davie. *Computer Networks: A Systems Approach.* Morgan Kaufmann, 1996. Third Edition, 2003.

[319] C. A. Phillips, C. Stein, E. Torng, and J. Wein. Optimal time-critical scheduling via resource augmentation. *Algorithmica*, 32(2):163–200, 2002.

[320] A. C. Pigou. *The Economics of Welfare.* Macmillan, 1920.

[321] H. Poorzahedy and M. A. Turnquist. Approximate algorithms for the discrete network design problem. *Transportation Research, Part B*, 16(1):45–55, 1982.

[322] C. Qin. Endogenous formation of cooperation structures. *Journal of Economic Theory*, 69(1):218–226, 1996.

[323] T. Quint and M. Shubik. A model of migration. Working paper #1088, Cowles Foundation, Yale University, 1994.

[324] B. Raghavachari. Algorithms for finding low degree structures. In D. S. Hochbaum, editor, *Approximation Algorithms for NP-Hard Problems*, chapter 7, pages 266–295. PWS Publishing Company, 1997.

[325] H. Raiffa. Game theory at the University of Michigan, 1948–1952. In E. R. Weintraub, editor, *Toward a History of Game Theory*, pages 165–175. Duke University Press, 1992.

[326] A. Rapoport and A. M. Chammah. *Prisoner's Dilemma.* University of Michigan Press, 1965.

[327] K. P. Rath. A direct proof of the existence of pure strategy equilibria in games with a continuum of players. *Economic Theory*, 2(3):427–433, 1992.

[328] J. Renegar. *A Mathematical View of Interior-Point Methods in Convex Optimization*. Society for Industrial and Applied Mathematics, 2001.

[329] C. ReVelle and D. Serra. The maximum capture problem including relocation. *INFOR*, 29(2):130–138, 1991.

[330] T. M. Ridley. An investment policy to reduce the travel time in a transportation network. *Transportation Research*, 2(4):409–424, 1968.

[331] A. J. Robson. The evolution of attitudes to risk: Lottery tickets and relative wealth. *Games and Economic Behavior*, 14(2):190–207, 1996.

[332] R. T. Rockafellar. Duality and stability in extremum problems involving convex functions. *Pacific Journal of Mathematics*, 21(1):167–187, 1967.

[333] R. T. Rockafellar. *Convex Analysis*. Princeton University Press, 1970.

[334] A. Ronen. *Solving Optimization Problems Among Selfish Agents*. PhD thesis, Hebrew University of Jerusalem, 2000.

[335] J. B. Rosen. Existence and uniqueness of equilibrium points for concave N-person games. *Econometrica*, 33(3):520–534, 1965.

[336] R. W. Rosenthal. A class of games possessing pure-strategy Nash equilibria. *International Journal of Game Theory*, 2(1):65–67, 1973.

[337] R. W. Rosenthal. The network equilibrium problem in integers. *Networks*, 3(1):53–59, 1973.

[338] T. Roughgarden. Designing networks for selfish users is hard. In *Proceedings of the 42d Annual Symposium on Foundations of Computer Science (FOCS)*, pages 472–481, 2001. Full version to appear in *Journal of Computer and Systems Sciences*.

[339] T. Roughgarden. The price of anarchy in networks with polynomial edge latency. Technical Report 2001-1847, Cornell University, 2001.

[340] T. Roughgarden. How unfair is optimal routing? In *Proceedings of the 13th Annual ACM-SIAM Symposium on Discrete Algorithms (SODA)*, pages 203–204, 2002.

[341] T. Roughgarden. The price of anarchy is independent of the network topology. In *Proceedings of the 34th Annual ACM Symposium on Theory of Computing (STOC)*, pages 428–437, 2002. Preliminary version of [343].

[342] T. Roughgarden. *Selfish Routing*. PhD thesis, Cornell University, 2002.

[343] T. Roughgarden. The price of anarchy is independent of the network topology. *Journal of Computer and System Sciences*, 67(2):341–364, 2003.

[344] T. Roughgarden. The maximum latency of selfish routing. In *Proceedings of the 15th Annual ACM-SIAM Symposium on Discrete Algorithms (SODA)*, pages 973–974, 2004.

[345] T. Roughgarden. Stackelberg scheduling strategies. *SIAM Journal on Computing*, 33(2):332–350, 2004.

[346] T. Roughgarden. Selfish routing with atomic players. In *Proceedings of the 16th Annual ACM-SIAM Symposium on Discrete Algorithms (SODA)*, 2005. To appear.

[347] T. Roughgarden and É. Tardos. How bad is selfish routing? In *Proceedings of the 41st Annual Symposium on Foundations of Computer Science (FOCS)*, pages 93–102,

2000. Preliminary version of [348].

[348] T. Roughgarden and É. Tardos. How bad is selfish routing? *Journal of the ACM*, 49(2):236–259, 2002.

[349] T. Roughgarden and É. Tardos. Bounding the inefficiency of equilibria in nonatomic congestion games. *Games and Economic Behavior*, 49(2):389–403, 2004.

[350] W. Rudin. *Principles of Mathematical Analysis*. McGraw-Hill, 1953. Third Edition, 1976.

[351] R. Sami. *Distributed Algorithmic Mechanism Design*. PhD thesis, Yale University, 2003.

[352] S. Savage, T. Anderson, A. Aggarwal, D. Becker, N. Cardwell, A. Collins, E. Hoffman, J. Snell, A. Vahdat, G. Voelker, and J. Zahorjan. Detour: A case for informed Internet routing and transport. *IEEE Micro*, 19(1):50–59, 1999.

[353] D. Schmeidler. Equilibrium points of nonatomic games. *Journal of Statistical Physics*, 7(4):295–300, 1973.

[354] A. Schrijver. *Theory of Linear and Integer Programming*. Wiley, 1986.

[355] A. Schrijver. *Combinatorial Optimization: Polyhedra and Efficiency*. Springer, 2003.

[356] A. S. Schulz and N. Stier Moses. On the performance of user equilibria in traffic networks. In *Proceedings of the 14th Annual ACM-SIAM Symposium on Discrete Algorithms (SODA)*, pages 86–87, 2003. Preliminary version of [93].

[357] A. J. Scott. The optimal network problem: Some computational procedures. *Transportation Research*, 3(2):201–210, 1969.

[358] D. Serra and C. ReVelle. Competitive location in discrete space. In T. Drezner, editor, *Facility Location: A Survey of Applications and Methods*, chapter 16, pages 367–386. Springer, 1995.

[359] Y. Sheffi. *Urban Transportation Networks: Equilibrium Analysis with Mathematical Programming Methods*. Prentice-Hall, 1985.

[360] S. J. Shenker. Making greed work in networks: A game-theoretic analysis of switch service disciplines. *IEEE/ACM Transactions on Networking*, 3(6):819–831, 1995.

[361] D. B. Shmoys. Computing near-optimal solutions to combinatorial optimization problems. In W. Cook, L. Lovász, and P. Seymour, editors, *Combinatorial Optimization*, pages 355–397. American Mathematical Society, 1995.

[362] M. E. Slade. What does an oligopoly maximize? *Journal of Industrial Economics*, 42(1):45–61, 1994.

[363] D. D. Sleator and R. E. Tarjan. Amortized efficiency of list update and paging rules. *Communications of the ACM*, 28(2):202–208, 1985.

[364] M. Slikker. Coalition formation and potential games. *Games and Economic Behavior*, 37(2):436–448, 2001.

[365] M. J. Smith. In a road network, increasing delay locally can reduce delay globally. *Transportation Research*, 12(6):419–422, 1978.

[366] M. J. Smith. The existence, uniqueness and stability of traffic equilibria.

Transportation Research, Part B, 13(4):295–304, 1979.

[367] M. J. Smith. The marginal cost taxation of a transportation network. *Transportation Research, Part B*, 13(3):237–242, 1979.

[368] M. J. Smith. The stability of a dynamic model of traffic assignment—an application of a method of Lyapunov. *Transportation Science*, 18(3):245–252, 1984.

[369] M. J. Smith. A new dynamic traffic model and the existence and calculation of dynamic user equilibria on congested capacity-constrained road networks. *Transportation Research, Part B*, 27(1):49–63, 1993.

[370] J. J. Spengler. Vertical integration and antitrust policy. *Journal of Political Economy*, 58(4):347–352, 1950.

[371] M. Spivak. *Calculus*. Publish or Perish, 1967. Third Edition, 1994.

[372] P. A. Steenbrink. Transport network optimization in the Dutch integral transportation study. *Transportation Research*, 8(1):11–27, 1974.

[373] R. Steinberg and R. E. Stone. The prevalence of paradoxes in transportation equilibrium problems. *Transportation Science*, 22(4):231–241, 1988.

[374] R. Steinberg and W. I. Zangwill. The prevalence of Braess' paradox. *Transportation Science*, 17(3):301–318, 1983.

[375] T. E. Stern. A class of decentralized routing algorithms using relaxation. *IEEE Transactions on Communications*, 25(10):1092–1102, 1977.

[376] D. Stirzaker. *Elementary Probability*. Cambridge University Press, 1994.

[377] P. D. Straffin. *Game Theory and Strategy*. Mathematical Association of America, 1993.

[378] C. Suwansirikul, T. L. Friesz, and R. L. Tobin. Equilibrium decomposed optimization: A heuristic for the continuous equilibrium network design problem. *Transportation Science*, 21(4):254–263, 1987.

[379] A. Taguchi. Braess' paradox in a two-terminal transportation network. *Journal of the Operations Research Society of Japan*, 25(4):376–388, 1982.

[380] R. E. Tarjan. *Data Structures and Network Algorithms*. Society for Industrial and Applied Mathematics, 1983.

[381] M. Tennenholtz. Rational competitive analysis. In *Proceedings of the 17th International Joint Conference on Artificial Intelligence (IJCAI)*, pages 1067–1072, 2001.

[382] M. Tennenholtz. Competitive safety analysis: Robust decision-making in multi-agent systems. *Journal of Artificial Intelligence Research*, 17:363–378, 2002.

[383] J. M. Thomson. *Great Cities and Their Traffic*. Gollancz, 1977.

[384] W. K. Tsai, J. N. Tsitsiklis, and D. P. Bertsekas. Some issues in distributed asynchronous routing in virtual circuit data networks. In *Proceedings of the 25th Conference on Decision and Control (CDC)*, pages 1335–1337, 1986.

[385] J. N. Tsitsiklis and D. P. Bertsekas. Distributed asynchronous optimal routing in data networks. *IEEE Transactions on Automatic Control*, 31(4):325–332, 1986.

[386] T. Ui. A Shapley value representation of potential games. *Games and Economic Behavior*, 31(1):121–135, 2000.

[387] V. V. Vazirani. *Approximation Algorithms*. Springer, 2001.

[388] A. Vetta. Nash equilibria in competitive societies, with applications to facility location, traffic routing and auctions. In *Proceedings of the 43rd Annual Symposium on Foundations of Computer Science (FOCS)*, pages 416–425, 2002.

[389] W. S. Vickrey. Congestion theory and transport investment. *American Economic Review*, 59(2):251–260, 1969.

[390] H. von Stackelberg. *Marktform und Gleichgewicht*. Springer, 1934.

[391] M. Voorneveld, P. Borm, F. van Megen, S. Tijs, and G. Facchini. Congestion games and potentials reconsidered. *International Game Theory Review*, 1(3-4):283–299, 1999.

[392] M. Voorneveld and H. Norde. A characterization of ordinal potential games. *Games and Economic Behavior*, 19(2):235–242, 1997.

[393] J. Walrand. *Communication Networks: A First Course*. McGraw-Hill, 1998. Second Edition.

[394] J. G. Wardrop. Some theoretical aspects of road traffic research. In *Proceedings of the Institute of Civil Engineers, Pt. II*, volume 1, pages 325–378, 1952.

[395] A. Weintraub and J. González. An algorithm for the traffic assignment problem. *Networks*, 10(3):197–209, 1980.

[396] D. Weitz. The price of anarchy. Manuscript, 2001.

[397] D. B. West. *Introduction to Graph Theory*. Prentice-Hall, 1996. Second Edition, 2001.

[398] W. Whitt. Counterexamples for comparisons of queues with finite waiting rooms. *Queueing Systems*, 10(3):271–278, 1992.

[399] R. T. Wong. Introduction and recent advances in network design: Models and algorithms. In M. Florian, editor, *Transportation Planning Models*, pages 187–225. North-Holland, 1984.

[400] S. Yagar. Dynamic traffic assignment by individual path minimization and queuing. *Transportation Research*, 5(3):179–196, 1971.

[401] H. Yang. Sensitivity analysis for the elastic-demand network equilibrium problem with applications. *Transportation Research, Part B*, 31(1):55–70, 1997.

[402] H. Yang and M. G. H. Bell. A capacity paradox in network design and how to avoid it. *Transportation Research, Part A*, 32(7):539–545, 1998.

[403] W. I. Zangwill and C. B. Garcia. Equilibrium programming: The path following approach and dynamics. *Mathematical Programming*, 21(3):262–289, 1981.

[404] W. I. Zangwill and C. B. Garcia. *Pathways to Solutions, Fixed Points, and Equilibria*. Prentice-Hall, 1981.

[405] D. Zhang and A. Nagurney. On the local and global stability of a travel route choice adjustment process. *Transportation Research, Part B*, 30(4):245–262, 1996.

Index

Printed in the United States
by Baker & Taylor Publisher Services